THE LAST PRINCE OF BENGAL

A Family's journey from an Indian Palace to the Australian Outback

Lyn Innes

AMARYLLIS

AMARYLLIS

An imprint of Manjul Publishing House Pvt. Ltd.
• C-16, Sector 3, Noida, Uttar Pradesh 201301, India
Website: www.manjulindia.com
Registered Office:
• 2nd Floor, Usha Preet Complex, 42 Malviya Nagar, Bhopal 462 003 – India
Distribution Centres
Ahmedabad, Bengaluru, Bhopal, Chennai, Hyderabad,
Kolkata, Mumbai, Noida, Pune

The Last Prince of Bengal by Lyn Innes

Maps by Lovell Johns.

Cover image: Nawab Nazim Mansour Ali Khan, the Last Prince of Bengal, c. 1870 © London Stereoscopic Company / Stringer / Getty Images.

This edition first published in India in 2024

ISBN 978-93-5543-740-2

Printed and bound in India by Parksons Graphics Pvt. Ltd.

LYN INNES is the great-granddaughter of the last Nawab Nizam of Bengal, Bihar and Orissa. Born in Australia, she later moved to North America where she earned a PhD from Cornell University and taught at the University of Massachusetts, Amherst. Innes became associate editor of *OKIKE: An African Journal of New Writing*, founded by Chinua Achebe, with whom she also co-edited two volumes of African short stories. Innes is currently Emeritus Professor of Postcolonial Literatures at the University of Kent, where she was the first Director of the Centre for Postcolonial Studies. Her publications include *A History of Black and Asian Writing in Britain, 1700–2000*

'A rich tapestry of family narrative … A masterpiece ... a spellbinding family history.' *Irish Times*

'A fascinating insight into the British Raj in India … Innes shows with unsettling effect how historical prejudices are still prevalent in modern times.' *Asian Review of Books*

'An eye-opening saga not only for its compelling plot but also for the truths it uncovers about the British Empire and the injustices faced by millions as a result of their regime.' *Indian Link*

'Lyn Innes explores her ancestors' history in moving detail, capturing the tragic story of the dethroned princes of Bengal.'
Shrabani Basu, author of *Victoria and Abdul: The True Story of the Queen's Closest Confidant*

'Lovingly researched and meticulously told, *The Last Prince of Bengal* is notable for its candid revelations of British colonial attitudes and hypocrisies across two centuries.'
Richard Holmes, author of *This Long Pursuit: Reflections of a Romantic Biographer*

ALSO BY LYN INNES

The Cambridge Introduction to Postcolonial Literatures in English

A History of Black and Asian Writing in Britain, 1700–2000

Ned Kelly:
Icon of Modern Culture Series

Woman and Nation in Irish Literature and Society, 1880–1935

Chinua Achebe

The Devil's Own Mirror:
Irish and Africans in Modern Literature

CONTENTS

INTRODUCTION

Who Did They Think We Were?

'But what is a black person then? And first of all, what colour is he?'
Jean Genet, *Les Nègres*

A hot summer day in February 1945, a few weeks after my fifth birthday. We had just moved from the slab hut near the road to our new fibreboard house on the hill, and I was watching my mother unpack. At the bottom of a trunk, wrapped in tissue paper, were several old photographs mounted on card. Looking straight out towards the camera in one were my father's Scottish parents: my grandmother in a high-necked long-sleeved dress, my grandfather in a tightly buttoned suit. There was another photograph of a man in profile – an elegant man with a fine, waxed moustache, prominent nose and broad forehead. In the sepia print he is only slightly darker than my Scottish grandparents.

This, my mother told me, was her father. He was Indian – no, not an American Indian but *from* India – and he was the man who had painted one of the two oil landscapes that hung in our freshly decorated living room. His painting is unobtrusive: a small, black-framed pastoral scene depicting a field with dark green trees, six inches by nine inches. The colours are sombre. There is no sunlight. Growing up I had assumed that the field was English since it did not look Australian. Examining the picture more closely now as it sits above the desk in my study in Kent, I see that the frame is not black but brown, that the trees in the foreground are a pine and an oak or chestnut, that there are brown cows in the field, and there is a suggestion of a ruined tower in the distance. The scene could be English or French.

This painting is the only thing my mother inherited from her father – or at least the only thing she had kept. He had died four years previously, just before my first birthday. To me then and now this quiet and unmistakably European rural scene evokes a distinctive and intriguing aspect of my grandfather's character: somehow, his Indian identity had to include being a painter of European landscapes. My mother later told me that her parents had lived in the suburb of Saint-Cloud, Paris, for several years; that her father had studied art there; and that his work had been exhibited in Paris. Once, she recalled, her parents had visited the Paris zoo, and on recognising an elephant as one that he had known as a boy in India, her father had called it by name and commanded it to kneel, which it did. She told one other story about my grandfather. When he was young, he and his older brother had caused outrage amongst the Hindu community in their neighbourhood by tying firecrackers to the tail of a cow and setting light to them. Their Muslim father had had to pay a large sum of money in compensation. It was a story my mother repeated several times in later life without, as far as I could tell, any concern for the cow.

Our own cows grazed quietly in the paddocks below the house on our isolated mountain farm, named by my father 'Rhu-na-Mohr', Gaelic for 'on the bend of the hill'. The nearest neighbours were three miles away, the nearest small town, Rylstone, twenty-one miles. From the windows of our new home we looked out over a wilderness of distant mountain ranges. We were taught at home with the aid of correspondence-school lessons and knew no other children. Since there were six of us, three girls and three boys, we did not miss the company of others. Nor did we experience the need to identify ourselves in social or cultural terms, although we were aware that our father was Scottish, and our mother English, and that this made both of them a little different from our neighbours on Nulla Mountain, at least with regard to the way they spoke. My mother's father and his Indian past existed as a vague footnote in the family story.

Soon after I turned seven my parents bundled us all into our 1928 Dodge car, and we drove the fifty miles of dusty roads for the first of several semi-annual visits to Glen Alice, where my grandmother lived on the property she and her husband had bought in 1926, soon after they had arrived in Australia. It was Easter and we began the visit searching for the small gifts that our grandmother had wrapped in yellow tissue paper and concealed behind the yellow and golden autumn leaves of the grapevines, rose bushes and shrubs which filled her English garden.

Indoors we were overawed by the elegance of the wide, verandahed house, and the sitting room with its polished parquet floors, leaded French windows, shining copper tables and crystal glassware. For these special family visits my grandmother dressed formally in a long, green taffeta dress with a white lace collar, and an amber necklace. In the sitting room I remember leafing delightedly through old copies of *Punch* magazine, looking for cartoons, and glancing through stacks of old newspapers, mostly the *Sunday Times*, which contained pictures of huskies and Eskimos. These pictures were illustrations for feature articles written by my grandmother and based on the experiences of an Arctic explorer. On top of a chest rested my grandfather's Qur'an, which we were told to treat with care – indeed, we were told that if one of us dropped the Qur'an, we would have to pay our weight in gold in compensation. We were not told to whom this payment should be made.

On a later visit my grandmother showed us her late husband's – our grandfather's – court dress and sword. I remember only that the tunic was made of bright green muslin, and that the long, slightly curved sword had a large green stone decorating its hilt. With it, there was a yellowed newspaper cutting from *The Times* dated 5 June 1914, that showed a photograph of my grandfather wearing an embroidered coat, the sword, and a cap with a feathered plume. There was a caption under the photograph: 'The Nawabzada Misrat Ali Mirza [sic] of Murshidabad, who attended court on June 5th. The Prince is the son of his Highness, the late Nawab Nazim of Behar, Bengal, and Orissa, and is the uncle of the present Nawab of Murshidabad.'

Although her husband's Qu'ran had a prominent place in my grandmother's house amid the leather bound volumes of Thackeray and Dickens and the more colourful covers of the books she herself had written, and although his dress clothes and family seal were there, not once did my grandmother ever speak to her grandchildren about him or about India. We were made aware of his status, but had no sense of

The Nawabzada
Nusrat Ali Mirza
of Murshidabad

him as a person. That very silence aroused my curiosity. Who was my grandfather and what kind of world had he and his ancestors inhabited?

As well as her newspaper and magazine pieces, my grandmother wrote fiction, mainly storybooks for children and teenagers, published under both her pen name, Elizabeth Marc, and her married title, Princess Nusrat Ali Mirza. These two identities existed alongside 'Mrs Mostyn', which is how she was customarily addressed in Australia. Sometimes, she used a large seal ring featuring a star and crescent and her husband's family motto, '*Nil desperandum*', to close her correspondence. Otherwise, everything about my grandmother, from her accent, garden, library and attitudes towards her neighbours to the repertoire of songs she encouraged us to sing together ('The Lincolnshire Poacher', 'Do Ye Ken John Peel') as I played her out-of-tune piano, impressed me as distinctively English.

To us, our grandmother seemed a somewhat imposing person, an upper-class Englishwoman whose attitudes towards our fellow Australians we could not share. As we gradually acquired the accents of our fellow students at school, she vehemently reprimanded us for 'sounding like Irish navvies'. She had deplored the fact that our father came from a 'trade background', worse still, a family of butchers.

However, our grandmother did share with us her love of books, and she was an enthralling reader; her rendition of *The Wind in the Willows* still echoes in my memory. Despite her un-Australian views, she appeared to us serene and settled in the comparative solitude of Tyar, seated on the wide veranda of the house she had designed, her beloved English collie Sandy beside her as she gazed out to the distant blue mountains.

The year I turned ten, my father's illness forced us to move from the farm he could no longer manage to a very small cottage on our grandmother's property, about one mile from her house. With this move came the dubious benefit of access to a school bus that could take us to a convent school in Kandos, a dusty cement-and-coal town twenty-five miles away. While my older brother was sent away to boarding school and my older sister stayed with our grandmother to study for her Intermediate exams (equivalent to Scottish Standard Grades or Intermediates) my three younger siblings and I left home at seven each morning to hurry down the two miles of dirt track to the bus stop.

I dreaded the bus journey. It lasted a stomach-churning hour and a half along winding roads, during which time we had to face the taunts of the other children. Most of all I dreaded Patricia, a plump, fair girl about my own age, whose parents lived on a nearby farm. When she and her brother boarded the bus she would push past the other children and stand over me, her cheeks red, her eyes glinting. 'How's the black princess?', she would sneer.

My initial bafflement as to what she meant amused everyone. The only 'black' people I had seen were the aboriginal boxers at the annual county show in Rylstone. Looking dishevelled, disdainful and formidable, they stood on a platform outside the tent that sheltered the boxing ring, daring the white lads to take them on. My father had shown me caves which had been decorated many years before by local aboriginal people, and I had once heard an elderly neighbour tell my mother how she had watched the men hunting down 'the last aborigine in the area', and seen him 'bounding over the fields like a kangaroo'.

Like my grandmother and my Scottish father, my siblings and I were all fair-skinned and blue-eyed. I tried sitting further back, but it became common practice for other girls on the bus to refuse me a seat next to them (to sit next to one of the boys would have been unthinkable, of course). I fought back, determined to retain my place on the bus, physically rather than verbally, because I did not know how to respond to the jeering. On some level, I realised that it was the particular combination of 'black' and 'princess' that Patricia and her friends objected to. I rejected both terms.

Eventually, I understood that the reference was to my grandfather, and that 'black' didn't mean 'black' but was intended as a generic term of disparagement that applied to anyone who wasn't white. It was on that school bus that I first realised that I was not only Australian, but also, in some sense, 'Indian'. Later, this realisation grew into determination to understand my Indian heritage, and to understand it in terms that took into account, but were not limited by, the attitudes of my Australian schoolfellows.

My brothers, sisters and I kept quiet about the fights on the school bus – the hair-pulling, the punches that I received and returned, all studiously ignored by the young male bus driver. Nor did we talk, even among ourselves, about our younger sister's travel sickness, or the embarrassment we faced during lessons for our lack of knowledge about Catholicism, or when we were caned for not knowing mathematical rules that the other children had learned years before. Our mother was struggling to run her small poultry farm, and both parents were growing increasingly anxious about money and our father's illness. The curiosity about my heritage did not feel so urgent in light of my more immediate need to acquire social codes expected of us by teachers and classmates. And then, following my father's death just over a year after we had moved to Glen Alice, my mother took up a position as a teacher in a one-room schoolhouse, in the tiny town of Naradhan 300-or-so miles west, where our ancestry was unknown. That same year I began secondary school as a boarder at St Scholastica's College in Sydney.

While my mother and younger siblings were living in Naradhan, I spent some weeks during my school summer holidays staying with my grandmother. I found those visits daunting, not only because of her insistence that we speak French, but also because she expected me to help with her large garden, pruning the roses and cutting back the periwinkle that straggled forlornly up the bank below her veranda. Those hours in the garden were hot and tiring; the rose thorns scratched, the hornets threatened, and the green and red ants ran over the dry, pebbly ground. Now every time I tend the periwinkle and the abundant roses in my garden in Kent I think of her and her determination to cultivate a truly English garden in the meagre soil of Tyar. It was in her house that I read every novel Thackeray and Galsworthy wrote, and began to glimpse the fictional world that sustained her and that she partly inhabited.

Boarding school was also daunting, with its rigid schedules and confined spaces. We were allowed to venture outside the school gates only one Sunday a month. Here religious affiliation superseded class and ethnic identities. Hierarchies were established that exalted religion first, ethnicity second. My classmates were O'Briens, Ryans, Murphies, McVeighs, Coogans, O'Connors and Lynches; occasionally a Kowalinski or Costello appeared on the name rolls, which were deemed acceptable 'New Australian' Catholic names, but lacking the status of good 'old Australian' Irish surnames. When, aged fifteen and home for the holidays, I attended my first public dance, I was rebuked for accepting an invitation to dance with an Italian immigrant: 'No decent girl would be seen dancing with a New Australian,' my older sister's friend told me.

Each morning our lessons imparted Irish nationalist history, including the persecution of heroic Catholics who stood up for 'the faith of their fathers' against English Protestants and Scottish Presbyterians. We were sternly discouraged from associating with Protestants and accepted that a 'mixed marriage' was a scandal. We pitied the children in Japan, Africa, China and India, devoutly offering our sixpences and our prayers for the salvation of their souls. I shared the widely accepted view that the few Papuan and Chinese Malaysian boarders at the school were special cases, who had been taken in as part of the convent's missionary zeal. In such a world, the possession of an Indian Muslim grandparent seemed both irrelevant and inadmissible.

The fact that neither of my parents had any trace of Irish Catholic heritage (both had converted to Catholicism shortly before I was born), and that my fees were subsidised by various scholarships and charities, made it all the more necessary to disassociate myself from other outsiders. Together with my classmates I joined the parades on St Patrick's Day, became a devout 'Child of Mary', and took 'the 'heroic pledge' to abstain from alcohol for life. Once, a fellow boarder who came from a rural town near Kandos, referred to a rumour that my grandmother was 'some kind of Swedish princess'. I did not disabuse her.

When I mentioned the report of our grandmother's Swedish identity, my mother suggested that I should not deny it if asked again. She had told me, without any apparent displeasure, that at school and university her friends had light-heartedly called her Mozzy (a play on Mostyn), Fuzzy or Golly. Her hair was now white and cut short and close to her skull, but I retained an image of her from some eight years earlier when her hair had been thick, black and frizzy. I had always thought that she looked and felt beautiful. Now I began to wonder what invisible scars those school nicknames had left, and remembered how disapproving she had been when as a very small child I had been given a gollywog by a family friend. A few years later, when studying at Sydney University, I mentioned to my mother in a letter that I had become friends with a male student from India. Her very prompt reply warned me that she was aware that 'Indian men can be very charming' but that I should beware of forming a deeper relationship.

During my teenage years, my grandfather's sister began writing to us from India. Great Aunt Vaheedoonissa had grown up in Murshidabad, her ancestral home in West Bengal. According to family lore (later proved incorrect), she had been betrothed at the age of five, but her husband-to-be had died before the wedding could take place, and she had remained in purdah all her life. I pitied her in her confinement and felt my good luck in being a liberated Australian female, seeing no contradiction in my growing ambition to become a nun in the very enclosed convent that housed my school.

The letters from my great aunt were written by her in Urdu and translated into English by a scribe. They conveyed family and political news, including events involving President of Pakistan Iskander Mirza, her cousin and ours. From these letters I learned that there were other perspectives on the Suez crisis than those advocated by the *Sydney Morning Herald*, the Australian Broadcasting Commission, and the Australian Prime Minister at the time, Robert Menzies, who was an ardent supporter of Anthony Eden and the British establishment. She bitterly denounced those who were responsible for the coup that ousted Mirza in 1958, and indignantly refuted claims that he was corrupt. Her letters brought both an awareness of and a connection to another world. Once along with a letter she sent a parcel containing silk scarves, ivory ornaments, and a little bottle of sandalwood-scented perfume. I claimed that bottle as my own, taking it with me when I moved to my student room at Sydney University. It has travelled with me through a series of American states and still exudes its special perfume here in Kent.

Those long-distance communications from my Great Aunt Vaheedoonissa began to make more tangible that other world to which my grandfather had once belonged. Everything was intriguingly different: the language, political histories, hierarchies, gender roles, clothing, smells and aesthetics. I became interested in my grandfather's Indian family and wanted to know about his parents. My mother explained that the British government's disapproval of my great-grandfather's marriage to an English governess had led to his abdication. My brothers, sisters and I were not discouraged from making analogies with the story of Edward VIII's abdication, a story kept alive by occasional articles about him and Wallis Simpson in Australian newspapers and magazines.

I was fascinated. What could it have been like for this young Englishwoman to travel to India, to work as a governess in an Indian palace, to be the wife of an Indian Nawab? *The King and I* was playing in local cinemas, but it was Thackeray's Becky Sharp rather than Deborah Kerr or Jane Eyre who informed my notion of a governess. Yul Brynner, however, seemed a desirable model for an oriental ruler, and to the strains of 'Getting to Know You' I embarked on the first of many attempts to imagine and write the story of my great-grandparents.

When I read many years later in a family history written by the son of President Mirza that my great-grandmother was not a governess but a hotel chambermaid, my interest increased. Humayun Mirza wrote: 'The Nawab Nazim embarked for England in February 1869 for what was planned as a short visit. As it turned out, he was to remain there for twelve years. By the time he returned to India, his weakness for servant girls and the pleasures of life in London gave the British the opportunity that they were waiting for to acquire Bengal, Bihar, and Orissa.'

Thus I learned that my own existence ensued from the Nawab's 'weakness for servant girls' and, in particular, of a seventeen-year-old chambermaid, Sarah Vennell, who happened to be working in the Alexandra Hotel in 1870. How did they meet, and was it this relationship that detained the Nawab in London for all those years? What was it like for Sarah to have been married to a Muslim nobleman? What was the British reaction that Humayun Mirza mentioned? These questions remained with me, but many years passed before I made my first visit to my great-grandfather's birthplace in Murshidabad and began to explore the story of the last Nawab of Bengal and the young English girl he had married.

Part I of this book, the exploration of the stories of the Nawab and Sarah, involved not only visits to Bengal but immersion in the history and politics of British and Indian relationships throughout the eighteenth and nineteenth centuries. Those relationships were well documented – from the British side – in the many volumes of letters, reports and official accounts gathered in the files of the India Office, now held in the British Library. However, when I turned to the story of their youngest son, my grandfather, my mother's memories and family photograph albums became the starting point of his story, informed also by memoirs, written and oral, passed on by my cousins. Consequently Part II of the narrative was shaped by personal experiences and encounters in a way that Part I could not be. Nevertheless, I was struck by ways in which both generations were involved in a resistance to and a dialogue with the political priorities, and the particular racial, and class attitudes that dominated Britain, India and Australia during their lifetimes: priorities and attitudes which continue to affect present generations in all three countries.

PART I

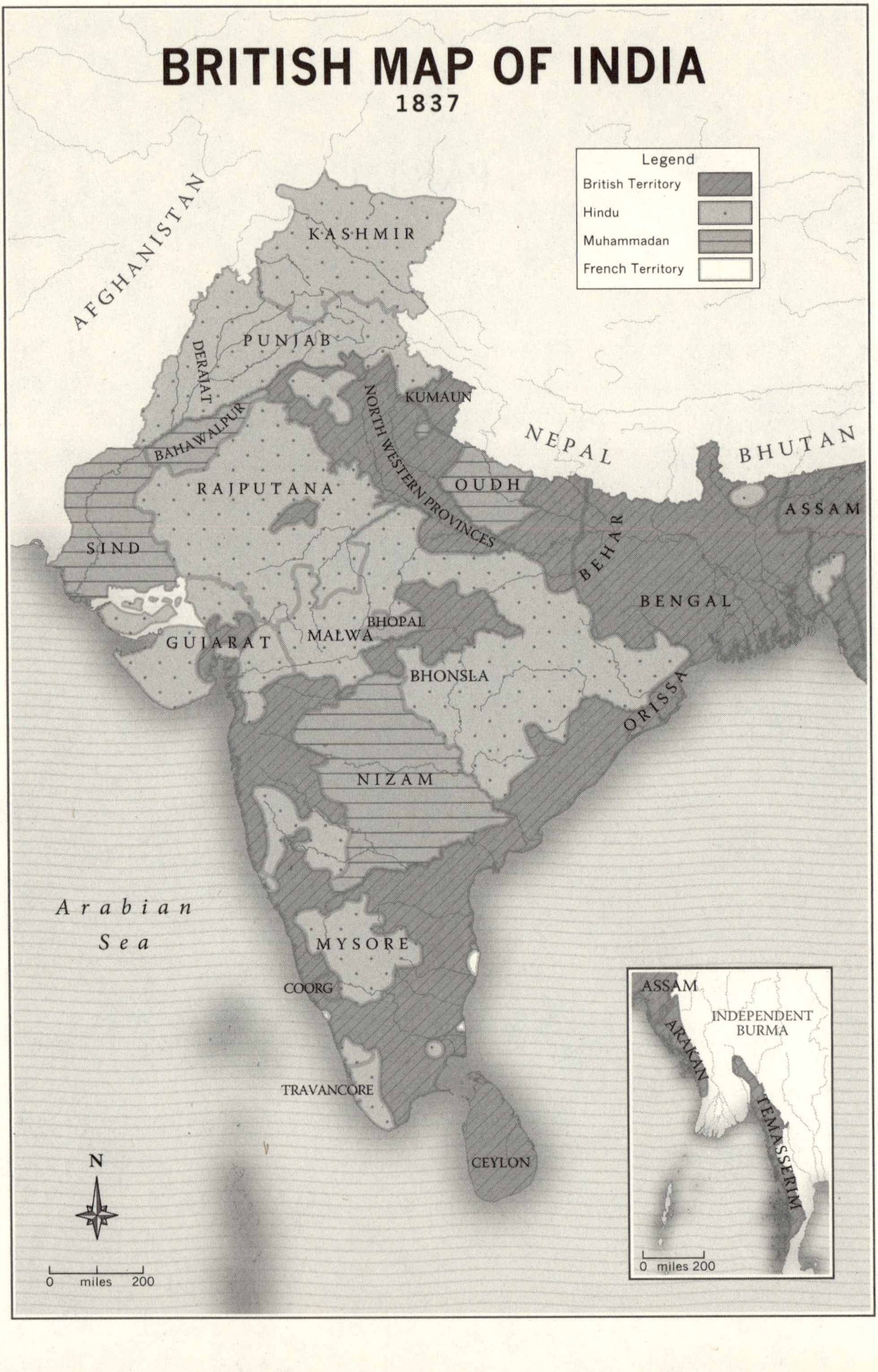
BRITISH MAP OF INDIA
1837
Legend
British Territory
Hindu
Muhammadan
French Territory
AFGHANISTAN
KASHMIR
PUNJAB
DERAJAT
BAHAWALPUR
KUMAUN
NORTH WESTERN PROVINCES
NEPAL
BHUTAN
ASSAM
RAJPUTANA
OUDH
SIND
BEHAR
BENGAL
GUJARAT
MALWA
BHOPAL
BHONSLA
ORISSA
NIZAM
Arabian Sea
MYSORE
COORG
TRAVANCORE
CEYLON
N
0 miles 200
ASSAM
INDEPENDENT BURMA
ARAKAN
TEMASSERIM
0 miles 200

CHAPTER 1

A Prince in Name

1838–1848

> *'My ancestors and the British Government made Treaties and the Government kept all the country, all the money, and left me nothing but the old and useless paper.'* Humayun Jah

Located 150 miles north of Kolkata, Murshidabad was once the capital of East India, and a focus for trade with the rest of India and other parts of the world. Granted a charter by Elizabeth I in 1600 for sole trading rights in India, the East India Company had become by the eighteenth century the world's most powerful and profitable commercial company, dealing in spices, silk, cotton, gold, silver and opium. By 1750 it had its own substantial army. When Robert Clive, Governor of the East India Company in the Bengal area, visited the city for the first time after the Battle of Plassey and appropriation of Bengal in 1757, he wrote in sheer surprise that 'the city of Murshidabad is as extensive, populous and rich as the city of London with this difference: That there are individuals in the first possessing infinitely greater wealth than the whole of the Lombard Street [the financial hub of London] joined together.'

Sadly, Murshidabad did not stay the power it was, and the city's pre-eminent status quickly declined under East India Company rule. The company was answerable first, foremost and solely to its shareholders. As with most corporations operating in this way and on this scale, it had no interest in the fair governance of East India or its wellbeing. Not long after the East India Company established itself in the region, as historian

William Dalrymple comments in his book *The Anarchy*, its rule 'quickly turned into the straight-forward pillage of Bengal and the rapid transfer westwards of its wealth'.

Today, Murshidabad is a small and dusty town with a population that has rapidly diminished from 250,000 in 1757 to just over 42,000. Remnants of its grand history remain in the entrance gates, mosques, decaying Mughal palaces, Jain, Sikh and Hindu temples, colonial residential buildings and the separate graveyards for the Nawabs of Murshidabad and their families, and the Dutch, French and British colonialists. The Hazarduari Palace, 'the Palace of a Thousand Doors', dominates the city, now as a state museum visited by crowds of tourists and schoolchildren.

The palace was designed by Scottish military engineer Lieutenant-Colonel Duncan MacLeod for the Nawab Nazim Humayun Jah in 1830. It was built in the European style and intended to impress as a grand venue for hosting durbars (court meetings) and other ceremonial events – rather than for domestic living. Inside and out, the palace declared the Murshidabad family's status as Indian royalty while implying equality with European royalty and aspirations. There are several galleries where paintings of various British officials hang – including a life-size portrait of King William IV – alongside the ancestral portraits of the Nawabs of Bengal, back to Mir Jafar, whom Robert Clive had installed as Nawab Nazim following the Battle of Plassey and the defeat of the then-ruling Nawab, Siraj ud-Dualah, Mir Jafar's nephew.

Among the paintings in the Hazarduari Palace is the earliest surviving image of my great-grandfather, the last Nawab of Bengal, who was also known as Mansour Ali Khan. It was painted to mark the completion of the Hazarduari Palace in Murshidabad in December 1837, when Mansour Ali Khan would have been seven years old. In this picture he wears embroidered red and white silk robes and a large gold necklace, identical to the one worn by his father, Humayun Jah, who stands beside him. My great-grandfather is watching his father intently.

Painted by William Henry Florio Hutchisson and titled *Handing over the Hazarduari Palace*, this painting hangs today in the entrance hall of the palace. It shows a crowded scene of featureless and indistinct Indians

Hazarduari Palace (The Palace of a Thousand Doors), Murshidabad

in white robes and turbans standing behind six seated Britons, four of whom are wearing military uniforms. Presumably their presence is intended to honour the occasion and the owner of the palace, but the British men appear to be engaged in rather desultory conversation with one another and are paying little attention to the ceremonial signing in the background. On the right side of the portrait, Lt-Col Duncan McLeod, the British officer who designed and supervised the construction of the palace, is seated at a small table holding a large scroll which is being signed, or perhaps sealed, by the splendidly robed Nawab Humayun Jah.

Less than ten months after the palace was completed, Humayun Jah was dead, aged just twenty-eight. Despite the fact that as a Muslim the Nawab abstained from alcohol, the British doctor blamed his death on over-indulgence in alcohol and luxurious living, although the usual palace rumours of poisoning circulated. And so, on his eighth birthday, 29 October 1838, Mansour Ali Khan was officially pronounced the new Nawab Nazim of Bengal, Bihar and Orissa: an area of East India almost three times the size of the British Isles. His ascension to the throne took place four months after Queen Victoria's coronation.

Almost immediately after Mansour Ali Khan's installation, he received a letter from the British Administration in Calcutta (the name by which today's Kolkata was known for practically all the period covered by this book). It congratulated him on his accession to the 'throne of his ancestors' and affirmed that 'the dignity and honour of the illustrious house you now represent will ever be an object of care and solicitude to this Government'. Some dozen volumes of laboriously handwritten files in the India Office Records demonstrate that, both before and during the young Nawab's childhood, and throughout his entire life, the British government's 'care and solicitude' was indeed unremitting.

Despite remaining the titular head of government for the region, the Nawab had very little power. After the Battle of Plassey, the Nawabs of Bengal had become in reality puppet princes. Robert Clive had installed Mir Jafar as Nawab, with a promised annual stipend of 5.3 million rupees (today equivalent to approximately 82 million pounds), drawn from taxes and revenue in Bengal, Bihar and Orissa. The East India Company at the same time exacted large payments for damages to people and property in Calcutta, salaries for the British troops, and 'gifts' to Clive himself. The real power was now held by the East India Company, which was in turn partly controlled by a British Parliamentary Council, with a Governor-General based in Bengal, appointed by the British Parliament and backed by a substantial army of British and Indian troops supervised by British officers.

Although Warren Hastings had moved the capital of East India to Calcutta in 1772, a British Agent to the Governor-General remained posted in Murshidabad. His role was specifically to oversee the management of the Nawab's estates and family. The Agent's salary and expenses, and those of his servants and clerks, were paid out of the Nawab's funds, as were all the allowances paid to the Nawab's numerous relatives and servants. Under the East India Company's management, the pension paid by the British administration from its Indian revenues to the Nawab decreased with each generation, often because the heir was not yet an adult, and the Agent deemed it unnecessary to allow him the full pension during his minority. Somehow the full amount was rarely reinstated when each new young Nawab's majority was reached. By the time Mansour Ali Khan, the ninth Nawab after Mir Jafar, ascended to the throne in 1838, the pension had been reduced from 5.3 million to 330,000 rupees, equivalent today to about three million pounds.

Mansour Ali Khan's father, Humayun Jah, had complained that his predecessors had made Treaties and the Government kept all the country, all the money, and left him nothing but the old and useless paper [treaties]. When the British Agent claimed that the Nizamut (the house of Murshidabad) was now degraded, Humayun Jah responded that this was because the English Government had broken its faith.

Humayun Jah had been a tall, proud, ambitious man, determined to ensure that his status was respected. Indeed, towards the end of his reign, he enquired several times about the possibility of being titled King (rather than Nawab), since the wealthy King of Oudh in a neigbouring province had been so honoured. The British Agent and Governor-General neither welcomed nor encouraged this suggestion. However, in 1836 the Nawab was pleased to receive from William IV, together with a life-size portrait of the king, a letter conferring on him the Grand Cross of the Hanoverian Royal Order. This was an honour created by George IV in his role as King of Hanover. Other recipients of the order included the Duke of Wellington, the explorer Sir John Franklin, and the King's own sons. The Nawab saw the order as confirmation from King William of his own high status and unique position in India and in the eyes of the world. The order might not be a hereditary title that induced the worldwide respect that 'King' would have secured, but Humayun Jah considered his position, and that of his family, assured.

When Humayun Jah's death was announced, the Governor-General's Agent in Murshidabad, Colonel James Caulfield, in consultation with the Governor-General and other British officials in Calcutta, immediately took steps to oversee the new young Nawab's education and control his finances. Caulfield emphasised the need to 'retrieve the affairs of the Nizamut from the state of disorganisation into which they had been suffered to fall by the late Nazim'. He also pointed out that, since in 1833 the Agent had become 'the channel through which all members of the [Murshidabad] family and their dependents receive their stipends', there was no need to appoint a Regent. Thus the British government gained even closer control of the young Nawab's affairs.

Ever since the Mughal conquests of North India in the sixteenth century, Persian had become the *lingua franca* for trade and government throughout the continent. It was also the court language in the Delhi imperial court as well as provincial palaces such as Bengal. Now, the East India Company officials and the British government sought to replace Persian with English as the official language. As the secretary to the Board of Control of India, Thomas Babington Macaulay, put it in his 1835 Minute on Education to the Governor-General's Council, through encouraging upper-class Indians to obtain a command of English the British could 'create a class who may be interpreters between us and the millions whom we govern; a class of persons, Indian in blood and colour, but English in taste, in opinions, in morals, and in intellect'.

For the 'Oriental branch' of the boy's education, Colonel Caulfield appointed Meerza Ali Azeem to tutor Arabic and Persian. In accordance with the new emphasis on a European education, Caulfied recruited Felix Seddon, a professor of Oriental Languages at King's College, London, for 'the more important duty of instructing [the Nawab] in English literature and European Science'. It was a well-paid job for Seddon, whose salary was 1,000 rupees a month, equivalent today to approximately £10,000. In comparison, Meerza Ali Azeem was paid 250 rupees each month to tutor the Nawab in Arabic and Persian – just one quarter the payment that Seddon received. Despite this it would seem that the tutors had a harmonious relationship with one another, and in one letter Seddon expresses considerable admiration for the learning and integrity of the Persian tutor, who he claimed was 'as good a man as I ever met and a sterling first-rate scholar'.

In the view of Robert Pemberton, who succeeded Caulfield as Government Agent in 1839, it was Seddon's role to offset the influence of Mansour Ali Khan's Indian tutors and steer him away from the women and eunuchs in the *zenana*, that part of the building reserved for them. Lord Auckland, then Governor-General of India, requested that Pemberton keep a diary 'showing how His Highness the Nazim … passes his time', recording his progress in his studies, and noting 'any particular traits of his general disposition and character' which might strike him as worthy of notice. Pemberton took it upon himself to examine the young Nawab every Monday morning in both English and Persian. 'Too much aware of his status', 'proud, unsteady and volatile' was Pemberton's report of the nine-year-old Nawab's character in 1839.

Those long and laboriously written reports from Seddon and Pemberton about Mansour Ali Khan's progress reveal varying degrees of conflict between the Agent, the tutors, and – above all – the young Nawab, who at first strongly resisted the insistence on learning English. 'Since his father did not learn English, his grandfather did not speak it, none of his ancestors spoke it, why should he?' Seddon reported him demanding. These Englishmen, these *angrezi*, had usurped his father's place, insisting on their right to direct and supervise him, but speaking a language he did not understand. Perhaps it is the voice of his Persian tutor, or his grandmother, we hear ventriloquised in his defiant questioning of the requirement to learn English.

Implicit, and sometimes explicit, in many of the reports and letters written by the British officials is an intimation of the different factions and interests striving to influence the young Nawab and keep him on side: his Persian tutors, the *molvis* (doctors of Islamic law) and other Muslim members of court concerned that he keep the faith of his fathers; his grandmother who seems to have been less willing than his mother to accommodate the British; his cousins and uncles; the eunuchs in the court, one of whom, an African, had been a respected member of the household and an advisor to the family for over sixty years. Pemberton reflected a typical British official distrust of those areas still managed by the women of the family when he complained that an 'adverse influence is still secretly exercised by those who have hitherto possessed a most pernicious influence over the minds and actions of his predecessors in office'. In the end it was the British who assumed the right to exercise major control over the child, and they had the power to do so.

The feelings and views of the young Nawab, his mother and relatives are rarely mentioned. Their language was Persian or Urdu, not English, and only the most formal documents in those languages have been preserved. It is the British records that have survived and which contain and interpret the Nawab's story in the light of British attitudes and assumptions, so that it is only by reading between the lines that we can try to glimpse his reactions to them.

Seddon was, as well as the first, perhaps the most sympathetic of Mansour Ali Khan's English tutors. As an orientalist who understood several Asian languages and had read a wide range of Persian and Arabic literature he was better able to communicate with the boy. He was sensitive to the Nawab's unique position and various pressures, conceding that 'one so young and so sensible that he is "monarch of all he surveys" cannot be treated quite like other children who feel more their obligation to do as they are bid'. His philosophy as a teacher was to follow the method of education advocated by the Swiss educational reformer Johann Heinrich Pestalozzi, a system that adjusted to and developed the child's innate qualities rather than imposing a pre-formulated curriculum. Several of his reports comment on the boy's interest in art, noting that, although he was often restless and recalcitrant during other lessons, he was willing to spend hours talking about pictures. Seddon wrote, 'He will look for hours at pictorial embellishments, and examine with a keenness of perception truly wonderful every part and atom of a picture with never ceasing enquiry and the utmost interest.'

Although the young Nawab at first made slow and reluctant progress in his ability to speak and write English, he quickly became proficient at writing Persian, and clearly enjoyed doing so. An early tutorial report comments that he would frequently stay on after his afternoon writing lesson 'and take up the reed and write his Persian copies, his little fingers sometimes forming strokes that would do little discredit to the most practised penman'.

There is a telling incident relayed in one report illustrating the frustration of both teacher and pupil, the boy's resentment and childish anger, as well as his need for affection and attachment. During the hot season, Seddon had forbidden the young Nawab to leave the palace in order to go out in the sun or to the *zenana* (which would be cooler and better ventilated), and he had locked the door. The young Nawab, on discovering this, had 'walked to the other end of the room, swelling with impotent rage'. However, within a few minutes, he apologised, saying 'I have behaved very ill, but you are my good tutor and you will I hope forgive me.' This sequence of events – the imposition of restrictions, the show of rebellion and frustration, followed by the capitulation to a paternal British representative – would be repeated throughout Mansour Ali Khan's life. It wasn't an isolated incident and throughout his education the Nawab clearly felt the burden of his position, even as a child. During another lesson the Nawab's Persian tutor sought to impress upon the young boy the importance of acquiring greater knowledge now because of the responsibilities he would take on at a later age. 'If this is the case, I will resign – I will give up the Nizamut,' was his reaction. It is the response of a small child of whom too much is demanded.

Robert Pemberton's death in June 1840 brought a change of regime. The new Agent, Major-General Felix Vincent Raper, had previously spent more than forty years in the Bengal Army; he considered Seddon too lax in his discipline. Seddon was transferred to become Principal of the Nizamut College, established in Murshidabad to offer schooling to the lesser members and dependents of the royal family. He was replaced by a new and stricter superintendent of studies, Captain G. D. Showers, who engaged James Cooper as the English tutor. Under the supervision of Showers, the now ten-year-old Nawab was required to study English, history, science, mathematics and geography from seven in the morning till one in the afternoon, and then, after a brief meal break, resume lessons in Persian till half-past five. In addition he was expected to go horse riding and take other physical exercise from daybreak till seven in the morning and from half-past five till half-past six in the evening, supervised by an English tutor. Following all these activities, Captain Showers reported, the pupil was 'too much exhausted to sit up at night and retires to his mother's *deori* [apartments]'.

Showers remarked somewhat defensively that he felt it necessary to allow a large portion of the afternoon to the Nawab's four Muslim instructors, saying he had done so because he considered it 'of importance that a Nobleman of his rank should possess a full share of Oriental acquirements … and also on account of the jealousy and suspicion which would be created by any appearance of partiality for a course of English instruction'. He noted with approval that the principal instructor, 'Meer Alee Azem', 'is a learned man, and tho' a recluse and a Sheea, he possesses sufficient liberality of principal to aid and assist me in all my views'. Nevertheless, Showers feared that any discussion of religion between himself and the young Nawab might be tricky, and so avoided including it as a formal part of his instruction. He hoped that science lessons would gradually lead the boy away from 'superstitious beliefs in Omens, Auguries, and Supernatural spirits'. Eventually he hoped to 'install in his mind those more exalted Notions of Omnipotence, and of an over ruling Providence'. That an 'exalted Notion of Omnipotence and an over ruling Providence' is fundamental to Islam seems to have escaped Captain Showers's notice.

Mansour Ali Khan's British supervisors ensured that he was more thoroughly acquainted with recent and contemporary English literature than boys of his own age in Britain, where the emphasis was on reading the Latin and Greek classics. In India, as in Ireland, it was British policy in the mid-nineteenth century to inculcate English culture and language. At the same time, however, the British sought to preserve the Nawab's status as Indian royalty, and as an ornament to the British Empire. As the Bengali historian J. Datta Gupta remarks, the Agent for the Governor-General had the difficult job of managing the Nawab's court and household, which was 'a latent threat to the Company's Government but which nevertheless had to be pampered and preserved, on administrative expedience, in an aura of respectability and splendour'.[1]

An August 1842 letter from Showers to the Governor-General's secretary expresses clearly this process of quarantining the Nawab against political contagion from any source that did not have the best interests of the British Empire at heart. He declares that, when he took over as Agent in 1840, 'the mind of the Nazim was essentially native, he was entirely under the Guidance of his relatives – suspicion of European [sic] was apparent in his manner'. Although the boy had been removed from the guardianship of his grandmother to that of

1 Gupta, 'Introduction', *West Bengal Records: Murshidabad Nizamut, Vol. II, 1834 –1870*, p.iii.

his mother, who seemed, or perhaps pretended, to be more willing to cooperate with the British Agent, Showers was anxious about what he claimed to be the very harmful influence of the mother's palace. Major-General Raper agreed that it was desirable to separate the boy from his mother and move him into a different building. Originally it had been agreed with his mother that her son should live with her until he was fourteen, but Raper and Showers determined that would be better to get him away from her as soon as he turned twelve. Showers and Raper decided to move the twelve-year-old Nawab and selected servants into a separate residence, the Mubarak Manzil, a palace and garden that had been bought and renovated by the Nawab's father in 1830.

Mansour Ali Khan's mother, Rais-un Nisa (also known as Dhoolin Jah Begum) had been a dancer and singer before her marriage, and seems to have been of independent and strong character, keen to see her son well educated in readiness for his future position as Nawab Nizam. But she was also willing to challenge the British officials, a trait which, together with her former profession, no doubt encouraged their view that she was not a good influence on her son. British Agent Colonel Mackenzie's wife Helen later described her as 'a very perverse person, who having been a dancing girl, stands to arms with a peculiar alertness in defence of her dignity and decorum'.[1]

Distrust of Indian women and the world of the *zenana* was common among British officials, as was shown a decade later when, following the annexation of the Punjab in 1849, the ten-year-old Maharaja Duleep Singh was removed from his mother and taken to live with Dr John Login, under whose influence he converted to Christianity. During the mid-nineteenth century, liaisons between British men and 'native' women, once almost accepted as natural, were increasingly regarded as shameful, something to be shunned and hidden. Very few of the women in the Nawab's household would have spoken any English. Did this contribute to suspicions of subversive talk and thought outside the British sphere of influence? British officers were certainly concerned about the mysterious world of Indian women and what happened

1 Helen MacKenzie, *Storms and Sunshine of a Soldier's Life, Vol II* (Edinburgh: David Douglas, 1884), p.219.

within their realm, about which they knew so little. It was the view of Richard Burton, the explorer and translator of the *Thousand and One Nights*, that Indian women were contemptuous of European men and found them sexually incompetent.[1]

We have seen the attempts to quarantine the young prince, but the files also contain much evidence of the British 'pampering' him. They allowed him expensive purchases, including many fine horses, which the teenaged Mansour Ali Khan liked inspecting, riding and racing. He also greatly enjoyed billiards and was a skilful player. Showers ensured that a billiard table was installed in the Mubarak Manzil, and encouraged the boy to become involved in planning extensions and decorations for the palace and gardens.

Yet, now that he had been moved away from his mother's apartments, the twelve-year-old boy's life was a lonely one, for he had no brothers, and was discouraged from spending time with boys 'below' his social status, unless they were British. One rather confused report tells of an incident that took place with the young Nawab and several teenaged, naval ensigns who had recently arrived. There was a scuffle between Mansour Ali Khan and a lad named Barlow, who hit him with a shoe. Aware that to be struck by a shoe could be regarded as a serious insult to a Muslim, let alone a Muslim Prince, the British officials who had produced the ensigns as temporary playmates were effusively apologetic. The young Nawab shrugged off the incident as mere play, and the report seems to suggest that he was uncomfortable that so much was made of it.

The India Office files for this period contain invoices for the books ordered for the Nawab. From these one gathers a fairly clear view both of his educational development and the curriculum the British considered appropriate for a young Indian prince. In his early teens he was studying Euclid's *Geometry*, *A History of Greece*, *A Life of Wellington*, the rules of cricket and other sports, and reading the collected poems of Byron. The reports note that he enjoyed reading the *Thousand and One Nights* both in Persian and in English translation, that his reading and comprehension of English advanced quite well after the first two or

1 Richard Burton as cited by Ronal Hyam, *Empire and Sexuality: The British Experience* (Manchester: Manchester University Press, 1991), p. 117.

three years, and that he was also afflicted with a stammer. Nevertheless, Showers reported in October 1843 that, when the then thirteen-year-old Nawab could be heard speaking in another room, 'his voice can scarcely be distinguished from that of an Englishman'. An examination report noted that he gave an expressive reading and sensible analysis of Tennyson's 'The Lady of Shalott'. As Mansour Ali Khan glanced down to the river flowing beneath the palace windows, perhaps vague comparisons with the Lady's plight occurred to him as he found himself reluctantly confined to his classroom with the assiduous Captain Showers: 'No time hath she to sport and play.'

Showers had expressed the hope that his educational regime, and his conversations with the young Nawab, would prove 'so agreeable to him, as shall lead him hereafter to associate the name of European gentlemen with many happy hours of his early years'. He did not perceive the boy's growing resentment of the regime and restrictions he imposed. 'I am obliged to do all that Captain Showers tells me,' the fourteen-year-old Nawab declared, 'because if I do not, he will not allow me to visit my mother.' Showers clearly thought his regime was rather more popular with the Nawab than it appears to have actually been. A letter from Showers to the Governor-General in 1844 expresses surprise that the Nawab's mother refused to see him, and later that the Nawab had asked the Governor-General's Agent to fire him.

As the young Nawab grew older, the struggles by his British guardians to maintain that 'aura of respectability' became more difficult and more frantic. There are letters berating him for keeping bad company, for visiting the bazaars, for encouraging relatives whose loyalty was questionable, for spending too much time in the women's quarters. This concern about visiting bazaars doubtless arose from courtesan households having had a presence there. Here, in addition to gaining and enjoying sexual experience, the young Nawab could appreciate the company of women dancers and singers, listen to poetry recitations in Persian and Urdu, and relax in a world far away from British scrutiny. Rather like Japanese geisha, the courtesans, known as *taiwafs*, were often highly educated and trained performers, sometimes writing their own poetry as well as reciting and discussing the poetry of others. And like the geisha they were independent women, controlling their own households and lives, although unlike the geisha the *taiwaf*'s status could sometimes be that of a mistress as well as an entertainer.

In the past young nawabs-to-be were sent to these *taiwafs* to learn good manners and become more sophisticated. Here they could be taught to appreciate good music and literature, and perhaps even practise the art of writing ghazals (a form of ode perfected by medieval Persian poets). This was the world to which the Nawab's mother had belonged before her marriage to Humayun Jah.

The agents in charge of his affairs were anxious to discourage Mansour Ali Khan's visits to the bazaars, where matters proceeded entirely independently of British influence. They were also no doubt distrustful of the bazaars on account of the sexual experiences that took place there. British officials were often puritanical in their attitude to sexual intercourse and saw themselves as upholding muscular Christian morals in India. Acceptance within courtesan households of same-sex relationships would also have been a cause of worry to them. Equally of concern to the British, the bazaars were a world where class and social boundaries were often blurred. As the Indian academic and author Ruth Vanita notes, 'While first marriages were arranged between equal-status families, men sometimes entered romantic second or third marriages with courtesans.'[1]

Concerned to keep the teenaged boy 'respectable', Major-General Raper now involved himself in negotiations for a suitable wife for the young Nawab. In early 1843, when the Nawab was still only thirteen, Raper approached the wealthy King of Oudh, ruler of the province adjacent to Bengal and Bihar, for a possible alliance with one of his daughters. After studying the young Nawab's lineage and assets, the King declined the offer. A marriage with Shams-i-Jehan was then negotiated, she being an aristocrat and a descendant of Mir Jafar's brother. Mansour Ali Khan was formally betrothed to her in 1845, at the age of fourteen. Their marriage was celebrated in May 1846.

Just three months after this marriage, one of the Nawab's mother's

---

1 Ruth Vanita, *Gender, Sex, and the City: Urdu Rekhti Poetry, 1780–1870* (Delhi: Orient Black Swan, 2015), p.227.

servants bore him a son. The servant was an Abyssinian slave girl named Hasina. The Nawab's mother, Rais-un Nisa, had several Abyssinians among her servants, originally purchased as slaves, probably from Ethiopia or Eritrea. Abyssinian or 'Habeshi' slaves were more expensive than ones from the Deccan. As in seventeenth- and eighteenth-century Britain households, African servants and slaves were something of a status symbol.[1]

The news of the birth of Nawab's first son with Hasina was greeted with dismay, not only by Shams-i-Jehan but also by the British Agent. Then, in January 1847, when the Nawab was still only sixteen, the birth of his second son (this one with Shams-i-Jehan) was announced. Soon afterwards a letter from Cecil Beadon, the Under-Secretary to the Governor of Bengal, encouraged the Agent in Murshidabad to try 'to divert the Nawab Nazim's thoughts from his domestic engagements, by rendering his studies as attractive as possible, and by engaging him in manly and healthy recreation'.

The Nawab's passionate involvement with Hasina, and his insistence on acknowledging their first child as his eldest son and heir, was to create bitter conflict with his first wife, Shams-i-Jehan Begum, her children and descendants, and the British government, all of whom maintained that Hasina and her children had no legal status. Interestingly, there is almost no reference in the records to Hasina's status as a former slave, nor to her identity as an African. What does bother the British officials is that she can definitely be categorised as 'lower class'. The Nawab's personal fund was used to pay stipends to his expanding harem and family, and the Agent ensured that the stipends paid to each concubine and her children from the fund were considerably less than the stipend paid to his official wives. Even after Hasina had become the Nawab's wife, in a formal marriage ceremony several years later, the Agent was reluctant to grant her an allowance equivalent to that of the first wife

1 In traditional Muslim law, a son is legitimate if begotten by a man and his wife, or a man and his own slave. Although 'wife' implies marriage, marriage may be entered into without any specific ceremony. For further information about domestic slavery in India with special reference to the Murshidabad households, see Indrani Chatterjee, *Slavery and the Household in Bengal, 1770–1880*, PhD Dissertation, School of Oriental and African Studies, University of London, July 1996.

since, in his view, Hasina, now known as Mehr Leka Begum, did not merit a stipend equivalent to that of the aristocratic first wife.

Throughout the young Nawab's childhood, the agents who controlled his affairs regarded his best interests as subordinate to those of the British Empire. Two full-length portraits of the young Nawab in the Hazarduari Palace, probably painted when he was eighteen and so had reached his majority, suggest the conflicting identities that survived his childhood and youth. One portrait presents him as the archetypal ruler figure, his stance a perfect replica of his father's as he stands left hand on hip, right hand placed on a table with a scroll written in Persian. He wears a rich scarlet, jewelled robe, a white turban, and gives us a searching look below finely arched eyebrows. The second portrait shows him seated, dressed in white silk, charmingly elegant and relaxed, looking away from the viewer and into the distance. But the Nawab would soon become aware, despite the image of glamour and status represented by these portraits, that his position was under further threat from a new Governor-General, as well as a new British Agent who had recently arrived to take over his affairs.

CHAPTER 2

Money, Power and Politics

1849–1859

'There is not a single prince, state, or potentate, great or small, in India, with whom [the East India Company] have come into contact, whom they have not sold, [nor] a single treaty they have ever made, which they have not broken. [Neither is there] a single prince or state, who ever put any trust in the Company, who is not utterly ruined.'
Edmund Burke, 'Speech on Fox's East India Bill', 1783[1]

Edmund Burke's denunciation of the East India Company and its treatment of Indian rulers was indeed applicable to the experience of successive Nawabs of Bengal. However, Burke does not mention the greater suffering that was experienced by the poorer Indians in the provinces of Bengal, Bihar and Orissa from 1769 to 1770. It was caused principally by devastating famine, but was further exacerbated by the unrelenting tax collections by the East India Company. It is estimated that nearly 10 million workers and peasants died after a failure of crops in 1769 when the tax collectors and revenue officers of the East India Company continued to seize and store grain while extracting high taxes at the same rate as before, causing thousands of families to become destitute.

Charles Fox's East India Bill, which called for British administration of Indian territories controlled by the East India Company, was defeated in Parliament in 1783, and so the Company continued its conquests and

1 Edmund Burke, 'Speech on Fox's East India Bill', 1 December 1783, *Selected Writings, Vol.IV.*

profiteering in India. Bengal had been only the starting point, and now many other states and principalities, small and large, were conquered by the East India Army. In each of these states the Company seized control of commerce, trading and taxation rights. Much land was cleared for the growing of cotton, tea and opium. It was a profitable army to serve in, with prize money and loot claimed by officers and soldiers.

In Murshidabad, first the Agent of the East India Company, and then the Agent representing the Governor-General, gained control of the administration of the Nawab's estates and family income and expenditure during his early years. Additionally, before 1821, the Indian Emperor in Delhi swore each new Nawab Nazim of Bengal into office. This link was broken in 1821, after which date each new Nawab had to be confirmed by the Governor-General of India instead. Thus, for the majority of royal families in India, the British sovereign replaced the Indian Emperor as the supreme authority. In Bengal, as in many other principalities, this authority also included acting as regent for monarchs who had succeeded to their thrones as minors.

Mansour Ali Khan had just turned sixteen when, in December 1846, Henry Whitelock Torrens replaced Major-General Raper as British Agent in Murshidabad. Unlike most other Agents, Torrens did not have a military background. He had arrived in India in November 1828, when he was twenty-two years old, and had been employed first as a clerk and then as a secretary with the East India Company in Meerut and Calcutta. The author of a prose translation of the *Thousand and One Nights,* as well as poetry, reviews, essays and not-very-short stories, Torrens served as Vice-President to the Asiatic Society of Bengal and saw himself as a man of letters. His was a florid style, laborious in its humour, and ambitious in its scope and range of literary reference. His biographer, James Hume, although an ardent admirer of Torrens as a writer and friend, admits that Torrens possessed a 'rather unpleasant surface'. Hume described his manner as 'a little coxcombical' for 'a strong feeling of self-satisfaction was too often exhibited in every look and tone and gesture'.[1]

---

1 Henry W Torrens, *A Selection from the Writings, Prose and Poetical*, ed. James Hume. Calcutta: Le. Page and Co., 1854 2 vols. P.cix

Torrens bitterly resented being posted to Murshidabad as Agent, believing he had been 'shelved' by an antagonistic 'Bengal clique', and that this was 'a job any fool could do, an appointment in which he had little or nothing to do beyond seeing that things were kept straight in the petty court of the Nawab, an office which the most ordinary person might have filled'.[1] Among his essays are two published under the pseudonym of 'Mark Matthews', purporting to be from 'the worst station' in Bengal, and giving immensely detailed descriptions of hunting expeditions in the company of numerous English officials and a Nawab Nazim.

Torrens also wrote about his travels in Egypt, whose Muslims he found much preferable to those in India, contrasting the 'pure form of Islam' followed in Egypt with what he considered 'the corrupt bigotry of the Indian mussulman, inoculated as he is with so much of the separatist spirit of Hinduism'.[2] Acknowledging an understandable bitterness on the part of Indians towards the British, who were 'a nation proverbial historically for insolent and overbearing demeanour among conquered or dependent races', Torrens at one and the same time condemns and displays the 'insolent and overbearing'[3] attitudes common in the reports and letters of British officials in India.

As a keen orientalist and translator of one of the Nawab's favourite books, Torrens had quickly won the trust of the young man. Torrens persuaded him to move his government securities amounting to nearly 2 million rupees (worth about £200,000 at the time, and equivalent to about 22 million pounds today) to a firm based in Calcutta. These securities were promptly cashed in by the firm and placed in an account under Torrens's name. When Torrens died six years later of dysentery, Mansour Ali Khan discovered that all the money was missing, and so too were many of the jewels belonging to the family and to the estate, including the Hanoverian Cross given to him by William IV. Some of these jewels later turned out to be in the possession of Torrens's mistress, Nina Baxter, who had been an actress in Calcutta's Sans Souci Theatre.

1 Torrens, pp. ci, cv

2 Torrens, 'Alexandria' in *A Selection from the Writings*, p. 77.

3 *Ibid.*

It was a terrible shock for the young Nawab to find that he had been so cynically betrayed and robbed, robbed moreover by a representative of the British government whose official role was to protect his interests.

Throughout the rest of his life, Mansour Ali Khan unceasingly contested the British government's handling of his finances, and what he saw as their appropriation of them and betrayal of the original treaty made with Mir Jafar. However, the then-Governor-General of India, Lord Dalhousie, appointed in 1848, had little sympathy with these claims. Under his rule, the Punjab and lower Burma were annexed, as well as other princely states, and the rule of the East India Company greatly expanded. Although Dalhousie sought to modernise India, and was responsible for the construction of railways and roads which could make more efficient the transport of British goods, his critics, including Mansour Ali Khan, claimed that he laid the foundations of the Indian Rebellion of 1857 and led the final transformation of profitable commercial operations in India into a money-losing colonial administration.

In Dalhousie's view, the very existence of Indian princes was a threat to British authority, and on behalf of the British government he laid claim to any lands or estates that did not have a direct heir when the title-holder died. He rejected the Nawab's claim that the annual stipend of 1 million 6,000 rupees (worth today about 10 million pounds), paid to him for his private use as originally agreed by the East India Company, was hereditary – although no one had previously questioned its payment to the Nawab Nazims who succeeded Mir Jafar.

Dalhousie also held the twenty-two-year-old Nawab responsible when, during a hunting party in 1853, two thieves died following a severe beating by his servants. Two servants were charged with murder but, when brought to trial, were found not guilty by the Indian Supreme Court in Calcutta. Ignoring this judgment, and seizing an opportunity to tighten his control, Dalhousie ordered the Nawab to sack the servants, and insisted that British police must accompany all future hunting parties. He also revoked treaty rights accorded by the East India Company, and several privileges traditionally conferred on Indian and other royalty, such as exemption from appearance in civil court. On a personal note, the Nawab deeply resented the loss of status implied in the Governor-General's reduction of his traditional nineteen-gun salute on official occasions to thirteen guns – so much so that he avoided any occasions that would have called for such salutes. Finally, the Nawab was also denied further supervision of the Nizamat Deposit Fund, which existed to cover expenses for the Murshidabad estate and public institutions. Control of this large portion of the Nawab's money had now passed to the very agency under whose remit he had just been so outrageously defrauded.

Nevertheless, the Nawab did not hesitate to supply elephants and members of his private guard to aid the British in suppressing the Santhal peasant rebellion in northern Murshidabad in 1855. The Santhals had decided to resist the extortionate taxes and corrupt moneylending practices supported by the local *zamindars* (landowners) and the British government. Over 15,000 Santhal tribesmen were killed, and dozens of villages were demolished.

Two years later, when the so-called 'Mutiny' began in Berhampore, just a few miles from Murshidabad, a member of his household encouraged Mansour Ali Khan to join in the rising against the British and wave the flag of rebellion, assuring him that he would instantly find at least 5,000 men prepared to fight on his side. Instead, the Nawab opted again to support the British, providing soldiers, boats, guns, elephants, camels and horses to help suppress the uprising. Given his disputes with the British one might have expected a different response. Indeed, he always insisted that Dalhousie was responsible for the rebellion. So why did Mansour Ali Khan not join the struggle for independence? Why did he choose to join with the British rather than his own people?

One reason may have been that he did not see the *sepoys* and peasants involved in the rebellion as 'his own people'. Rather, like many other Indian princes, he identified with the landowners whose property rights had been secured by the East India Company, and members of the aristocracy who, following the Santhal rising, saw the peasantry and *sepoys* (many of whom may have been dispossessed from their land) as a threat. It is also true that, from the Nawab's early childhood, the British in Murshidabad had cast themselves in a paternal role; they had replaced the father he had lost. Besides, he had come to admire and appreciate many aspects of British culture. And so the conflicts with the British bore a resemblance to the conflicts between a strict father and his sometimes-recalcitrant son; but patricide was unthinkable.

Or perhaps it was simply that the Nawab believed that the British were too powerful to be beaten, and it was in his interest to remain on their side. Such considerations would have been strengthened by the British conquest and annexation of the Punjab in 1849. Moreover, in 1856, Dalhousie had ordered the annexation of the neighbouring kingdom of Oudh (Awadh) on the grounds of misgovernment by Nawab Wajid Ali Shah. Doubtless Mansour Ali Khan also hoped, indeed expected, that his loyalty to the British would be repaid by the restoration of his hereditary pensions and rights, the pursuit of which became a focus of his activities in the second half of his life.

Such expectations were reinforced immediately after the suppression of the uprising. In August 1858 the British Parliament published the Government of India Act, abolishing shared power with the East India Company, with its distinct presidencies in Calcutta, Bombay and Madras, and its nominal subservience to Mughal rule. The last Mughal Emperor in Delhi was exiled to Burma, and his two sons and grandson murdered by Major William Hodson, a commander of the Light Cavalry, thus ending even the illusion of Mughal rule in India. Now all authority was invested in the British Crown, and a Viceroy responsible for all Indian subjects and territory replaced the Governor-General. The newly appointed Viceroy, Lord Canning, publicly thanked the Nawab for his assistance to the British, although he did not restore his exemption from court appearance.

The historian Kenneth Ballhatchet remarks on the perplexity among British officials with regard to social precedence in India at this time, following Queen Victoria's declaration on the rights, customs and religious beliefs of her Indian subjects, as well as the treaties made with Indian princes. The latter, she said, were 'Not members of the ruling race, yet they ruled by right of birth.' Yet British officials in India assumed that political and social hierarchies should correspond, and tried to make it clear through all kinds of ceremonial customs such as gun salutes and required dress that it was the British who belonged at the top.

Helen Mackenzie, who was the wife of the British Agent appointed to Murshidabad in 1858, recounts an episode that illustrates both the rigidity and the pettiness of the British determination to reinforce a sense of rank in the hierarchy. In 1859 her husband accompanied the Nawab to Calcutta in order to officially pay his respects to Lord Canning. However, a problem arose when it was discovered that the Nawab's shoes were neither European nor black, and Lord Canning insisted that black European shoes must be worn in his presence; the Nawab's dress slippers worn in Muslim courts were not acceptable. Nor could the requirement for black shoes be waived for Shi'i Muslims (who avoid wearing black except during the month of Muharram and other times of mourning). And so Mansour Ali Khan had to send out for a pair of black boots. He was also made to present a symbolic tribute of mohurs (gold coins) to the Viceroy, a tribute formally paid only to the Mughal Emperor of India in Delhi.

On this occasion, following his visit to Lord Canning, the Nawab was forced to remain in Calcutta for a further three weeks before the Viceroy deigned to return his visit, and then on condition that he 'did not speak on business', although the Nawab had much business he was very keen to discuss. However, on the day of his departure, the Nawab was pleased to receive an acknowledgement of his own relatively significant position in the hierarchy when the Viceroy sent a message letting him know that his right to a nineteen-gun salute had been restored.

Despite Canning's autocratic behaviour, relations between the British government and the Nawab seemed at first to become more equitable. The new British Agent for Murshidabad, Brigadier Colin Mackenzie, supported the Nawab's case, believing he had been shabbily and unjustly treated, and advocated that the personal stipend of £160,000 should be restored. However, the British government still refused to accept that the stipend was hereditary, and Mackenzie was reprimanded for his report on the Nawab's affairs.

Mackenzie and the Nawab's relationship during the first two years of

Mackenzie's appointment was reasonably friendly, although Mackenzie was a devout Christian and Mansour Ali Khan a devout Muslim. Mackenzie had been a hostage during the First Afghan War (1839–42) and took pride in being a man of honour who 'understood' the Afghans and obeyed his parole conditions when sent as an envoy to the political agent at Jellalabad. When Mackenzie returned to England in 1842 after the war, he had an imposing full-length portrait painted of himself wearing Afghan dress.

Mackenzie's actions as commander of a Sikh regiment during the Second Anglo-Sikh War (1848–49) had been rewarded by Lord Dalhousie, who appointed him a Brigadier-General in charge of a division in Hyderabad. Like Torrens, Mackenzie regarded the posting to Murshidabad as a demotion; unlike Torrens, he sought to fulfil his role as Agent in an upright and honourable way, even incurring the displeasure of his superiors in defending the Nawab's cause.

The Mackenzies found the Nawab amiable and attractive, but 'easily led',[1] although he proved to be not so easily led by Mackenzie. His court and retinue were indeed cosmopolitan: his Diwan, or chief financial minister, was a Bengali, his coachman a Scot from Aberdeen, his master of ceremonies a Persian, while the commandant of the Nawab's bodyguard was an Irishman. All were in attendance, and made their salaams to the Nawab, at a durbar held in the Hazarduari Palace soon after the Mackenzies' arrival in March 1858. Helen Mackenzie gives a vivid account of this durbar:

> The Brigadier gave [the Nawab] his arm (as to a lady) and led him in. He came up to be introduced to me, and then took his seat. He wore a plain white dress and turban, without a single ornament. His little sons all came to be introduced; they were covered with jewels, especially magnificent emeralds and pearls, then the ceremony began. Everyone of the Nawab's court presented him with *nazzar* or gift of homage, generally of money, which he took and handed to a deaf and dumb Abyssinian on

1 Helen Mackenzie, *Storms and Sunshine of a Soldier's Life* (Edinburgh: David Douglas, 1884), p. 192.

> his right hand. His relations he embraced, and they kissed his arms … A crowd of *chobdars* [attendants] at the end of the room continually shouted his titles… A filigree flower was offered to the Nawab, which he very courteously presented to me. At the conclusion he decorated the Agent with a sort of chain, made of gold tinsel ribbon, and sent similar ones, which the Agent then put over the heads of the ladies and officers. His Highness then bestowed chains with his own hands on everybody, and Major Mackenzie finally led him into the drawing room, where we sat and talked a little.[1]

Helen Mackenzie's biography of her husband gives glimpses of Mansour Ali Khan's life with his wives and children at this time. His first wife, Shams-i-Jehan Begum, whose marriage with the Nawab had been arranged by Major-General Raper, was aristocratic, pretty, but 'exceedingly bland', in Helen Mackenzie's view, while his second wife, Malika-uz Zamani Begum, appeared to be 'quite sickly'. Neither wife was able or willing to make any conversation with the Agent's wife, nor, it appeared, with the Nawab. They were, he told Helen Mackenzie, 'equal in rank and in his affection, except that the first had precedence', but they were not accustomed to speaking before superiors such as his sisters, his mother, or himself. He wished they would talk to him 'as English ladies do'. The children were more lively, although very well behaved. All were overseen by Darab Ali Khan, an eighty-year-old eunuch, originally from Africa.

The Nawab's pleasure in the company of English ladies who 'would talk to him' is glimpsed in another episode that Helen Mackenzie recounts. During a long safari, the Nawab refrained from hunting on a Friday, being 'exceedingly strict in observing the Musulman Sabbath', and so spent most of the day teaching her to play chess, as they sat on the floor of her carpeted tent.[2]

Mansour Ali Khan went to considerable trouble and expense to entertain and please the British officials stationed near Murshidabad,

---

1 *Storms and Sunshine,* pp.192–3.

2 *Storms and Sunshine*, pp.214–217.

and not just through hunting parties. On the festival of Bera, which takes place in the autumn on the banks of the Bhagiratha River to honour the river god, the Nawab gave a dinner party, and watched and conversed as the 'Christians' ate at his table, before all adjourned to watch a magnificent display of fireworks and illuminations. As Helen Mackenzie recalls the scene:

> It was a clear, still, dark night; a beautiful illumination like a fort was on the opposite bank of the river, and when the Behra, the procession of rafts of all sizes, made of plantain stems supported on earthen pots, came floating down the river bearing ships, castles, and palaces traced in coloured fire, some of them throwing up rockets as they passed, with other tiny ones like fiery swans, – the effect was magical.[1]

There were also the musical evenings, with performances of ghazals by professional male and female singers, and ragas played on sitars accompanied by intricate rhythms on the tabla. The Nawab and his courtiers would become immersed in the music, sometimes joining in the well-known ghazals, or murmuring 'wah, wah' in appreciation. Helen Mackenzie makes it clear that for Europeans like herself these long sessions – with the intricate but repetitive dances, stylised expressions, and endless variations – seemed interminable. It was with difficulty that they stifled yawns, or giggles, before leaving as soon as they could without giving offence.

As a break from their day-to-day duties the Mackenzies and other Britons preferred pig and tiger hunts. For these the Nawab provided forty or more elephants for the participants to make their journey, as well as tents and provisions for eight or more days, and multitudes of attendants. The elephants would advance in a line, wading across patches of mud, then swaying over the rough hard ground beyond, before crashing through the thick and tangled mass of vegetation. There was the roar and trumpeting of the elephants, the mahouts shouting '*Lugge! Lugge! Lugge!*', the squealing of boars as they broke cover and ran, or

1 *Storms and Sunshine*, pp.214–217.

were pierced by a spear thrown by a man galloping on horseback.

On such occasions, instead of his usual plain white tunic, Mansour Ali Khan donned a green silk coat and white muslin skullcap. He also wore his gold-rimmed spectacles, but upside down, as this apparently made it easier for shooting. And indeed, he proved himself to be a crack shot, on one occasion killing in one day a brace of partridges, several deer, and two boars as the line advanced, in addition to a tigress and one of her cubs.

But in 1861 the relationship between Colin Mackenzie and the Nawab turned sour, partly over the issue of who should control the Nawab's finances. Mackenzie thought highly of the Diwan, Raja Prosunnu Narain Deb, a Hindu Bengali. However, Mansour Ali Khan began to feel that the Diwan was not handling his affairs well, and, given his disastrous experience with Torrens, the close relationship between the British Agent and the Diwan increased his uneasiness. Further annoyed by what he regarded as impudence and lack of due respect, Mansour Ali Khan dismissed Raja Deb from his position as Diwan, and declared that the Nizamut affairs should from now on be handled by his two oldest sons (the sons of Hasina and Shams-i-Jehan).

Mackenzie insisted that the Nawab 'had no power to dismiss the Diwan without the consent of the British authorities', and that he was acting in defiance of the British government. In reply the Nawab claimed that the Diwan was insolent, incompetent and insubordinate, and alleged that he was misusing funds. The British Agent then refused to pay the Nawab's stipend, declaring that only the Diwan could authorise the payment. Mackenzie's letters to the Nawab at this point became both blunt and threatening. The apparently cordial relationship and show of respect for the Nawab were revealed to have been merely a very thin veneer, covering intense contempt and overt racism. Mackenzie wrote:

> But my office here is not only to protect the interests of the Nizamut, but also by advice and by other means (if necessary) to keep you, the Rais, and the inferior members of your family, male and female, from committing gross errors and follies, alike injurious to yourselves and scandalous in the eyes of the

> British Government, who protects you, and without whose protection and favour, your family would in a very short time principally through the utter absence in themselves of true dignity, commonsense, and honourable principals of action, fall to ruin, and be swallowed up by the population of the City of Moorshedabad who are notoriously the scum and refuse of Bengal.[1]

After this extraordinary diatribe, combining outright insult and blatant threat, Mackenzie went on to mention gossip in the Bazaar about the Nawab's disreputable behaviour, and particularly warned him: 'It remains [to be seen] what view the Supreme Government will take of your having put yourself so completely within the hands of your mother.' He also reminded the Nawab that the Agent carried 'the full authority of the Governor-General and Council, and that in defying the Agent you have literally defied the British Government'. Moreover, he lamented the Nawab's adherence to Shi'i Muslim rather than Sunni Muslim practice and belief.

The Nawab's response to missives such as this from Mackenzie, as well as to earlier British Agents who paid him insufficient respect, was to limit all further correspondence to the Persian language. The recourse to Persian was not merely a means of insisting on communicating in his own terms, but it was also a reminder of the courtly tradition and culture that had long preceded the intrusion of the British. Mackenzie's antagonism was stoked further by this ploy. He informed the Governor-General that it was not possible for him to investigate the Nawab Nazim's claims about the misuse of Nizamut funds during his minority, and declared that in his view 'the assumption by Her Majesty, of the direct sovereignty and rule of India, leaves His Excellency the Viceroy … at full liberty to continue, alter, or abolish the hitherto existing relations between the British Government and the Nizamut, including of course the Rais or Chief, the Nazim.' Mackenzie's view was fully in line with that of the former Governor-General, Dalhousie,

1 Murshidabad Nizamut: letters issued/edited by J.Datta Gupta and Sanat Kumar Bose. (Calcutta: Superintendent Govt. Print, West Bengal, 1965–67), p. 545.

and it would be the view informing future Viceroys and Secretaries of State for India.

For the time being, however, a compromise was reached whereby the Diwan was to become the employee of the British Agent and answerable to him rather than the Nawab. Thus Mansour Ali Khan was not forced to personally re-employ or deal with the Diwan. However, he also lost further control over the Nizamut estate finances.

With the advice and assistance of a series of English private secretaries, the Nawab wrote several long letters to the Indian Viceroy and his officials setting out his claims for compensation and restoration of his status. He was particularly aggrieved that his contribution of elephants, boats and soldiers to help put down the 'Mutiny' of 1857 was insufficiently acknowledged, and that the behaviour of the Governor's agents was patronising and high-handed. He expressed his indignation that minor European royalty were treated with greater respect than he was. He complained that his funds had been reduced to one tenth of the original amount promised, and noted that, while rewards had been heaped upon those who were merely 'not flagrantly rebellious' during the Mutiny, he, as 'the oldest ally of the British Government is forgotten ... And yet,' he went on to declare, 'I never swerved from my allegiance, and my services have been repeatedly acknowledged by Government. So far as I can ascertain my rank is even higher than that of a peer of the realm, and yet Peers and Peeresses are exempt from arrest.' He asserted that his status was equivalent to that of a dethroned sovereign, and hence he had the right to be forever treated with the same privileges and marks of respect accorded junior members of the British and European royal family. He wrote:

> If it was thought right to secure this position to the Prince of such a very small territory as Hollern Zollern, how much more should the rights of the family who brought to the Crown of Great Britain the Sovereignty of three such provinces as Bengal, Bihar, and Orissa, be maintained! It is my desire to be to her Majesty the QUEEN the first, as I have always been the most loyal, of her Indian subjects, and it is to her most Gracious Majesty that

> I appeal for the fulfilment of the pledges, so repeatedly given, to maintain 'my dignity, rights, and interest,' the splendour of my court, and my ease, comfort, and prosperity.

Mansour Ali Khan makes very clear here his awareness that he is not regarded in the same light as a European prince, nor treated equally, and his consequent resentment. Throughout his life he experienced and wrestled with the curious 'doublethink' that characterised the language and actions of almost all the British officials who imposed themselves on him, and which became explicit in that letter from Colin Mackenzie reminding him of his subordination to the British, and the presumed inferiority of the people of Bengal. Yes, he could be acknowledged as a royal prince, but since he was Indian (and Muslim), he could not be regarded as having the status of European royalty.

In response to a later reiteration of his complaints, the Governor-General's aide acknowledged in 1865 that the Nawab had been a loyal supporter of the British government throughout the Santhal rebellion and the 'Mutiny', and had not only supplied troops and elephants, but had used his influence in Murshidabad to prevent any uprising. It seems that this acknowledgement was the only ground that the agents were prepared to give to the Nawab. Further letters and petitions to the Governor-General went unanswered or were blocked by the British Agent in Murshidabad.

CHAPTER 3

Passage from India

1859–1869

'He is but a prince in name – a shadow of a shade.'
Illustrated Times, April 1869[1]

Since 1859 the Nawab had been planning to visit England to see the country about whose wonders he had read and heard so much. He also wished to pay his respects to Queen Victoria, and to lay his claims for compensation before the British government, claims for which he believed his support for the British during the two uprisings would serve him well. He clung to the conviction that British justice would eventually triumph, that in Britain itself his status would be recognised, and there he would receive a fairer hearing than he had received from British officials in India.

There was little to detain the Nawab in Murshidabad. His beloved Hasina had died in May 1858, and he seemed to have relatively little affection for his other surviving wives, of which he had many. Like other Shi'i men of ample means, the Nawab had two kinds of wife. Shi'i law allowed up to four *nikah* wives at any one time – who were permanent and enjoyed a sense of status that *mutah*, or 'pleasure wives', did not. A *mutah* marriage involves a temporary contract between both parties to enjoy a sexual relationship, although under Shi'i law any children born of the relationship are legitimate and should be supported by the father. There is no limit on the number of *mutah* wives a man may take, but no more than four concurrent *nikah* wives are permitted at any one time.

1 *London Illustrated Times*, 14 April 1869, p.227.

With the death of Hasina, the Nawab now had three *nikah* wives.

In fact, neither the Nawab nor the British officials seem to have paid more than the most cursory attention to the Nawab's wives, except to name them occasionally as the recipients of stipends in the quarterly accounts for the Nizamut. Here one can find their names, and only by careful and continuous scanning of the accounts, year by year, can one note the addition of a new wife and the disappearance, presumably the death, of another. And it is the accounts that reveal, or at least suggest, which of the wives had been married in a formal *nikah* ceremony (and thus given a permanent legal status), and which were *mutah* or temporary wives. Nor is there any mention of the Nawab's daughters, although later genealogies reveal that twenty-two daughters survived, and almost as many died in childhood. What we learn from the records is that it is the sons who matter, and it was the sons who were the focus of the Nawab's affections and fatherly concern.

Reading through these records one begins to glimpse the plight of these women, whose status and wellbeing was wholly dependent on remaining in favour with the Nawab (and the British Agent). And when one finds in the later genealogical records that the first wife, Shams-i-Jehan, bore thirteen sons, twelve of whom died in early childhood, one cannot help feeling the terrible poignancy of her situation, for the pain of her loss of each child is compounded with the desperate need to provide the Nawab with a male heir. In this record of repeated loss one might also see the source of the Nawab's deep attachment to his living sons. But at the same time he took seriously his responsibility to see that the women and the daughters they bore were well cared for.

Mansour Ali Khan's attachment to his sons was strengthened by a hope that his heirs might regain some of the power and respect that his father and ancestors had bargained away. Evidence of his affection and his lack of inhibition in demonstrating it is recorded by Colonel Charles Herbert, whose task was to supervise three of the sons on a grand tour of Europe and Britain. Thwarted year after year by the refusal of what he deemed adequate funds for his own travels in proper state and comfort, the Nawab finally decided in 1865 that his three oldest sons should undertake the trip without him. Accompanied by Colonel Herbert, the two oldest sons, now both aged nineteen, and a third son, who was fifteen years old, set off from Calcutta on 9 March 1865. Herbert records with some distaste the Nawab's tearful leave-taking of the three:

> His Highness was very much affected at the parting, apparently putting no restraint whatever on his feelings; and it was with much trouble that I eventually succeeded in leading him on shore, when the friends of the passengers were warned to leave the vessel.

When the ship reached the port of Galle, Sri Lanka, eight days later, a telegram from the Nawab awaited them, enquiring after his sons' welfare. Herbert reported that he was 'glad to be able to reply they were well and happy'. He also remarked that they had 'already shown themselves to be amiable gentlemanly-feeling lads [who] had made a pleasant impression, not only on me, but on our fellow passengers generally'.

At the end of their yearlong travels, which were recorded day by day, Colonel Herbert gave a general summary of the boys' characters, a summary revealing much about British colonial stereotypes which existed alongside and in the same consciousness as more human and generous individual attachments. Of the eldest youth, Hassan (Burra Sahib), Hasina's son, Herbert wrote:

> I found him amiable, steady, and desirous to learn. I think him truthful and less inclined to deceive than usual among Asiatics, and capable of strong attachment. This he probably inherited from his mother, an Abyssinian.

The other two boys were, in Herbert's eyes, a little too 'Asiatic', and he found Hussan, the son of the Nawab's first wife, too aware of his status, but at the same time rather unforthcoming.

The trio returned to Murshidabad in March 1866, and regaled their father with accounts of their visits to the pyramids and Cairo, Malta and Gibraltar, the Crystal Palace and Westminster Abbey, the opera and the theatre, Margate and the races at Derby, their meetings with nobles and royals, and then their return via Paris, Rome and Pompeii. The Nawab determined that he would put off his long-desired visit to Europe no longer. Moreover, his complaints about his mistreatment by British officials in India had been either rebuffed or unanswered. He would go to the top officials in Britain, and indeed call on Queen Victoria herself, to ensure that his claims were given a hearing.

Between 1861 and 1868, Mansour Ali Khan had repeatedly sought permission to visit England, and was repeatedly prevented from doing so. Whenever his freedom of movement was at issue the stark contradiction between the Nawab's supposed status as an Indian monarch and his actual power became evident. His every movement was monitored, and he had to send a written request (in English) to the Agent for the Governor-General if he wished to leave Murshidabad to visit Calcutta or other places in Bengal. Except for an occasional ceremonial visit to Calcutta to meet the Governor-General, his movements and activities were restricted to official duties nearby, such as attendance at entertainments given for the soldiers stationed at Berhampore, eight miles from Murshidabad, or brief hunting excursions in the company of British officials. Some Agents were more easy-going than others, but nevertheless the Nawab was dependent on their goodwill for permission to embark on a great many activities. These restrictions also extended to his immediate family. It took several letters from her British doctor before the Agent would allow the Nawab's mother to take an excursion on the Ganges for health reasons. Her first request had been refused as an unnecessary 'indulgence' by the then-Agent, Henry Torrens, in 1847, and she did not gain permission until Colin Mackenzie took over in 1856.

Moreover, the Agent kept firm control over visitors, and especially discouraged the Nawab from meeting Europeans who were not officially approved by the British government in Calcutta. In October 1861, Major Colin Mackenzie forbade the Nawab from admitting William Austin Montriou, a distinguished English lawyer, to the palace compound, nor was he permitted to 'hold direct intercourse with the gentleman'. And when the Nawab wished to employ Montriou as his secretary,

Mackenzie wrote to inform him that he could not 'appoint any officer, or indeed a European of any rank to an office in the Nizamut, without the sanction of Government and the recommendation of the Governor General's Agent.'[1] In fact William Montriou, whom the Nawab did eventually employ in defiance of Mackenzie and his threats, was well qualified to advise and serve him. In 1856 he had published a translation of the first chapter of the Persian classic *The Gulistan*, a chapter that focuses on advice for kings. Montriou also wrote several books about Indian legal matters and gave a series of lectures to law students at Presidency College in Calcutta.

Such restrictions and frequent reminders of his powerlessness can only have strengthened Mansour Ali Khan's determination not only to obtain a hearing for the grievances the Viceroy refused to discuss but also to escape the claustrophobic world of British officialdom in Calcutta and Murshidabad. In 1868 the opportunity finally came; permission to visit England was granted, although the requisite funding for what the Nawab thought proper for someone of his status had to be negotiated. Which British official should accompany him (or be his 'minder') was also a concern for both the Nawab and the British officials. Finally it was decided that the Nawab would travel with Colonel Layard.

Colonel Frederick Peter Layard, brother of the explorer Henry Layard, had long been resident in Bengal, first serving with the Indian Army there, and then becoming head of public works in Bengal. From 1849, when Mansour Ali Khan was eighteen, he was a frequent visitor to Murshidabad and, although only twelve years older, seems to have had a paternal but friendly relationship with the Nawab. Layard was also an amateur artist, and published a fine collection of 'Bengal Sketches'. The Nawab had always been interested in art and throughout his reign accumulated an outstanding collection of European and Bengali paintings and carvings for the palace. The shared interest in art may well have encouraged their friendship.

Frederick Layard had written to his brother Henry sympathetically

1 Murshidabad Nizamut: letters issued/edited by J. Datta Gupta and Sanat Kumar Bose. (Calcutta: Superintendent Govt. Print., West Bengal 1965–1967), p.644. Montriou also appears as Montrion in some records.

about the Nawab's case for restoration of his privileges and full pension in 1858, when Henry had been sent to investigate the causes of the 'Mutiny'. In 1865, when contemplating a move to Murshidabad and wondering whether his wife would be permitted to share his residence there, Frederick wrote:

> There might be a little difficulty about Ida and the children living with me, but the [Nawab] Nazim begs I will allow my wife to reside in the same house, telling me how much benefit (I wish I could see more of it!) he derived from the kind advice of Mrs Showers when he was a lad.[1]

Frederick concurred with advice that Henry, now Under-Secretary for Foreign Affairs, sent the Nawab, and declared:

> It is a sad pity that he does not realise the fact, that he might become a useful and respectable member of society by a little energy and toil in keeping up his [position]. I have many times tried to induce him to work for admission into Council, but he looks on this as *infra dig*, telling me that it is no place for a Prince of his rank when Mr Jennings, the man of business at Messrs Osler & Co., crockery and glass shop, would be on an equality with him as a member!

Despite these differences with Colonel Layard about how he could best 'become a useful and respectable member of society',[2] and how best to retain his status as Nawab, Mansour Ali Khan had been keen that Layard should be the person who accompanied his sons on their tour of England and Europe in 1865. He was bitterly disappointed and aggrieved when the aforementioned Colonel Herbert, a stranger, whose previous role as superintendent for the deposed King of Oudh most likely did not commend him to the Nawab, was appointed instead. Layard expressed his own disappointment, and his wife's, at not being

---

1 Supplementary Layard papers, Vol. 1, ff. 164. Add. MS 58152 1843–1891.
2 *Ibid.*

able to go on this trip, and asked Henry to assist the boys, commenting:

> The Nazim, with all his faults and weakness, is kind-hearted and loyal to our government. I have for 20 years received much kindness from him and should be glad to see the young lads improve themselves and make the best of their opportunities in England. I had hoped to do much for them both for their sake and for their father's.[1]

In November 1868 the Nawab wrote formally to the Agent, indicating his plans for the journey and visit, should Layard be authorised by the Viceroy to accompany him. His intention was to travel to Allahabad the next month and proceed from there by rail to Bombay, where he would embark for Europe. 'I would much like to go to Brindisi,' his letter continued, 'and thence, after visiting all places of interest in Europe, so arrange to reach England about the month of April.' He did not expect his stay in England to last longer than nine months, although he noted that it would 'depend on circumstances whether my stay will be for a longer or shorter period'.[2]

But there were further delays. The sum allowed for his expenses had to be negotiated. It was not till late December that the Viceroy finally granted permission for Colonel Layard to take leave for a year as the Nawab's companion and mentor.[3] The Agent then had to assign a further allowance for Colonel Layard's expenses. In the end, the Nawab was granted an allowance of four lakh rupees (worth nearly 4 million pounds today) from the Nizamut Deposit Fund. This allowance also had to cover expenses for his sons as well as his large retinue of courtiers, secretaries and servants. Colonel Layard's personal allowance of 1,000 rupees a month (in today's currency, equivalent to over £110,000 a year) was also drawn from the Nizamut Deposit Fund. The British Agent noted that 'this is the highest rate of allowances which has ever been allowed to officials similarly deputed'.

1 Supplementary Layard papers, Vol. 1, ff. 164. Add. MS 58152 1843–1891.
2 L/PS/ 6/565/169.
3 *Ibid.*

Since the Nawab was determined to arrive in England in time to be presented to the House of Lords on 9 April, he decided to forgo his tour of Italy and, leaving his wives in Murshidabad, sail from Calcutta to Marseilles. So, on 15 February 1869, the Nawab and his entourage set out on their journey. The Nawab's companions included his eldest son, Prince Ali-Kudr-Hassan-Ali-Bahadoor, now twenty-three, and thirteen-year-old Prince Suleiman-Kudr-Wahid-Ali Bahadoor, known respectively as Hassan and Suleiman. Both of these young men were the Nawab's sons with Hasina. Together with Colonel Layard, they boarded the SS *Mongolia*, a combined sail and steamship built just four years earlier for the Peninsular and Oriental Company (P&O). The SS *Mongolia* was constructed to accommodate wealthier passengers and upper-level civil servants travelling to and from India and Europe, a journey taking just over five weeks. Its relatively spacious cabins and staterooms could accommodate 130 first-class passengers, while the servants would share the few second-class cabins, holding forty-one passengers altogether. The Nawab's entourage occupied a large segment of both kinds of accommodation, for it included four courtiers – a scripture reader, two scribes and a eunuch – and a group of servants consisting of three valets, a butler, a musician, a compounder of medicine, a barber and a cook. In addition, the Nawab was accompanied by his European private secretary, Mr W. D. Fox.

They reached Marseilles on 22 March. This was the Nawab's first view of a completely European city, and he was entranced by the grand buildings, all brightly lit by chandeliers, as well as by the squares and promenades which contrasted so much with the small, winding, dusty or muddy streets of Murshidabad and its crowded bazaars. On that first night in Marseilles, his party attended the theatre. Although the Nawab and his sons understood little of the language of the singers and actors, they nevertheless admired the ingenuity of the scenery and lighting, as well as the liveliness of action. The music, however, must have seemed rhythmically and melodically primitive and simple compared to the complex ragas that entertained them in the Murshidabad court, although the orchestra had many instruments new to the visitors.

A week later, Mansour Ali Khan arrived in Paris. There he was met by Lord Lyons, the British Ambassador to France, and formally presented to the Emperor Napoleon III and other members of the nobility, including the Marquis de la Valette, a member of Napoleon III's government and French Ambassador to Britain.

The Nawab stayed in the Grand Hôtel du Louvre, noted for its luxury and steam-powered lifts, and next to the fashionable shopping Galeries du Louvre. Here numerous visitors came to pay their respects. Among them was Louis Rousselot, who in 1867 had travelled to Murshidabad and sought permission to visit the Nawab, but had been refused, as he had not been given an official endorsement. In Paris, Rousselot now observed, Mansour Ali Khan was delighted to find his title of Nawab taken seriously by the Parisians and even by the government. No longer did he need permission to meet Europeans. 'The worthy Bengali now receives in state at the Grand Hôtel numerous visitors who come to pay their respects,' Rousselot wrote, 'and, very proud to have his title as Nawab taken seriously by the Parisians and by the government itself, he has considered it appropriate, in order to emphasise his majesty, to abandon his usual every-day clothing and dress himself as an Indian prince.'[1]

In Paris the Nawab gave several extensive interviews with French journalists who, while giving fulsome descriptions of his glamorous status, appearance and entourage, also saw him as an individual. One reporter introduced him as a 'great lover of paintings, a keen hunter, and a very skilled marksman'. 'The Nawab is a small man,' this reporter continued, 'slight, with a grey moustache, and [skin] the colour of Victor Cochinat' [a well-known Parisian writer and lawyer of mixed race from Martinique]. But what really struck the reporter was the Nawab's enormous round spectacles, 'such as a grandmother or notary might wear'.[2]

Together with Colonel Layard, the Nawab and his sons visited the Louvre, several museums, the theatre, and went shopping in Paris. They were fitted for and ordered fur coats, shoes and boots. One night it

1 Louis Rousselot, *L'Inde des Rajahs.* (Paris: *La Hachette,* 1874), pp. 737–8.

2 Joe Trezel, 'Curiosites Parisiennes: Le Nabab de Bengale', *Le Gaulois*, 1 April 1869, p.1.

snowed, and they all, together with their servants, went out into the street to look at and touch the flakes as they fell. They attended a banquet given by Lord Lyons, and sat at the table through the many courses and servings of drink refusing the wine and all the dishes, since halal food was not provided. Back in the hotel, Mansour Ali Khan and his sons ate a simple dish of rice and mutton, provided by the Nawab's own cook.

Responding to keen interest on the part of the British public, the Nawab's arrival in France and imminent journey to England was reported widely by the British press in both London and the provinces. British newspapers varied in their willingness or ability to transcribe non-European names and honorifics. In English papers and reports, the Nawab is sometimes referred to as 'Synd' [Mansoor] Ullee Meerza, more often as 'Syed Ullee Meerza', which was the name he himself used in official papers. In Bengal he was and still is more usually referred to as 'Mansour Ali Khan', or as Feradan Jah (his official title). Many of the reports simply stated the fact that the Nawab of Bengal had arrived in Marseilles, or Paris, or Calais, but some commented on the purpose of the Nawab's visit and on his glamorous appearance.

While the French reporters viewed the Nawab with a certain degree of sympathy combined with irony, some British reporters were more inclined to sneer. The Paris Correspondent for the popular weekly magazine *The Illustrated Times* wrote:

> Just now we have among us the rich Nabob of Bengal, Synd Munsoor Ali, with a vast number of other queer looking names, at least when written in Roman characters. The Prince is not a very imposing person, but his costumes and those of his two sons are picturesque and attractive – the long silken robe with gold-embroidered sash, the religious green turban, chains, and rings.[1]

But whereas British officialdom in India had demanded that the Nawab shed his oriental slippers and wear black leather shoes, this British correspondent deplored and mocked the acquisition of such footwear by the Nawab and his sons, noting that 'Christian civilisation has already

1 *Illustrated Times,* 14 April 1869, p.227

invaded the Indian legs and feet', and that they had 'adopted the odious trousers of Christendom and highly varnished boots'. The writer went on to confirm the implication that the Nawab of Bengal represented more show than substance, concluding that he was 'but a prince in name – a shadow of a shade'.

Such snide comments were not typical of the press reports during the Nawab's first two or three years in England. Numerous British papers respectfully announced the Nawab's arrival at Calais on 6 April, and his departure for Dover on 8 April 1869. More characteristic of the reports on the Nawab's presence and activities is this short announcement in the 9 April 1869 issue of the *Morning Post*, immediately following the court news, that 'His Highness Synd Munsoor Ali Nawab Nazim of Bengal, Behar, and Orissa; Prince Alee Kudr Hassan Ali Meerza Bahadoor; Prince Soleiman Kudr Wahid Ali Meerza Bahador; Colonel F. P. Layard, political agent with his Highness the Nawab Nazim have arrived at the Alexandra Hotel.'[1] The same court news also announced that Her Majesty had held a drawing room reception that afternoon, had afterwards gone for a drive with Princess Beatrice and Lady Campbell, and that HRH Princess Louise had honoured the painter George Watts with a visit to his studio.

The journey from Dover to London by train could not have provided a favourable introduction to the city, as they passed what another Indian traveller at that time described as 'a collection of mean black houses and smoky chimneys'. However, their short coach journey to the Alexandra Hotel in St George's Place revealed wider streets and larger houses. On the way they would have passed the Green Park Arch topped by the huge statue of the Duke of Wellington on his horse Copenhagen. It was quite close to the Alexandra Hotel, an elegant and extensive building overlooking Hyde Park.

The morning the Nawab arrived in London, 8 April 1869, was a day of grey skies and cold drizzle in London. At the Alexandra Hotel the Nawab and his entourage were greeted with suitable bows and respect. The servants were directed to their quarters in the rear of the hotel while the Nawab, his sons and courtiers were taken to several of the

1 *The Morning Post,* 9 April 1869. p.5.

suites on the second floor. As soon as they had all been settled and had warmed themselves by the coal fires in their suites, Colonel Layard and Wlliam Fox set about confirming arrangements for the Nawab and his sons to be presented to the House of Lords. Fox also sent out briefings informing the press of the Nawab's presence and case for reparation.

The next day was a Friday. Mansour Ali Khan and his sons changed from the simple white cotton clothing they all wore for the communal Friday prayers held at noon with their servants and attendants, and drove through a thick London fog to the Palace of Westminster, peering through the carriage windows to make out the shapes of the buildings they passed. No doubt the cold and damp seemed to penetrate even through the fur coats they had bought in Paris, and which they reluctantly removed once they entered the House of Lords. They were escorted to their seats in the Distinguished Strangers' Gallery.

The Nawab and his sons were dressed in full court costume, featuring elaborately embroidered cream silk tunics and golden chains. The sons wore jewelled ornaments on their fezes; the Nawab's turban vaunted a magnificent cockade covered in rubies, emeralds and sapphires. His dress sword displayed above its sheath a large emerald. Even amid the robes of the peers and the red velvet lavishly adorning the Lords' Chamber they stood out, and felt themselves under intense observation as they were formally presented by the Secretary of State for India to the assembled peers. Although it was a Friday, there was a good attendance, since Earl Russell's proposal that a limited number of life peerages could be created to allow for wider representation was scheduled for debate in the House. Russell sought to reverse the 1856 decision that life peers (as opposed to hereditary peers) could not sit or vote in Parliament. To avoid the danger of too many peers being appointed by the crown, Russell proposed that the number of life peers should not at any one time exceed twenty-eight, which was about the number of the Irish representative peers and also of the English bishops, who were peers for life.

Issues regarding the status of hereditary as opposed to life peers and the category to which the Nawab of Bengal and his ancestors belonged, would later be central to the debates concerning Mansour Ali Khan's claims.

During the next few days numerous papers throughout the United Kingdom, including even the *Dundee Courier* and the *Greenock Telegraph and Clyde Shipping Gazette*, carried this news item:

> His grace the Duke of Argyll [Secretary of State for India] had the honour of introducing a great Eastern potentate into the House of Lords on Friday afternoon. The distinguished stranger was none other than the Nawab of Bengal, who was accompanied by his two sons and suite, all arrayed in gorgeous oriental garments. Their presence attracted much attention.[1]

Throughout the next months the Nawab's schedule was a remarkably busy one and the press reported every activity: his visit, together with the Duke of Argyll and Colonel Layard to have an audience with the Queen in Osborne House on 28 April; his presence that same day at a reception held by the Duchess of Marlborough, attended also by such grandees as the Earl and Countess Stanhope, the Duke of Norfolk, the Duke of Wellington and the Russian Ambassador; his appearance at a performance, in Italian, of Rossini's *William Tell* on 1 May. The following week, the Nawab and his sons were listed among the guests at a 'Reunion' and musical entertainment hosted by the Duchess of Marlborough, as well as a reception held by Mrs Gladstone at the Gladstone family residence in Carlton Terrace. On 13 May they were among the many guests listed at an afternoon tea party hosted by the wife of Archbishop Tait at Lambeth Palace. Two days later readers of the indefatigable *Morning Post* learned of the Nawab's visit with his sons to Crystal Palace to see a dioramic picture of St Peter's, painted by a 'Mr Matt. Morgan'. On 19 May they went to see a display at the Royal Botanic Society, together with the Prince and Princess of Wales. Numerous papers reported their attendance at the Queen's levees – her private receptions – on 11 May and 1 June. Also on 1 June the Nawab went to a horse show with the Prince of Wales and Colonel Layard and bought a brown hunter named Handcuff for 182 guineas. That same

---

1 The *Dundee Courier* 12 April 1869; *Greenock Telegraph and Clyde Shipping Gazette*, 10 April 1869.

evening he entertained friends, including several former Agents who had served in Murshidabad, the Marquis of Huntly, and Henry Layard, at the Alexandra Hotel.

In most reports of the Nawab's presence at receptions, balls and other social events, his name headed the list of distinguished aristocratic guests, and particular attention was given to his glamorous 'oriental' appearance. A characteristic item appeared in the *Leeds Mercury* after the Nawab and his sons went to see the Derby races on 26 May:

> Another great point of attraction was very near the Royal box. It was a portion of the ground on which were placed the carriages of the Nawab of Bengal and his suite. These dusky Orientals, clad in gorgeous silken vestments, and glittering with gold and jewels, formed a strange contrast to the occupants of the carriages around them. To the multitude at large they were the subject of the most profound wonderment; and some idea of the view generally taken with respect to their identity may be gathered from the fact that the gazers repeatedly asked each other, 'which is little Theodore?' Evidently under the impression that the swarthy strangers formed a part of the spoils of the Abyssinian campaign, and had been generously sent down to Epsom by the government to add to the attractions of the day.[1]

The confusion of 'the multitude at large' is a reminder of the concurrent campaigns of conquest and control that the British were undertaking across the globe, and what details of those campaigns the British press was sharing with the public. 'Little Theodore' was the son of the Emperor of Ethiopia, Tewodros II, who committed suicide when a British punitive expedition defeated his forces in 1868. Theodore (Dejazmatch Alemayehu Tewodros) was then eight years old and was brought back to England where Queen Victoria became interested in his education. Given that the Nawab's two sons visiting England with him were the sons of his Abyssinian wife, and hence had some North-African features, the question about their identity might not have been

1 *Leeds Mercury*, 27 May 1869, p.3.

The Nawab's Turban Jewel

as absurd as the reporter suggests.

Mansour Ali Khan had expected his visit to England to last less than six months; his plan was to present his memorial (as the statement of factual basis for a petition was termed) to the British government, receive an immediate hearing, and then return to India in October 1869. Before the Nawab's departure from Bengal, the then-Viceroy, the Earl of Mayo, had written a private letter to the Scottish peer and Secretary of State for India, the Duke of Argyll, suggesting that the Nawab should be treated with deference and his mission given attention without delay.

> While he is in England he should see Her Majesty as soon as possible. He is a good sportsman, speaks English well and is going to take the moors in Scotland this autumn. If your Grace could put his people in the way of getting a place where there are plenty of grouse you would do him a great kindness.[1]

1 Private Letters from the Earl of Mayo to the Duke of Argyll, 1869. Mss Eur. pp.54-55.

Based in India, Mayo characterises Mansour Ali Khan as one who shares the interests, and even the attributes, of English and Scottish aristocrats. The Nawab's provision of elephants, horses, tents and provisions for British safaris hunting tigers and pigs in India is to be repaid with 'getting a place where there are plenty of grouse'. The letter to Argyll suggests a sense of class obligation, and perhaps also a concern to placate the Nawab in view of the likelihood of his mission being unsuccessful. In public the Nawab was treated with deference, and as an exotic celebrity in the media; behind the scenes, however, the politicians saw him as a problem to be managed and as a threat to their overall control of India.

In order to progress his mission as quickly as possible, the Nawab had received permission to send his papers directly to the Secretary of State for India in Westminster, and this he did in July 1869. However, protocol required that the papers be seen and commented on by the Viceroy in India, and so the British India Office sent them to Calcutta – but not until November 1869, where they languished unacknowledged and unclaimed at the P&O wharf for over four months. It was only in March 1870 that Viceroy Mayo became aware of the petition, or so he claimed.

In response to his many anxious inquiries, Mansour Ali Khan was told that his petition, with its detailed statement of his grievances, was under consideration and that he would soon have a reply. It is unclear whether this long delay was simply the result of shambolic disorganisation within the India Office, or if it involved deliberate delaying tactics, perhaps in the hope that the Nawab would simply give up and go away. A reporter for one of Western Ireland's more substantial newspapers, the *Tralee Chronicle*, cynical about the British government but sympathetic to the Nawab, suggested the latter, and that the temporary loss of the papers in Calcutta was no mere oversight:

> This 'accident' has had the – of course, unexpected – effect of delaying for a whole season in India the judgement of Lord Mayo on the facts. It also involved detaining the Nawab in England for another year at a ruinous expense, to say nothing of the peril of the Northern climate to an Eastern constitution. More than all it

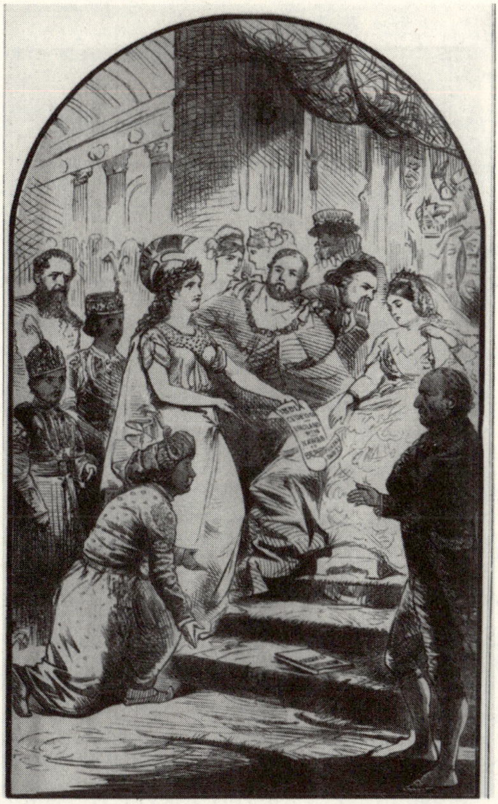

'Be Just and Fear Not' by Matt Morgan. The Nawab kneels with Britannia to petition Queen Victoria, his two sons standing behind him.

> has a result of tiding over to the chances of another session, and the possibility of another Secretary of State for India, or another Governor General, all questions of the policy pursued by the Indian government in regard to the native princes of India.[1]

By late March 1870, Mansour Ali Khan had realised that he would need to stay in England for at least another year in order to press and see through his petition for the restoration of his rights, monies and status as Nawab Nazim of Bengal, and safeguard these for his sons. One result of this realisation was a campaign of political and journalistic lobbying to win the sympathy of politicians and the general public for the Nawab's cause. In the first week of April the following notice for a book detailing the history of British mistreatment of the Nawab of

1 *Tralee Chronicle*, 17 May 1870, p.1.

Bengal's family appeared in dozens of newspapers and journals:

> This day is Published, Price 1s, BRITISH POLICY IN INDIA, With Special reference to the Nawab Nazim of Bengal. BY AN ENGLISHMAN. London: J. Burbridge & Co., 351 Moorgate St., EC.

A few weeks later another series of advertisements and reviews appeared in the papers for a second book billed as '*THE WRONGS OF THE NAWAB OF BENGAL. INDIAN RECORDS, with the Nawab's Memorial and Portrait*. Cloth 5s. C. Bubb, 167, New Bond-street, London, W., and all Booksellers ...'

The prolonged stay also created opportunities of another kind. Assuming that he would be absent for no more than six or nine months, the Nawab had left his wives and concubines in Murshidabad. He was a man who enjoyed the company of women; and, with the prospect of a much longer absence from Bengal, he looked for that company in England.

Mansour Ali Khan was now thirty-eight years old; his hair and large moustache were turning grey, and he was no longer the slim, handsome youth who had gazed from the full-length paintings in the Hazarduari Palace gallery. But contemporary portraits show that he was still attractive. He was consistently portrayed as a glamorous figure with his 'gorgeous oriental garments', his jewelled turban and coat, his royal status. Here in England he welcomed the society of women of all classes. Soon there were rumours about such associations: according to one report he was seen 'spinning around the city in a baroucheful of prostitutes' (a barouche being a four-wheeled carriage).[1] No doubt he also received women in his apartment in the hotel. That the Alexandra Hotel placed no obstacles to its male guests receiving female visitors and having private meetings and meals with them is apparent from reports of the then notorious Bagot case, which tell how the wealthy Christopher 'Nugget' Bagot received midnight visits and had 'jovial

1 Sylvia L. Collicott, *Connections: Haringey local-national-world links* (Haringey Community Information Services, 1986), pp. 96–98.

suppers' in the Alexandra Hotel with the two Misses Verner.[1] In the Bagot case, marriage between one of the Misses Verner and Mr Bagot was arranged 'at length', and Miss Verner 'drew up a list of measurements of her features, body, and limbs, which was read in court, and was not of a very delicate character'.

During his stay at the Alexandra Hotel, Mansour Ali Khan took note of the maids who worked there. One girl in particular attracted his attention shortly after she took up a position as chambermaid at the hotel in 1869. She was a sixteen-year-old East Londoner, and her name was Sarah Vennell.

1 *Northern Territory Times and Gazette,* 17 August 1878, p2.

CHAPTER 4

A Cinderella Story

1852–1870

A young Christian girl from one of the poorest areas of East London, Sarah Vennell cannot have imagined that she would ever become acquainted with a Muslim monarch from India. And yet both their worlds had been shaped by the tortuous relationship between Britain and India.

When Sarah was born on 18 July 1852, her parents were living in Rotherhithe, about three miles upstream from the East India Docks. From these docks the larger cutters departed for the Indian subcontinent, and returned with cargoes of tea, spices, silks, jute and Persian carpets. The East India Docks were among the busiest in London, with the annual number of ships using them increasing from about fifty in 1810 to 400 by 1866. Their crews included many sailors recruited or press-ganged from India, Ceylon and China. Owing to the immense wealth brought by the East India Company following its involvement with Mansour Ali Khan's ancestors the previous century, and Britain's dominance of world trade and rapid industrialisation, London was a city that was fast developing. The docklands were crucial to that development.

Sarah Vennell's family were among the many who had moved from rural England to find a living in the city. Her father, Josiah Godfrey Vennell, was born in Sandhurst on the border of Kent and Sussex; he sought employment as a tailor in London, probably at first as an apprentice. Tailoring was a popular profession in the early nineteenth century and by 1851 tailors represented the fifth largest occupation for males in London. It was a profession that required relatively little investment in terms of space and capital. Moreover it could be a family business, supported by wives and daughters. Josiah had paid five pounds to join the Company of Spectacle Makers in February 1845, so that he could 'set up business as a Tailor' and trade freely in the City of London.

By 1845 Josiah Vennell and his wife, Mary Ann, had four young children. Their fifth child, Louisa, was born in Southwark in 1847, and it was there also that their first child, Josiah Henry, became a victim at the age of ten of a major cholera outbreak the following year. The 1851 census recorded the family living at 5 Medway Terrace in Southwark. Here their neighbours were employed in trades associated with the docks. Records show that they included several mariners, a boatswain, a bricklayer and a sawyer. Josiah identified himself as a master tailor, employing one man. They now had one son, William, aged eleven, and four daughters, the youngest of whom, Mary, was just ten months.

1851 was the year of the Great Exhibition held in the huge glass-and-iron Crystal Palace in Hyde Park, displaying goods and artefacts from all over the world. Half of the exhibition was devoted to Britain and her colonies. Among the most spectacular displays was the exhibit from India, featuring gifts sent to Queen Victoria by Josiah's future son-in-law, the Nawab of Bengal. They included an ivory howdah, complete with elephant trappings, worked in gold and silver, as well as a throne with a silver framework canopy. The exhibition catalogue also lists fine carpets and rugs, together with silks, ivories and marble from 'Moorshedabad' and other areas of Bengal.

More than 6 million people attended the Exhibition between the opening day on 1 May and its closing in October, a majority of them members of the working classes from London and the rest of Britain, for whom the entry price was lowered to one shilling after 24 May. It is very likely that Josiah and Mary Ann Vennell were among them, and the India exhibit would have long been a talking point.

Tailoring was a seasonal trade. Few orders came in the three months following Christmas, when trade would pick up again after Easter until early summer, before dwindling again until November. Most semi-skilled workers in London took on a variety of jobs at different times of the year and Josiah was among the many who, in addition to tailoring or some other work, set up shop to supplement his earnings and provide for his growing family. In April 1854, Josiah and Susannah, his eldest daughter, appeared as witnesses at the Old Bailey, testifying against a twenty-one-year-old soldier, James Alexander, charged with 'unlawfully uttering counterfeit coins' that he had tried to use as legal tender in their shop. Twelve-year-old Susannah's evidence was clear and to the point:

> My father keeps a tobacconist's shop at Rotherhithe. On Sunday, 29 January, the prisoner come for half an ounce of tobacco, and gave me half a crown. I gave it to my sister [Catherine, aged eleven] to give my father, to see if it was good, and gave the prisoner the change. As soon as he heard my father say, 'try it', he ran out.[1]

Josiah corroborated Susannah's evidence and added that he had given the suspect coin to his daughter to try in the detector, which bent the coin, proving it was counterfeit. Josiah chased the soldier and his companion (another soldier); he overtook them, and asked them to return to the shop with him. 'It is respecting your passing a bad half-crown I wish you to return,' Josiah told the court he had said. But this very civil request was met with an oath and a further attempt to escape. Thereupon Josiah managed to hold both young men, call the police, and give the accused into custody.

The policeman who was a witness at the trial confirmed Josiah's testimony, including how he managed to capture both soldiers. It suggests that at this stage in his life Josiah was a fit man for his thirty-five years, able to outrun and hold on to two men some fifteen years younger than himself (although it is possible the two soldiers were drunk. Josiah mentioned that one soldier 'left in haste; so much so, that he fell out the door'). Hard-working and determined to provide for his family, Josiah maintained both the tobacconist's shop in Medway Terrace and his place of work as a tailor (at first in Newgate Street and later near St Martin's Le Grand) for several years.

1 *London, England, Proceedings of the Old Bailey and Ordinary's Accounts Index, 1674–1913*. Provo, UT, USA: Ancestry.com Operations, Inc., 2016.

With the birth of Sarah's younger brother George in 1855, there were now seven children aged from a few months to fifteen years. When Sarah was five years old, Mary Ann Vennell died, and the seven children were left motherless. In addition to helping out in the shop, and perhaps with small tailoring jobs, Susannah, Catherine and Louisa would have taken on the tasks of looking after their baby brother and two little sisters during their mother's illness and after her death. The family was not long to be without a mother however; within six months after his first wife's death, Josiah remarried. Sarah's stepmother, also named Mary Ann, was Mrs Cousins, a widow two years older than Josiah.

By 1861, the Vennells had moved to Lambeth. William, the oldest of the children, found employment as a draper's assistant. Competition in the tailoring business had greatly increased, and thousands of tailors are listed in the commercial directories for London in the early 1860s; Josiah is no longer among them. In Lambeth Josiah rented a chandler's shop, the equivalent in the mid-nineteenth century of a grocery and general store, at 38 East Street (the street where Charlie Chaplin was born twenty-eight years later). Chandler's shops took and sold at a very small profit the goods left over from the street traders nearby. They were regarded as the last resort for the poorest residents in the district, since they gave credit where other kinds of shop, such as the baker's or butcher's, would not.

What can we surmise about Sarah's life during this period? She lived with her family in the small building which housed the shop, first in Medway Terrace and then in East Street, sharing one of the two small upstairs rooms with her four sisters, while little George's cot was probably placed in her parents' room. As a very small child she might be found lingering in the tobacconist's shop, close to her parents and older sisters. Later at the chandler's she learned to take and give change to the customers, to weigh out small portions – a few ounces of flour, a half ounce of tobacco, a button and a needle, a little bundle of matches, two or three elderly potatoes, a small bunch of wilting spinach, one candle. As she grew older, Sarah learnt which customers could be given credit, deciphering their names and laboriously writing the amounts on small pieces of paper. Unfamiliar customers seeking credit would have to speak to one of her parents.

When it was not too wet or cold, she could escape outside to the street, charged with looking after George. There she could sit or stand with the women and children from the adjoining houses, listening to the gossip and laughter and complaints. During winter, the thick fog and smoke from chimneys shrouded London and the streets became too dank and cold for outside gatherings. On hot days the acrid smell from the nearby tanneries and pickle factories hung in the street. Sometimes the stench from the river could be overpowering. An exceptionally hot summer in 1858 produced 'the Great Stink' in London, a smell so foul that the windows at Westminster were draped in curtains soaked in chloride of lime so that the Members of Parliament could breathe. At last the use of vast quantities of slaked lime and several days of rain caused the Great Stink to dissipate, but not before it had displaced the 'Indian Mutiny' as the chief topic of conversation.

Sarah was not quite five years old when the so-called Indian Mutiny erupted in Bengal in May 1857, and for a year the newspapers were filled with reports of 'savage' Indians attacking 'brave' British men and 'terrified' British women. Such images had little connection with the few Indians Sarah would have seen in East London. Some would have lived and wandered through her neighbourhood as pedlars for the most part, as lascars looking for work locally or waiting on the docks for their next ship. Some joined the ranks of beggars of varying nationalities on the London streets. Sometimes one of the *ayahs* might be seen, the children's nurses hired in India, brought to accompany wealthy families on their long voyages to England, and then abandoned, left to find shelter in cramped and squalid lodging houses nearby. One report from 1858 referred to a lodging house accommodating more than thirty *ayahs*, each paying sixteen shillings a week rent while they tried to find families going out to India and in need of their services.

Occasionally, Sarah and her neighbours must have encountered Indians selling religious tracts, an activity the journalist and social reformer Henry Mayhew regarded as a 'line peculiar to the Hindoos'.[1] He records other Indians sweeping crossings, busking as musicians,

1 Rozina Visram, *Ayahs, Lascars, and Princes* (London: Pluto Press, 1986), p.57.

trading as herbalists. His prejudices against 'Asiatics' were doubtless shared by many Britons. Mayhew described the 'Hindoo' beggars and traders as 'snake-eyed', 'cunning', characterised by 'a mendacity that never falters, hesitates, or stumbles, but flows on in an unbroken stream of falsehood'.[1] Mayhew also remarked on the colourful and conspicuous costumes worn by these men, who would 'do anything where their picturesque appearance, of which they are proud and conscious, can be effectively displayed'.

Schooling was not compulsory, but George, the youngest child in the family, received enough education to find employment as a clerk by the time he was sixteen. For the girls, attendance at school was encouraged but considered dispensable, and often Sarah and her sisters might have preferred to stay at home. In winter the schoolroom was bitterly cold. When it was foggy, the room was not only cold but dark, and the weak gaslight could be heard hissing all day. During the long hours spent on needlework at school, more often than not making shirts for the boys, the girls complained that their fingers were sometimes too frozen to hold the needle.

Sarah and her sisters were quite good at arithmetic, as they got practice in the shop, but they often struggled to keep up with reading and writing, especially after missing school when they were kept home to help look after little George, or their mother when she became ill, and sometimes they were needed in the shop. In their early teens the girls were encouraged to leave school and find work.

Domestic service was one of the best and most widely available options for young women. It was particularly desirable if it involved living out in another household, and so relieving the family of keep while freeing up a little space in the home. Sarah's oldest sister, Susannah, found a position as a nursemaid in Notting Hill Square, looking after the two small sons of Frederick Battam, an artist for a china manufacturer. Louisa, five years older than Sarah, probably met her future husband, William Blackman, while in service. William was in 'public service' working at the exclusive Brook's Club in St James's Street, where he eventually became head waiter.

---

1 Visram, pp.57–8.

Opportunities to work in 'public service' – service in hotels and clubs, as opposed to private service with a family – were growing in the 1860s. London's reputation as a fashionable shopping centre, featuring inventive and well-lit displays behind plate-glass windows, drew many tourists from the country regions and abroad. Tourism from other regions of the United Kingdom was enabled by the development of the railway system, and large hotels such as the Great Western at Paddington and the Great Northern at King's Cross were established at the railway terminuses in the city. Writing in 1863, the physician and author Andrew Wynter commented on the welcome changes in accommodation for travellers, from rooms providing 'funereal four-posters' and 'musty old corner washstands' to the grandeur of the Grosvenor Hotel, where the rooms featured 'private closets', and surpassed even Parisian hotels in splendour and comfort.[1] During the 1860s many grand hotels sprang up in the West End. The inaugural day for such hotels was often a scene of pomp and ceremony, such as that of the Langham in Portland Place, which was opened in 1865 by the Prince of Wales, and featured 600 rooms and suites and its own fire brigade.

The hotel industry brought new kinds of employment for both men and women, but especially for women. In 1871 there were 12,700 male servants working in hotels and inns, and 4,300 women. Thirty years later, the number of men working in hotels had doubled, while the number of women had swollen to an almost equal number to the men.[2] British newspapers dating from the 1860s display numerous advertisements for servants, including chambermaids, in both private and public service. Some of these advertisements were for specific but unnamed hotels, such as this notice, which appeared in the *Clerkenwell News,* 20 July 1870:

> CHAMBERMAID wanted for an Hotel. Apply at 11, Ryder-street, St James's.

1 Quoted by Jerry White, *London in the 19th Century* (London: Vintage Books, 2008), p. 194.
2 White, p. 195.

A hotel in Rochester sought 'a Chambermaid or Upper Housemaid', offering wages of £12 'and all found'[1] – 'found' meaning all accommodation and other necessities, as well as food. Advertisements for barmaids, waitresses, chambermaids and 'Young Ladies for Shops'[2] also emanate from agencies like 'Mrs Morgan's Old-established Registry' in Cavendish Square.

Sarah's father and stepmother might have questioned Sarah's decision to enter 'public' rather than private domestic service – hotel chambermaids, like other, especially lower-class, women working in public venues, were often seen as not quite respectable. As one hotel chambermaid wrote in the 1880s: 'I know the public service has a bad name, but that is because some hotels keep fast girls to bring gentleman about the place …'[3] However, service in hotels had the attraction of greater independence, and in some cases greater glamour. Moreover, salaries were supplemented by tips, which could almost double a chambermaid's annual income. The same chambermaid who commented on 'fast girls' in public service also told her readers:

> I have been in my present place five years, and before then I was in another hotel three years, so I can speak for public service, which is very different to private service, and much better to my mind. I had twenty-five rooms to do in the other place, but here I have only thirteen. I get £17 a year, which is the wages, I think, everywhere for chambermaids. Last year I made over £25 by 'tips,' and another girl got £30. I don't know how she did it, for she is in the back wing, but she is a bit flighty. I know chambermaids that make more than that, but our hotel is very select, and since I've been here only one girl has been turned away for being flighty.[4]

---

1 *Daily Telegraph,* 14 January 1871, p.8

2 *London City Press,* 1 October 1870, p.8.

3 Quoted in Michelle Higgs, *Tracing Your Servant Ancestors,* (Barnsley: Pen and Sword Family History, 2012), pp.22–23.

4 Quoted in Michelle Higgs, *Tracing Your Servant Ancestors,* (Barnsley: Pen and Sword Family History, 2012), pp. 22–23, from Toilers In London; Or, *Inquiries Concerning Female Labour in the Metropolis*, being the second part of 'Tempted London' by the 'British

The Alexandra, which had opened in 1864, was one of the most select hotels in London. An imposing building, overlooking Hyde Park and Rotten Row, it offered apartments and suites as well as rooms, and advertised its 'ascending room' (elevator) to all floors. Many members of the board of the Alexandra Hotel Company belonged to the social elite, including the diplomat Sir William Gore Ouseley, Vice-Admiral Sir George Lambert, and Prince Albert's former equerry, Sir Charles du Plat. However, shares in the company were also held by local tradesmen and servants and employees of the hotel.

In August 1864, the hotel management reported that during its first London season every room had been occupied, and applications for apartments had been overwhelming. In addition to advertising its location as 'one of the most cheerful, healthy and pleasant in London', the Alexandra featured an elegant coffee room for ladies and was also a popular host venue for wedding breakfasts. It soon became the hotel of choice for foreign nobility, including the Sultan of Zanzibar and Baron Anselm Rothschild from Austria, as well as wealthy Americans, landowners and gentlemen farmers visiting London from across the United Kingdom. For Sarah Vennell, gaining a job as chambermaid at the Alexandra Hotel must have seemed a considerable achievement.

Whereas there are numerous portraits and sketches of the Nawab in Murshidabad and in the French and British journals, sadly I have found no pictures or photographs of Sarah, nor any physical description of her or her early life. Entries from contemporary school logbooks in East London are among the sources which have allowed me to imagine her childhood. From the portraits of her son I assume that she had the large blue eyes he inherited. I assume also that she must have been strikingly attractive to have so specially caught the eye of the Nawab. Who knows where or how their paths crossed in the hotel? Perhaps he had found her making up the fire in his suite when he rose for early morning prayers, and they had spoken together. Other visitors from India during this period noted the willingness even of lower-class English women to take part in conversation and discuss politics. The diplomat, author

---

Weekly' commissioners, edited by the author of *Out of Work, etc* (London: Hodder and Stoughton, 1889).

and traveller Hafiz Ahmed Hassan, writing about his stay in England in 1870, expressed his amazement at finding members of the lower classes reading and discussing newspapers and public events. 'What are you to think of a country where a common charwoman is able to converse about the war in France, and evince a considerable knowledge of geography?' he wrote.[1]

In this respect, Sarah may have proved a welcome contrast with the Nawab's Indian wives, who had been taught to remain silent and submissive before male and female 'superiors'. Like Queen Victoria, who could enjoy more informal relationships with John Brown and her Munshi, Abdul Karim, the Nawab may have found it a relief to escape in Sarah's company the formality of relations and expectations that marked his meetings with British officials and nobility. Did Sarah insist on marriage before any sexual association, or was the Nawab so entranced by her that he proposed marriage so that she could not become any other man's partner? Oral tradition within my family maintains that Sarah insisted on marriage and on the Nawab seeking her father's consent, a requirement under Islamic Law.

In April 1870 the Nawab paid a visit to Josiah Vennell to seek his consent to the marriage. Family tradition also maintains that Josiah stipulated that the marriage should be a legal one – that is, that it should be a permanent *nikah* marriage contract, not a temporary *mutah* one. Under Sharia law it was permissible for a Muslim to marry a 'woman of the book' – that is, as well as a Muslim, a Christian or a Jew. Sarah later declared that she was not aware that the Nawab already had three wives in India, although the presence of the Nawab's two sons suggests she must have known of at least one prior marriage. However, they were Hasina's sons, and Hasina had died twelve years previously. Whether either Sarah or her father was fully aware that the marriage could not be regarded as legitimate under English law is uncertain. It was to become a crucial issue later.

Traditionally a *nikah* marriage would be preceded by an agreement between the couple as to the terms of a marriage settlement, or *mahr*,

1 For example, Hafiz Ahmed Hassan, *Pilgrimage to the Caaba and Charing Cross* (London: William Allen, 1871) p.136.

which might involve a gift of money and also fulfilment of other obligations, such as care of the wife's family. In Sarah's case, the *mahr* promised a dowry of £10,000 (which she never received) and must also have involved provision for her parents and for her siblings, including her younger brother, George. Shortly after the marriage took place, Josiah was able to retire from running the chandler's shop in East Street, Lambeth, and move with his wife and nineteen-year-old daughter, Mary, to a larger house and more salubrious area at 195 Bulwer Road, Barnet, in North London. George, who was then sixteen years old and working as a clerk, was given the funding to return to school and then train as a lawyer. It is probable that Sarah's other siblings also received financial support.

The marriage itself took place in the Alexandra Hotel on 15 May 1870. It was a quiet and simple ceremony, overseen by the Nawab's scripture reader or one of his courtiers, who would have recited a passage from the Qur'an, traditionally the first verses. He would also have spoken in Arabic on the bride's father's behalf words to the effect, 'I have given away in *nikah* the woman who has thus appointed and authorised me, to the man who has authorised you, on an agreed *mahr*.' The Nawab's response would have been a simple '*Qabiltun Nikaha* (I have accepted the *nikah*).'

And thus Sarah Vennell became the Nawab's English wife, the Nawab Sarah Begum, his fourth living *nikah* wife. She also became a stepmother to the Nawab's many other children, including the two princes who were accompanying their father on his London trip: Hassan, who was six years older than Sarah, and Suleiman, four years her junior. Both of the young princes would always address her as 'Mother' in their letters written to her in later years. Like Cinderella she had been quite suddenly elevated from domestic servant to princess. But the Cinderella story always ended with the marriage; what happened afterwards remained to be told.

The Nawab in Court Dress

CHAPTER 5

Battling Parliament and the Press

1869–1873

His marriage to Sarah Vennell made little change to the Nawab's life at first; he remained a resident of the Alexandra Hotel and he continued his busy round of social and political activities. On Monday 16 May 1870, the day after the wedding ceremony, Mansour Ali Khan was guest of honour at the Royal Theatrical Fund dinner, where he was seated between the Prince of Wales and the Duke of Sutherland. *The Liverpool Daily Post* reported how Lord Lennox toasted the visitors, remarking that 'since his arrival, the Nawab had shown himself a generous supporter of English charities ... and was so great an admirer of Shakespeare that even Mr Buckstone [the manager of the Haymarket Theatre] might be satisfied. The one thing he regretted was that he had not seen Shakespeare more frequently acted.' The Nawab's reply, displaying his command of formal English, was quoted in several papers:

> Your Royal Highness, my lords and gentlemen, I thank you for the cordial manner in which you have associated my name with a list of distinguished visitors present at this festive board. I may add that since my arrival in England it has afforded me much pleasure to visit the several dramatic institutions of the metropolis, and to there witness a display of talent and theatrical art which I suppose is unsurpassed in any other part of the world.

Mansour Ali Khan's eminent status, his generosity and his manifest appreciation of English culture made him a desirable guest at aristocratic gatherings. The next day he and his sons 'assisted Her Majesty' at the

Queen's Drawing Room, a reception also hosted by the Prince and Princess of Wales, and the Duke of Cambridge. On Wednesday 18 May, the Nawab attended the annual charity dinner for the Metropolitan Free Hospital. Along with the Prince and Princess of Wales he visited the Botanic Gardens on 19 May. He and his sons were among the guests at the Queen's levee on 1 June, the second Queen's levee that the Nawab had attended since he had been in England, as well as an assembly held by the Countess of Clarendon for the Queen's official birthday celebration on 2 June. He also attended a fancy dress ball in the club known as Willis's Rooms on 7 June. Such social engagements, including travel to Birmingham, Worcester and Portsmouth, continued at this pace throughout the year.

Sarah was not included in any of these outings. Many of them were all-male affairs, although occasionally, as in the case of the Theatrical Fund dinner, ladies were allowed to sit in the galleries, or a female singer might be invited to provide musical entertainment for the assembled guests. But wives did attend other social and ceremonial occasions. Not Sarah. She had risen in status to become the Nawab Begum, but she had also become the wife of a Muslim man, although it seems she remained a Christian. Her new status brought many changes. The long hours and drudgery of work as a servant had been left behind; now she was served by others. She had the time and leisure to visit her family and friends, and to enjoy seeing the benefits her marriage had brought them. And, as Helen Mackenzie and others have testified, the Nawab could be charming and affectionate, treating her with a courtesy and respect that she had not encountered before. Moreover he was also a very experienced lover.

In the midst of his packed schedule, the Nawab found time to attend the annual meeting of Royal Literary Fund. Formed to assist impoverished writers and their families, the RLF had been strongly supported by the Royal Family since its foundation in 1790. As guests of honour at the AGM, the Nawab and his sons were seated immediately to the right of the presiding president, Lord Stanley (whose son was six months later to become the first Muslim peer in the House of Lords). Lord Royston sat on Lord Stanley's left. Among those present was the novelist Anthony Trollope, and it is perhaps no coincidence that Trollope's next 'Palliser' novel, *The Eustace Diamonds*, first serialised in 1871, includes a running reference to the grievances of 'the Sawab of Mygawb'. In Trollope's novel the Sawab's claim against the British government aggravates the conflict between the Liberal Under-Secretary of State for India, Lord Fawn, and the Conservative MP and lawyer, Frank Greystock, as Fawn supports the Sawab's case, and Greystock argues against it. And as in the main plot of the novel, which hinges on whether or not the diamonds should be seen as an heirloom or as a disposable gift, the Nawab of Bengal's claim rested on whether or not his pension and estate were inherited or were a gift at the disposal of the British government.

However, as the fictional title Sawab of Mygawb suggests, the Nawab of Bengal was not the only member of Indian royalty whose claims were being debated during this period. For example, the case of the Nawab of Tonk, who had been exiled to Benares and disinherited from his kingdom by the Governor-General of India, came before Parliament in 1870. Members of Parliament sympathetic to the Nawab of Tonk raised concerns about other Indian Rajahs and Nawabs whose titles had been abolished. They included Prince Azeem Jah, whose title and kingdom of Carnatic had been confiscated when Dalhousie was Governor-General; the King of Mysore, whose chosen heir the British refused to recognise; and Duleep Singh, whose father had ruled the Punjab.

Why then does the Nawab of Bengal feature so prominently in an array of British newspapers, and why do those same newspapers rarely mention the other disinherited Indian princes? One reason could be the significance of Bengal as the setting of Britain's first occupation of India as a puppet state, rather than a trading partner, and with it the celebration of Clive of India and the notoriety of 'The Black Hole of Calcutta'. Bengal was also the scene of the first actions in the 1857 'Mutiny', and Calcutta the capital of the British Raj and residence of the Governor-General. Many British families had relatives who had served in Bengal as civil servants or soldiers, and so Bengal was a place whose name conjured up a multitude of mixed associations, a name that could immediately arouse interest when seen in the papers.

The Nawab's presence at the Royal Literary Fund dinner may

suggest another reason for the constant publicity relating to him and his activities. Here he would be seen by many of the most influential writers and journalists in England; their awareness of and sympathy for his cause could be very useful. His aptly named secretary, Mr Fox, would have been keen to encourage the press hounds to take up the chase, preferably to bark rather than bite.

The publication of the Nawab's memorial (see chapter 3), detailing the history of Britain's mistreatment of the Nawb's family, had sparked a flurry of notices and comments on the Nawab's activities and claims. Financial incentives may also have encouraged sympathetic reviews and articles. In 1877, when the Nawab's extensive debts were being reviewed, several payments for 'literary services' were listed. Some of these seem to have been one-off payments to specific journals, journalists and politicians.

One named journal was *Vanity Fair*, which received payments of £40 and £100. It printed several articles supporting his cause. *Vanity Fair* also published a caricature of the Nawab on 16 April 1870, which did not meet with the Nawab's approval. According to a later report in the *Huddersfield Daily Chronicle*, Mr Fox was summoned to the Nawab, to be confronted with the offending caricature and the Nawab's outrage at what he regarded an impudent, ugly and libellous depiction. Mr Fox struggled to explain the tradition of caricature in British journals and sought to appease the Nawab by assuring him that only the most important people, such as the Prime Minister and the Archbishop of Canterbury, were chosen to be the subject of caricatures in *Vanity Fair* or *Punch*. Indeed, Mr Fox contended, to be caricatured should be regarded as an honour rather than a mark of disrespect.

In general the mixture of paid adverts and genuine sympathy for the Nawab in the press worked. By far the majority of British publications favoured the Nawab's cause and fostered his image as a prestigious, exotic Indian royal. Whereas in Murshidabad British officials sought to wean Mansour Ali Khan away from what they saw as 'Asiatic excesses', in England and Europe his role was to be an oriental celebrity – any display of Western dress or behaviour was met with displeasure. He probably shared the experience of the Nawab of Tonk's representative, Hafiz Ahmed Hassan, who noted that while 'officials in India are haughty, rough and

'A Living Monument to Injustice',
Vanity Fair, 16 April 1870

overbearing in behaviour to natives of all classes, including the native gentry', by contrast he encountered in England 'much kindness, affability, and courtesy from various members of the aristocracy and gentry'.[1]

But not all were sympathetic. Some journalists sneered at the expenses incurred by the Nawab and his retinue, and were openly racist in their comments on 'Hindoo habits'. The Irish papers tended to be either ardently supportive of the Nawab and indignant at this continuing story of British injustice, or critical of the Nawabs of Bengal as collaborators who had betrayed their own people. The support and intervention of Irish politicians would become significant in later years. However, in 1870, one Irish nationalist paper dissociated itself from the temptations

1 Hafiz Ahmed Hassan, *Pilgrimage to the Caaba and Charing Cross,* p.138

of money and oriental glamour which had, in its view, seduced the British press. *The Nation*'s reporter later wrote:

> When, in 1870, the journals of England were absolutely 'reeking with sympathy' for the aggrieved Nawab Nazim of Bengal, we were able to tell pretty accurately the origin of that feeling. A poetical squib, written in the character of an indignant Englishman (there were some such persons, perhaps) appeared in one of the publications issued on the *Nation* office at that time, which contained the following lines:
>
> What shall we do at all, at all
> With this here Nawab of Bengal?
> We've something else to mind today
> Besides the Nawab and his pay.
> But turn to read where'er we will,
> The Nawab's name confronts us still.
> Some purchased puff before us lies,
> Some venal 'leader' meets our eyes,
> Marked with a pen or pencil scrawl.
> About this Nawab of Bengal.
>
> Oh, foolish Nawab of Bengal,
> You should not linger here at all;
> In vain to clamour for redress
> You hire our glorious British press;
> In vain you pay for friendly words
> From poor M.P.'s and needy lords;
> Your time and cash are spent in vain,
> For what we've gripped you'll not regain;
> Home from our shores you'd better flee
> Before you've lost your last rupee,
> And off to jail the lawyers haul,
> The Nawab Nazim of Bengal.[1]

1 *Nation*, 13 January 1877, p.14. See also *The Kent Courier*.

In July 1870, Mayo had sent his response to the Nawab's petition and memorial, dismissing the Nawab's claim to hereditary rights. He informed the Duke of Argyll that the Nawab Nazim had 'no right or title whatsoever to any alliance by treaty', and that it was pointless to discuss the morality or policy of British government or East India Company actions, 'since they were in substance a conquest of Bengal by the Company'.[1] This was a striking contrast in tone and substance to the private letter sent the previous year by Mayo to Argyll. It was also a significant rewriting of history by the Earl of Mayo and his advisors. As Major (Thomas) Evans Bell, a persistent critic of British imperialism, wrote at the time, 'A confederacy with Native nobles and ministers, and a campaign carried out with Native troops, ending in the installation of a Native Prince [Mir Jafar], can hardly be called a conquest.'[2]

Six months later, the Duke of Argyll informed the Nawab that his title could not be regarded as hereditary, and his complaints were rejected. Nor would the government reconsider the Torrens case and disappearance of the family funds or the reinstatement of his right not to appear in civil court. Moreover, the title of Nawab Nazim of Bengal, Bihar and Orissa would be abolished, and his successor would be called the Nawab of Murshidabad, receiving a stipend not exceeding four lakh rupees (today equivalent to about 2.5 million pounds) per annum. The Duke wished, however, to indicate that the British government graciously forgave the loan of 300,000 rupees given towards the expenses of his visits, and would now regard it as a gift. Such a minor concession must have seemed both offensive and demeaning in the face of the news that the Murshidabad family's status, fortune and privileges were all about to be so radically diminished by the British government.

The Nawab not only had failed in his mission to restore his family's rights and fortune, but was now faced with their near-total obliteration. He was devastated. His reward for support and loyalty to the British before and during the 1857 Indian Rebellion had been, over the period of his reign, the loss of the equivalent of over 16 million pounds and many of the precious jewels stolen by Henry Torrens, as well as the

1 Mirza, *From Plassey to Pakistan*, p.97.

2 *The Bengal Reversion* (London, 1872), p. 45

reduction of his annual stipend from the equivalent of 7 million pounds to 2.5 million pounds. Worst of all was the abolition of his eminent status as Nawab of Bengal, Bihar and Orissa, an area more than three times the size of Great Britain; and the revoking of almost all marks of his status as a monarch, including the nineteen-gun salute and the right not to appear in a court of law. From now on, the British government proposed, his successor would be titled Nawab of Murshidabad, a small province in Bengal.

However, Mansour Ali Khan now had one more option, a direct appeal to the House of Commons for the restoration of his rights and hereditary stipend. Argyll was Secretary of State for India, and Gladstone's liberals were not anxious to retain strong links with India, except where trade was concerned; given these factors, such an appeal would be difficult to win. Nevertheless, the Nawab's secretary, William Fox, encouraged him to follow this procedure, and continued his campaign of issuing press releases, distributing pamphlets, and lobbying Members of Parliament. Members and supporters of the Liberal party carried on a counter campaign in Parliament and in papers such as the *Pall Mall Gazette* and the *Illustrated London News*, drawing attention to the Nawab's lavish lifestyle and his association with lower-class women, while also claiming that he had no claim to a hereditary royal title.

A private letter from Argyll to Mayo, dated 17 March 1871, indicates that the outcome of the appeal was not certain, and indeed that – off the record – the Nawab's case might have some merit:

> The Nawab Nazim's case is to come soon in the Commons. There is much in that position – history of that Nizamut fund that is anomalous and uncomfortable – and easily capable of being misunderstood and misrepresented – and the action of the House of Commons on Indian affairs is not easily calculated. The Tories will vote for anything which has a chance of putting the Government in a minority.[1]

Six weeks later Argyll wrote again, expressing more anxiety: 'All the

1 Private Letters from the Earl of Mayo to the Duke of Argyll, 1869. Mss Eur, pp. 54–5.

discontented Indian Princes get themselves friends in the House of Commons – a great many of the radicals have an inherent proclivity towards nations hostile to the Government of India ... Northcote is away, and until he returns we have no one on whom we can rely on our side of the house to keep it right on Indian matters.'

The motion to consider the Nawab's appeal was debated in the House of Commons on 4 July 1871. Edmund Haviland-Burke, a descendant of Edmund Burke and a supporter of Irish Home Rule, moved that a select committee be set up to investigate the Nawab's complaints. Speaking on behalf of the government, M. E. Grant Duff argued that the Nawab Nazim's title and income were merely personal awards by the East India Company and British government; even if they were hereditary, the British government need no longer be bound by treaties made before 1857. The Nawab's loyalty to the British during the 1857 uprising was irrelevant, Duff went on to argue, since if he had been disloyal then the British would simply have removed him. When the motion to investigate the complaints was finally moved, sixty-four MPs, mainly Irish, voted in favour, and 122 MPs voted against.

Argyll was triumphant. His aim now was to remove Mansour Ali Khan from Britain as quickly as possible, and send him back to India. He wrote:

> You will have seen that we beat the Nawab – with the aid of your friends. But the radicals generally vote against the Indian Govt as a matter of course. We shall now try to get the Nawab to go home. But he is an obstinate Brute [*sic*] and difficult to deal with.[1]

For Mansour Ali Khan the defeat was a bitter disappointment. However, he was indeed obstinate. Not only his own status but that of his sons and his whole family was at stake. He would stay and continue to fight his cause. Moreover, a return to Murshidabad would be humiliating and an admission of failure. His life there would be even more constricted and closely monitored than it had been before. In Britain he was free to travel whenever he wished and without prior permission, and he was

1 Private Letters from the Earl of Mayo to the Duke of Argyll, 1869. Mss Eur, pp. 79–80.

treated with greater deference. His new wife was reluctant to leave her family and travel to India, particularly with a three-month-old baby. The Nawab decided to send his eldest son, Hassan, back to Murshidabad to take care of affairs there, while he himself would remain in London with Sarah and with Hasina's younger son, Suleiman. In fact it would be another ten years before he finally left England and returned to India.

CHAPTER 6

The Nawab's English Family

1871–1881

Sarah's transformation from lowly chambermaid to the wife of an Indian monarch brought an extraordinary change for her and her family. She was treated with a courtesy and respect she had not encountered previously. Nor had she ever possessed the jewels, the fine clothes, the servants and the leisure time that the Nawab now provided for her. At first even more bewildering was the fact that, although she remained a Christian, she had become part of a Muslim world, where the religious observances, the language, the food, the music, the clothing, the social codes were all unfamiliar.

How much Sarah knew about the sons, daughters and co-wives back in India is not clear; she would later claim that she was unaware of any other wives living at the time of their marriage, and she seems to have assumed that her new husband would regard her as his one and only wife. Hasina's two sons had accompanied the Nawab to England, so she was certainly well aware of them, but Hasina had died in 1858. Hassan, Hasina's oldest child with the Nawab, would have been just eleven at the time of his mother's death, while Suleiman, now twelve, must have been less than two years old.

Humayun Mirza – the descendant of Mansour Ali Mirza's first *nikah* wife Shams-i-Jehan Begum – indicates in his book *From Plassey to Pakistan* that in the Murshidabad palaces these two young men were seen as the children of an 'upstart' Abyssynian slave woman who had usurped the affections of her husband and the inheritance of her own son. Neither Shams-i-Jehan nor the Nawab's other wives were likely to have concealed their resentment of the Nawab's preference for Hasina and her children. The Nawab may well have feared for the safety of Hasina's two sons if they were left behind in Murshidabad while he was in England. Frequent accounts exist where deaths of children in the palaces lead to suspicions of poisoning at the hands of jealous wives, who hoped their own children would gain precedence if older children with more direct claims to inheritance were 'removed'.

Sarah's feelings towards Hassan and Suleiman are not known. However, having lost her own mother when she was only five, and gaining a stepmother soon afterwards, Sarah must have had some awareness of how the Nawab's sons might feel with regard to the mutual loss of a parent at a young age. She knowingly accepted the Nawab's two sons as part of the marriage contract, and it would have been clear to her that any children she bore would not be competing for her husband's title when he died. Suleiman was only a year or two younger than her brother George; so her relationship with him would have included both motherly and sisterly elements.

Hassan and Suleiman were accustomed to a world where their father accumulated wives and mistresses, and where they themselves accumulated stepbrothers and stepsisters. In Murshidabad they had, like their father, been well tutored in the English language and had known many European officials and servants, including Colonel Layard and Mr Fox who accompanied them to England. The peculiarly English attitudes towards different strata of class would have been foreign to them despite their royal status in India. For Sarah, accustomed to the offhand casualness of her own family life and the brusque or dismissive attitudes of hotel guests and supervisors, the civility and deference with which they treated her must have been a new and welcome experience.

But the role of mother in this new family was at first uncharted. This was not the kind of mothering Sarah had previously experienced as a child or when looking after her younger brother and her neighbour's small children. To begin with she was not living with her husband and his sons. Even when she later began living in the same household, the everyday practical matters, which in her worldly experience would have defined a motherly role, were removed. Now it was the servants who arranged what clothes should be worn for each occasion, prepared the food, dealt with the children when they fell ill. Not that she could have attempted to cook the kinds of food her husband and stepsons preferred; nor would she have known how to look after and arrange their elaborate clothes. Nevertheless, a bond grew between Sarah and the Nawab's sons. A letter from Hassan to Sarah a few years after he had returned to Murshidabad in 1871 closes:

> … I convey my affectionate kisses towards my brothers and sisters,
> I shall feel very happy to get yours and their photographs.
>
> We are all well here hoping you are doing the same.
>
> I remain, my dear mother, your affectionate son.
> Hassan Ali Meerza[1]

His letters to her in later years continue to address her as 'Mother', and express his respect, fondness, and concern for her.

Neither the Nawab nor Sarah would have considered it appropriate for her to live with him in the Alexandra Hotel, where she had been one among the many servants who still worked there. Like many upper-class Muslim wives, Sarah Begum had been settled in her own women's household. This was White Lodge, a small house in Keppel Street, Chelsea (now Tryon Street), a street known for its gardens and plant nurseries, about one mile from the Alexandra Hotel. Once owned by the photographer and inventor John Charles Stovin, who had migrated to New Zealand, the house was now occupied by Stovin's wife, Elizabeth. At the time of the 1871 census Elizabeth's fellow residents included Sarah, Sarah's older sister Louisa Ann Vennell, and a second Sarah, a servant called Sarah Rowhen. Here, in April 1871, eleven months after her marriage, Sarah Begum gave birth to her first child, Miriam. Reports of the infant's birth and the Nawab's marriage to Sarah now reached Murshidabad, where it caused dismay. The British Agent wrote, 'The effect which the news of these proceedings has had on the minds

1 IOR/LS/P/13.

of the disconsolate Begums at Moorshedabad can easily be imagined.'[1]

Following Louisa's marriage and departure from the Keppel Street household in May 1871, Sarah took up residence in 20 Brompton Square, just a few blocks from the Alexandra Hotel. It was a four-storey Georgian terrace house, facing a pleasant tree-lined park. The Nawab visited his wife and baby when his social and political life left him free to do so. Sarah was soon pregnant again; another baby girl, named Sara, was born just one year after Miriam. But little Sara did not survive; her mother watched helplessly as her tiny near-namesake grew weaker and weaker from diarrhoea and convulsions until she died on 24 July 1872, just three months old. She was buried nearby, in Kensal Green cemetery. A third baby girl, Hajerah, was born in March 1873. Notice of all three births was sent to Murshidabad.

Meanwhile Mansour Ali Khan had formed a brief liaison with a young woman living in Chelsea, called Emma Hallett. She gave birth to their son, Freddie, in June 1874. Although Emma very soon after married Israel Mohsin, and the child was registered as Abraham Mohsin, the Nawab acknowledged responsibility and secretly provided maintenance for his first England-born son (who in India Office files remained identified as Freddie Hallett). Humayun Mirza believes that Sarah was unaware of this liaison and Freddie's existence,[2] but it is possible that Sarah either knew or suspected that her husband was visiting other women. Given the pressure from the British government that he should quit Britain, she may also have feared that he might return to India and leave her and her children unprovided for.

While Sarah was recovering from this almost continuous series of pregnancies and births – and, with the assistance of a nursemaid and servants, attending to her infant girls – Mansour Ali Khan was recovering from the disappointment of Parliament's refusal to consider his petition. In late 1871 he had resumed his campaign to restore his family's status and fortune. With the assistance and encouragement of his secretary William Fox and other well-wishers, he sought more publicity and the support of influential Englishmen and women for his cause. Now his tactics

1 Quoted in Mirza, *From Plassey to Pakistan,* p.96.

2 *From Plassey to Pakistan,* p.103.

were slightly different. Instead of sending out the Nawab's own detailed memorandum to newspaper editors and Members of Parliament as they had done in 1870, his staff and supporters turned attention to a series of books that addressed the wider question of British dealing with India, drawing on the history of the Nawabs of Bengal as a particularly telling example of policies which were misguided and in bad faith.

Three books were published in 1872: *The Princes of India, Their Rights and Duties* by F. W. Chesson; *The Bengal Reversion: Another 'Exceptional Case'* by Thomas Evans Bell; and *Empire in Asia: How We Acquired It: A Book of Confessions* by W. T. McCullagh Torrens (no relation to Henry Torrens, the British Agent who had misappropriated the Nawab's money and jewels two decades previously). Chesson and Evans Bell specialised in writing books that exposed imperial wrongdoing in South Africa as well as various principalities in India, while Torrens made a practice of raising the Nawab's case in Parliament, and later led a delegation to ask the Duke of Argyll, Gladstone's Secretary of State for India, to reconsider the issue. Each of these books received long, serious, and generally favourable reviews in British journals and newspapers. Both Torrens's and Chesson's books were given particularly sympathetic reviews in the Irish *Freeman's Journal*, which drew detailed comparisons between the British government's treatment of its Irish and Indian subjects.

As part of the strategy to encourage a wider understanding of the issues, the Nawab joined with the Maharajah Duleep Singh and others to create a venue where upper-class Indians and English people could meet. The 12 January 1872 *Morning Advertiser* carried the following announcement:

> ORIENTALS IN LONDON – As the number of Orientals resident in London increases, the want of an adequate or regular means of social intercourse between them and educated Englishmen becomes more apparent. To remedy this, a social meeting once a week at rooms to be engaged, the expenses of which reunion would be defrayed by a small annual subscription. Many influential persons have given their adhesion to this movement.[1]

1 *Morning Advertiser,* 12 January 1872, p.2.

The *Morning Advertiser* also mentions but does not name 'several distinguished ladies' as supporters of the group. In addition to the Nawab of Bengal, these 'influential persons' included the Liberal Lord Chancellor William Page Wood; former Viceroy of India Lord Lawrence; former Secretary of State for India Charles Wood; former Governor of Bombay Sir Bartle Frere; and Maharajah Duleep Singh.

The Maharajah Duleep Singh had lived in the United Kingdom since he had been brought there as a child in 1854 following the British conquest of Punjab, and both he and the Nawab were frequent guests at Queen Victoria's levees and at receptions held by English and Scottish aristocrats. However, neither of them had previously made common cause with other disinherited Indian princes. Both had declared themselves loyal subjects of the Queen and seemed to have identified themselves not so much with India and other Indians but rather as specifically belonging to the Punjab or Bengal. Duleep Singh had converted (or, some would argue, had been converted) to Christianity when he was fifteen, but was now developing an interest in Sikhism; the Nawab remained a firm believer in Islam. Until now they may have considered that there were more differences than similarities between them. But in British eyes they shared a common identity as 'Orientals' and as members of Indian royalty, an identity which obscured and carried more weight than regional affiliations or religion. Having now spent almost three years in Britain, Mansour Ali Khan became increasingly aware of others like himself who had suffered loss of status and property under British rule in India.

During 1872 both Duleep Singh and the Nawab attended lectures by sympathisers such as Chesson, and joined in discussions with 'educated Englishmen' and 'distinguished ladies'. The Nawab was also present, along with Charles Dickens and Benjamin Disraeli, at the Royal Literary Fund dinner, that year hosted by the King of Belgium. His presence at court and other aristocratic gatherings such as the Annual Liberian Ball was noted in the papers, and his status as a celebrity seems not to have diminished. His attendance at the Lyceum Theatre (to see Henry Irving in *The Bells*) was news, as was his presence in March as a spectator of the Oxford/Cambridge Boat Race, despite heavy snow. On none of these occasions was Sarah reported as present, although the wives of other grandees, including Duleep Singh's, often were. Sarah's almost continual 'condition', whether pregnant or recovering after childbirth, may have been a sufficient reason for her absence. However, the Nawab was probably aware that his marriage to a working-class Englishwoman would not be well received in the upper-class circles where he and his sons were welcomed. At this point the marriage does not appear to have been public knowledge.

When a thanksgiving ceremony was held at St Paul's Cathedral on 27 February 1872 for the recovery of the Prince of Wales from typhoid, Mansour Ali Khan was among those who attended. A report of this occasion in the *Bedfordshire Times and Independent* gives a list of eminent persons proceeding in their carriages to St Paul's, including Mr and Mrs Gladstone and the Archbishop of Canterbury. The newspaper comments that 'many of these distinguished persons were cheered by the crowd; Mr Disraeli and the Nawab of Bengal especially so'.[1] That coupling of Disraeli and the Nawab being cheered 'especially so' is intriguing; was it because both were seen to be in opposition to Gladstone's government? Or was it for the seemingly disparate causes that Disraeli would later unite when he came to power in 1874 – sympathy for the stark inequalities experienced by the working classes together with the allure of the British Raj? Or was it the exotic glamour they both represented that so appealed to people whose everyday lives were drab and colourless?

Many reports in the newspapers make much of the Nawab's apparent opulence – his clothing glittering with gold leaf and jewels, his purchase of a racehorse, his generous gifts to charity. But his expensive life style could not be maintained; he was deeply in debt and the creditors from whom he had raised loans in India were demanding repayment. The monthly stipend of approximately £2,500 a month (equivalent to over £160,000 today) sent to the Nawab from the Nizamut fund was neither sufficient for his current expenses nor sustainable, given dwindling income from the Murshidabad estates. The Nawab asked his son Hassan to sell some of the jewels that were then in Murshidabad, but the British

1 *Bedfordshire Times and Independent*, 5 March 1872, p. 7.

government objected, claiming that these jewels belonged to the State rather than the family.

In November 1873, the British government took over management of the Nizamut finances, including the stipend for the Nawab Nazim, 'in order to preserve the dignity and honour of an exalted Indian family and that public sentiment may not be hurt by their fall into utter poverty[1].' From the Nawab's point of view, however, 'utter poverty' was precisely what was about to hurt him. On 1 January 1874, his monthly stipend was cut by 80 per cent, from 25,000 rupees to 5,000 rupees: worth then around £550 and today equivalent to about £35,000. Meanwhile, the British government and corporations continued to profit from its revenues from Bengal. During just two months in 1875 'the receipts from three sales of Bengal opium', mainly to China, came to £136,701, equivalent in today's money to nearly 9 million pounds.

Groups of sympathetic MPs led by Torrens attempted on several occasions to reopen the Nawab's case in Parliament, but were met with rebuffs from the Duke of Argyll each time. After one such attempt, the London correspondent for the *Belfast Telegraph* reported that the Duke was 'very abrupt in his manner, and very summary in his mode of disposing of the delegation, [declaring] that he had too much regard for the ratepayers of India to hold out the faintest hope that his Highness's income would be increased'.[2] The papers did not mention whether the Duke had equal concern as to whether ratepayers of India and England were happy to contribute so heavily to the enormous expenses of the English royal family and the British administration of India.

Following the sudden death in October 1873 of William Fox, the secretary who had been so zealous in promoting his cause, the Nawab realised that his efforts to recover his full stipend were unlikely to succeed, and his present lifestyle in London could not continue. Argyll hoped he would now return to India, but the Nawab was unwilling to do so. In Murshidabad he would be besieged by creditors, and constrained by condescending British officials. In England he could enjoy relative freedom, variety and respect. Moreover, he was very much attached to

1 *From Plassey to Pakistan*, p.101.

2 *Belfast Telegraph*, 12 July 1872, p.4.

Sarah, and she may have been reluctant to leave England and lose all contact with her own family.

By the end of 1873, the Nawab had found it necessary to leave his expensive apartments in the Alexandra Hotel. Hassan, the Nawab's oldest son, had returned to Murshidabad the previous year to try to look after the Nawab's interests there; Suleiman, his younger son with Hasina, was at boarding school in England. These changes may have been for the Nawab a matter of regret, but for Sarah it meant she could now live openly with her husband. Following the example of the Maharajah Duleep Singh, who owned a country estate in Norfolk, they rented a twenty-one-room Elizabethan mansion on the Borde Hill estate near Cuckfield, Sussex. For the first time in her life, Sarah was not living in London. The space, the lack of crowds and traffic, the sounds of farm animals and birds were all a novelty. Borde Hill House was surrounded by 224 acres of farmland and woods, and the front room with its ornate green wallpaper looked out over the Sussex Downs. From that room one could glimpse the great Balcombe Viaduct and swirls of steam and smoke as the London train puffed its way towards Brighton. It took less than two hours for friends and family to travel by train to nearby Balcombe. And from Balcombe, one could also take the train to Brighton and see the Royal Pavilion with its imitation oriental palace and gardens.

Sarah had now become part of a Muslim household, where halal food was served, pork and ham forbidden, and the five daily prayers followed an orderly sequence. At home in the summer her husband wore a simple white cotton tunic and trousers, and each morning he rose at dawn and faced east to say the Fajr, or morning prayers. Hearing the Indian servants talking among themselves she might gradually have learnt a few Urdu words and Muslim greetings – 'acha', 'tik', 'shukriya', 'ji-nahin', 'asalaam Aleikum' ('good', 'all right or fine', 'thank you', 'yes', 'peace be with you'). This too was where she experienced her first Ramadan, which Mansour Ali Khan, his courtiers and his Muslim servants observed that October and November. She ate on her own or with George during the daylight hours, and joined her husband each evening when he broke the fast with a sweet kajool date. Eid al-fitr was

The house on Borde Hill, Sussex

on 12 November, and the feast that day was lavish, with several kinds of sweet milky pudding prepared by the Indian servants. The Nawab gave everyone, including the servants, gifts. It was probably on such an occasion that Sarah received one of the several pearl and diamond rings she possessed.

Five days later the midwife was hastily summoned from Cuckfield to help deliver Sarah and the Nawab's fourth daughter, Vaheedoonissa, on 18 November 1874. Eighty years later that same Vaheedoonissa, my great-aunt, would send letters about events in Bengal and Pakistan to my mother in Australia, along with the tiny bottle of perfume from Murshidabad that I still possess, and which has travelled with me from Australia to America and England, and so back to Vaheedoonissa's birthplace.

Sarah might have found this new household and its surroundings difficult to adjust to, but she did have the familiar company of her young brother, and doubtless an English nursemaid and other servants. George, now twenty, had become the Nawab's secretary, and was enjoying the pursuits of a country gentleman. That he was new and rather unskilled in such pursuits is indicated by a short news item in the *Kent and Sussex*

Courier reporting that George, 'when hastily discharging his gun at an unexpected rise', had accidentally shot a young beater named Winter in the head. Fortunately for George and his victim, 'the young man [was] said to be going on favourably[1].' Another report noted that the Nawab had himself accompanied Mr Winter in a carriage to his mother's house in nearby Cuckfield and waited while the doctor extracted 'a good many of the shot'.

At the end of the twelve months for which the Nawab had rented Borde Hill, the family moved back to London. Here it was easier for Mansour Ali Khan to pursue his political lobbying for his traditional rights and fortune, and here also he could enjoy a more varied social life with the aristocratic families who continued to invite him to their gatherings. Now he rented another Elizabethan mansion, Pymmes House, in Edmonton, North London. In earlier times it had been the home of the Tudor statesman Robert Cecil and his descendants. Like Borde Hill, Pymmes House was surrounded by parkland, with ponds and gardens shaded in the summer by great chestnut and oak trees.

From Pymmes House, Sarah could more easily visit her father and stepmother, just over an hour's carriage ride away in New Barnet, where the Nawab had bought them a newly built villa, much larger than the cramped little house over their shop in Lambeth. Still only twenty-two, she was now the mother of three small girls and mistress of a large household of servants, both English and Indian.

When they moved to Pymmes House Sarah was again pregnant. Already the mother of three children, and perhaps aware of her husband's affair with Emma Hallett, Sarah persuaded the Nawab to make a declaration before Robert Carden, the acting Lord Mayor of London, testifying to their marriage and its legitimacy under Muslim Shi'i law, and acknowledging their three living daughters as 'the fruit of his loins'. The declaration, signed on 26 August 1875, read:

> I, Syud Munsoor Ullee Nawab Nazim of Bengal Behar and Orissa, a Mahomedan native of India of the Sheah Sect and of the Ossullee branch of that sect at present resident temporarily

1 *Kent and Sussex Courier*, 23 October 1874, p.3.

Pymmes House, Edmonton. Home of the Nawab, 1875–1878

at Pymmes Park Edmonton in the county of Middlesex in England, do hereby formally and solemnly declare that on the fifteenth day of May in the year one thousand eight hundred and seventy, I entered into a marriage and duly contracted such marriage according to the law and forms of the Sheah sect of Mohamedans as required in the case of a marriage with a Kitabeeah woman with Miss Sarah Vennell (hereinafter giving her separate declaration) the daughter of Josiah Godfrey Vennell of No. 1 Colyton Villas, Bulwer Road, New Barnet, Herts, and with his (her father's) express consent, she being at the time a single or unmarried Kitebeeah woman professing the Christian religion, and I hereby state and declare that on the date and location of the marriage above mentioned, I and the said lady mutually declared our acceptance of each other as husband and wife respectively by the usual and customary words as prescribed to be used on such an occasion of marriage by the above law and with the intention of binding ourselves as husband and wife, and I further in like manner state and declare that the said marriage was afterwards

> in due course consummated by me and the said lady and that I and the said lady ever since have lived together and are still living together as husband and wife.[1]

Kitabeah is derived from *kitab*, Urdu for book, hence a *kitabeah* was a 'woman of the book', i.e. a woman who is a Muslim, Jew or a Christian and whose faith derives from the Bible. The Nawab's declaration was followed by Sarah's sworn statement affirming her assent to his testimonial and declaring that she had 'by the required words at the time and occasion of the marriage' accepted the Nawab Nazim as her husband.

Additionally, two days before this declaration, the Nawab signed an indenture affirming that Sarah had been endowed £10,000 (the equivalent today of over £600,000) as part of the marriage contract, and promising that each of his three daughters and any subsequent children should be paid £5,000 when they attained the age of twenty-one, this sum to paid out of the Nizamut deposit fund. The indenture also specified that these payments were conditional upon the children being brought up and educated as Shi'i Muslims. Moreover it affirmed that it was 'the special consideration and agreement of this agreement that it will be lawful for His Highness if he shall be so minded exclusively and irrevocably to have and exercise all control over the said children now living and such after-born children (if any) as aforesaid both as relates to their education bringing up and religious teaching and to all other matters whatsoever.' Such conditions that gave full control to the children's father, although impossible to consider now, were in accord with English law and custom in the 1870s. This document was signed by Syed Mansur Ali, Sarah Begam, George Vennell and James Lyster O'Beirne. It was witnessed by the Nawab's new secretary, Valentine Holt, and Mowbray Walker, a lawyer who would later become a guardian for the children.

On 26 October 1875, Sarah gave birth to her first son, named Syed after his father's nomenclature on official documents. Twenty months later, on 22 June 1877, my grandfather, Nusrat, was born. The Nawab

1 OIR/L/PS 13.

was especially pleased by the arrival of his two 'English sons'. For almost three years Sarah and Mansour Ali Khan enjoyed with their five children the spacious elegance and rural attractions of Pymmes Park. There the Nawab could also be seen as an eminent benefactor within the local community for whom the estate could be made available on special occasions. A July 1877 report in the *Tottenham and Edmonton Weekly Herald* tells of one such occasion when a group of nearly 300 Sunday School children from the Edmonton Congregational Chapel enjoyed games and tea in Pymmes Park 'kindly lent for the occasion by His Highness the Nawab-Nazim of Bengal'. During the afternoon the Millfield House Band 'played at intervals ... in their usual excellent style'.

When the lease on Pymmes House expired in March 1878, the advertised auction by Mr George Cowles, 'honoured with instructions from His Highness the Nawab Nazim of Bengal', gives a glimpse of the world the family had occupied:

> Pymmes Park, Edmonton, near Silver Street Station. – About 10,000 very superior Bedding and Greenhouse plants, including several fine Orange and specimen Banana trees, two shorthorn Cows, handsome Bay Cob, Black Horse, Pony, Poultry, Dogcart, Basket Chaises, Double and Single Harness, Farm and Garden Implements, Tools, boarded Pheasantry ...[1]

Additionally, the furniture was advertised as the contents of 'sixteen Bed and Dressing Rooms, Drawing, Dining, Morning and Billiard Rooms, Library, Domestic Offices, Dairy, etc.'. Specific items included a full-sized billiard table, oak dining and library suites, 'valuable oil paintings', and some 'very richly Engraved and Handsomely Cut Glass'.

However, the Nawab's dwindling finances and mounting debts now forced them to find a smaller house in the city. The year after Nusrat's birth, the family moved to 42 Bedford Square, one of a series of elegant four-storey Georgian dwellings facing a small private park. Sarah sought appropriate furnishing for this house. An affectionate letter sent to her

1 *London Evening Standard,* 19 March 1878, p.8.

by Hassan, her oldest stepson, from Murshidabad in December 1878, responds to her request for a tiger-skin rug:

> My dear Mother,
>
> I have received your kind note of the 17th November last in due time – I am sorry to learn that Miriam Begum is not in good health – I expect her recovery by the time this letter reaches you. You have desired me to send you the skin of a tiger killed by me in chase. I would have gladly done so if I had any with me now. If I succeed in getting one next time when I go out for hunting, I will lose no time in sending it to you.[1]

In late 1879 Sarah became aware that her husband had started a relationship with Julia Lewis, a maid employed in the house; that he had made her pregnant, and he now proposed to give her the status of a *mutah* wife. Under Shi'i law at the time, a male Muslim could not have more than four *nikah* wives concurrently, but there was no limit to the number of *mutah* wives he might have. In 1879 Mansour Ali Khan had four living *nikah* wives (three in Murshidabad, and Sarah in England). During his entire lifetime he had six – before he married Sarah, two previous *nikah* wives had died, Hasina in 1858, and the other in 1865. He had had more than twenty *mutah* wives in total. When he proposed to make her a *mutah* wife, Julia was eighteen years old.

Mansour Ali Khan may have been taken aback by Sarah's reaction to his proposal to accept and live with a second wife. His other wives in Murshidabad had not been pleased when he told them of new additions to the *zenana*; they sometimes sulked, but they were fatalistic, and accepted the changes as the Nawab's prerogative. Sarah was distraught. She had believed that the marriage ceremony in 1870 and the declaration before the Mayor in 1875 implied an exclusive relationship, and she had been faithful to her husband. The very notion that she would agree to sharing him with another wife, or even a mistress, was demeaning and humiliating. There were angry scenes in which she

1 IOR/L/PS/13.

accused her husband of betrayal. The doctor was called; he judged Sarah to be hysterical, and advised her to seek rest and respite away from the Nawab and Julia. James Lyster O'Beirne, the Nawab's private secretary and trusted advisor, encouraged Sarah to leave, suggesting it was her only alternative. Sarah took refuge in her father's house in New Barnet. The children remained at 42 Bedford Square with their father and their new stepmother. Given this arrangement, it became difficult for George Vennell to remain part of the Nawab's close circle, and so O'Beirne became the Nawab's chief advisor.

James Lyster O'Beirne belonged to a line of advisors and officials, like Henry Torrens, who won the trust of the Nawab and went on to enrich themselves at his expense. Like Torrens, O'Beirne fancied himself as a literary man, but he had first trained as a solicitor in Ireland, and had then gone on to be elected as a Member of Parliament for Cashel. In 1869 he was found to have bribed voters, his election was declared void, and the borough of Cashel was disenfranchised. In London he became editor of the *Court Journal*, belonged to the Fielding Club (a favourite haunt of Thackeray's), and charmed young literary men as a mentor and man about town.

Together with the Nawab, O'Beirne took part in negotiations with the British government. Deeply in debt, and with failing health, Mansour Ali Khan now wished to leave England. His mother sent messages appealing to him to return to Murshidabad. Julia, renamed Mohamadee Begum, was willing to go to India with him. O'Beirne suggested a deal with the government involving an annual stipend for the Nawab of £14,000, allowing him to live somewhere in the Middle East, and guaranteeing provision for all his dependents. In response, Horace Cockerell, Secretary to the Government of Bengal, wrote in scornful dismissal to the Secretary to the Government of India, Viscount Cranbrook:

> Now, the present Nawab has of his own free will entirely abdicated his position as Nawab Nazim and head of the Nizamut Family of Moorshedabad. He has left his country, deserted his wives, children, family, and friends, and has shown no wish to return and

> again occupy the position, for the maintenance only of which a large stipend was allotted to him. He has in England led a life of debauchery, and has disgraced his rank and position to such a degree that he is entirely excluded from all respectable society, and he has formed a connection with an English woman of low extraction, and lives with her in a suburb of London in a manner entirely unfitting to the position of a Mahomedan nobleman, and certainly in a manner which is inconsistent with his position as Nawab Nazim.[1]

It seems that the liaison with Julia was as yet unknown to Cockerell. He also was unaware or chose to ignore the fact that the Nawab continued to be received in the higher ranks of society in 1878 and 1879. Mansour Ali Khan did, for example, join by invitation a large party of English and European aristocrats and diplomats invited to watch the April 1879 boat race. Disgusted that the Nawab should 'form a connection with an English woman of low extraction' and actually *choose* to live in a suburb, Cockerell further dismissed the likelihood of the Nawab's returning to India, and thought it undesirable that he should do so. This was common practice by the British government in such situations. Duleep Singh was actually prevented from visiting India when he tried to return some years later, and arrested by the British at Aden in 1884. It was feared his presence might stir up hostility to British rule. The Nawab's decision not to return had made the job of the British government much, much easier.

Cockerell advocated the abolition of the title Nawab Nazim of Bengal, Bihar and Orissa, and the status that accompanied it, as had been recommended in Argyll's response to the Nawab's petition in 1871. It was Cockerell's view that a stipend of £8,000 a year (just over £500,000 in today's currency) would be more than sufficient to maintain the Nawab in England, and that, after his Indian wives and children had been provided for, no further pensions should be granted. In short, contrary to Queen Victoria's promises of recognition in 1858, his recommendations were a return to Dalhousie's policy of abolishing

1 *From Plassey to Pakistan,* p.105.

Indian princely states and attaching their revenue to the British government.

The negotiations continued. Mansour Ali Khan held out for a better deal, but in the end the British government defeated him. He was forced to abdicate and renounce all claims on the British government. His title would lapse; his successor would be known simply as Nawab of Murshidabad and would receive neither the gun salutes nor other privileges which had traditionally belonged to the Nawabs of Bengal. Nor would his successors be referred to as 'His Highness' – although old habits die hard, and his sons were recognised by this title in practice, if not in law.

In return for 'accepting' his abdication, Mansour Ali Khan would receive a lump sum of £83,000 (worth today about £5,500,000) and an annual stipend of £10,000 (today, a little over £600,000). His 'English sons', Syed and Nusrat, would each receive 10,000 rupees a month (c. £165,000 today) for life, and his surviving English daughters, Miriam and Vaheedoonissa, were allotted one-off sums of 20,000 rupees (c. £330,000 today) to be administered by trustees. There was no mention of provision for either Sarah or Julia. The government of India insisted that no pension should be given to Sarah, as in its view 'the connection was a discreditable one[1].' The remainder of the Nizamut Deposit Fund was transferred to the British government. It was worth £500,000 at the time; equivalent to around 55 million British pounds sterling today.

While these negotiations and preparations were proceeding, Mansour Ali Khan sought to maintain communications with Sarah, who was convalescing at the Greyhound Hotel, Hampton Court. On 17 April 1880, the Nawab wrote to her from Bedford Square

> My dear wife,
> I was very pleased to hear from George that you were better, and trust you will soon regain strength. The boys are progressing favourably. Miriam and Vaheedoonissa Begum are quite well and send their love and kisses to you.
>
> The night air did not affect my chest. I arrived home quite

1 *From Plassey to Pakistan,* p.106.

safely – Soobah Sahib sends his love and [plans] to come down to see you tomorrow.

I remain,

Your affectionate husband, Syud Munsoor Ullee.

It is unclear from the documents we have how frequently Sarah was seeing the Nawab at this time, if at all. Humayun Mirza states that, after Sarah went to her father's house in 1879, she never saw her husband again, but this letter with its reference to arriving home safely and not being affected by the night air suggests that Mansour Ali Khan may have just visited her at the Greyhound Hotel where she was staying. The Nawab makes no mention here of the death of their six-year-old daughter Hajerah from scarlet fever, just six weeks previously at 42 Bedford Square, although his assurance that the other two girls are well may indicate an awareness that Sarah might be concerned lest they too might have caught the fever.

The Nawab also refrained from saying anything about the birth of Julia's daughter, Amina, in January 1880, or about preparations to send the remaining children to India with Julia. When Sarah found out about the plans later that year, she begged O'Beirne to intervene. He told her that, if she tried to prevent the children from going to India with their father, no provision would be made for them in the future. In fact, the agreement to provide for them had already been signed, but this fact was kept from Sarah. Like the Nawab, Sarah also became the victim of devious and self-serving advisors.

In November 1880, Sarah's four surviving children, Miriam, Vaheedoonissa, Syed and Nusrat, together with their new stepmother Julia (now renamed Mohamadee), were taken on board the SS *Eldorado* to travel to India. They arrived at the Murshidabad Palace on 2 January 1881. Thus a decade which for Sarah and the Nawab had begun with hope, excitement and the promise of a new kind of life, now ended in hurt, humiliation, and grievous loss for both of them. At the age of seventeen Sarah had suddenly been transformed from a chambermaid to a princess, and she was to become the mother and stepmother of princes and princesses. Now aged twenty-seven, Sarah had lost her husband, her livelihood, and all her children. She did not accept defeat, however; she would insist on retaining her title as Sarah Nawab Begum, and her fight to regain her children had only just begun.

CHAPTER 7

Leaving England

1880–1884

On a cold, grey London day in November, 1880, Sarah's four children, together with Julia and her baby daughter, were handed into carriages which took them to the East India Docks, close to Sarah's birthplace. They were accompanied by the Nawab's fourth surviving son, Prince Assad Ali Mirza (Subah Sahib), whose mother was the Nawab's second *nikah* wife, Shams-un-Nisa. Prince Assad had been studying art in London during the past year. Valentine Holt, one of the Nawab's English secretaries, also travelled with them.

For the children this was the bewildering end to a troubled year. First they had left behind the familiar animals and gardens at Pymmes Park and had moved to a new house in the relatively densely populated Bedford Square. There their mother was often in tears, and then had gone away. They were told that Julia was their new mother. Then their sister Hajerah, who was nearly ten, became ill and died. Now they were going to India with their new mother and baby sister Amina, and Subah Sahib, their older brother. It was two days before Vaheedoonissa's sixth birthday; Miriam was nine and their younger brothers Syed and Nusrat were aged five and three. The children knew little about India except that it was far away, that the weather would be hot, and that there would be lots of elephants and monkeys. They had also been told that their grandmother lived there with their other brothers and sisters, whom they had never met.

But first they had to get the boat from London. Together with the servants the children stood bewildered on the wharf deafened by people talking and shouting, with hundreds of bodies pushing urgently past them, and porters trundling trunks. Looming over them was the *El Dorado,* its chimneys belching black smoke. Subah Sahib, Mr Holt and two of the servants led them up the gangway, onto the deck and down steep stairs to two cabins with bunk beds. Vaheedoonissa and Miriam would share one cabin with one of the servants; Syed and Nusrat were to sleep in the other with another servant. Julia needed to have her own cabin with little Amina and the *ayah*. During the long six-week voyage, those cabins became a familiar refuge.

Four days before they reached Calcutta, the crew and most of the passengers celebrated Christmas. Miriam and Vaheedoonissa could remember their previous Christmas in London with their mother, when the park in Bedford Square was covered with snow and they had to put on their fur coats and boots. Now they were wearing the loose silk pantaloons and tunics bought when the ship had stopped at Colombo. They did not receive Christmas presents, but Subah Sahib told them it was a special day for Eesa, the prophet the English called Jesus, and they should say their Namaz prayers.

At last they reached Calcutta. The heat, the noise, the bustle were overwhelming. Nusrat and little Amina had to be carried down the gangway to the wharf; Miriam, Vaheedoonissa and Syed followed them, guided by the servants. The next day they boarded a much smaller boat on the Hooghly River, and sailed to Murshidabad. They could see the sloping riverbanks on each side, where sometimes there were women in brightly coloured saris washing clothes and small children splashing in the water. They passed dozens of small fishing boats and, as the journey progressed, saw large white-and-black birds with long curved beaks by the water. These, they later learned, were called ibis. And once Suba Sahib pointed out a group of monkeys clambering up a bank towards a group of mulberry trees.

Murshidabad was their new home, a home where Vaheedoonissa and Miriam would remain for the rest of their lives. Together with Julia the children were taken to their grandmother's palace. Their grandmother was Nawab Rais-un Nisa Begum Sahiba, whom they were told was the Gaddanashin Begum, or First Lady; now over seventy years old, she was treated with great deference. She spoke to them in Urdu and the children understood very little of what she said. Their older stepbrother, Hassan, who was now in charge of the Palace and estate, greeted them in English and explained who everyone was.

In the Palace, the Nawab's 'English' wife and daughters were the focus of much curiosity. Growing up in England with a large household of servants and private tutors, Miriam and Vaheedoonissa had assumed that it was perfectly normal to have an Indian father and an English mother. Now they found that they were pointed at and sometimes pushed aside as *angrezi larkhian* ('English' or 'foreign' girls), and the few Urdu words they had learned from their father and stepbrothers or the servants were inadequate. When they asked questions in English or tried to use Urdu the other children and their mothers just stared or giggled.

The boys were allowed to stay at night with their grandmother and their sisters, but had to spend most of the day with Mr Holt and another secretary in their apartments in the Hazarduari palace. Years later, Nusrat could recall only fragmentary memories of his life from the age of three to eight in Murshidabad: the sound of the muezzin in the early morning; long hours sitting cross-legged with the other boys learning and reciting verses from the Qu'ran; the trumpeting of the elephants in the elephant house and watching them bathed and sprayed themselves in the pool nearby. In one of the palace rooms there was a stuffed crocodile with its gaping mouth and big teeth. There was also a mirror that showed not the viewer, but anyone standing behind it, where Nusrat and Syed particularly liked trying to catch each other out.

Writing about his childhood nearly forty years later, Nusrat told how once a magician came to his grandmother's palace and he was allowed to watch through the shutters in the room next to the *zenana*. The magician sent a small boy climbing up a rope and then apparently chopped him to pieces. Nusrat was horrified, but suddenly the boy got up again and was perfectly whole. As a small boy Nusrat preferred the trick where the rope turned into a mango tree, and the magician gave them all fresh mangoes to eat. Another vivid memory was of the pilgrims coming to the long white Imambara opposite the palace, with the sound of drums and chanting during the Muharrum festival – and then the fireworks, and the boats all lit up on the river. And he told his

The Imambara (pilgrims' hostel) built by Mansour Ali Khan in 1846.

daughter how very angry his older brother Nawab Hassan was the time when he and Syed tied a firework to the tail of one of the cows lying in the street. Although it was Syed's idea to fasten the firework, they both got into trouble.

Sometimes Nusrat rode with his family in a tonga (one-horse carriage) drawn by a small pony through the dusty streets of the city and out through the large gate, past a forest of tall mulberry trees. When a cow lying in the middle of the road blocked their way, they had to be patient until it decided to move aside.

Meanwhile, their father remained absent. After sending his English family to India, the Nawab had taken a three-month tour with his chief secretary and advisor James O'Beirne round Europe, returning to London in April 1881. He stayed at the Albemarle Hotel, Piccadilly. Here Mansour Ali Khan received the news on 15 June that Julia had given birth in Murshidabad to a son, Mohammed. In July he travelled to Paris, and then back to England again. He finally left England in September 1881, accompanied by one of his legal advisors, Mowbray Walker, arriving in Bombay in October. Unwilling to return to Murshidabad where he would be watched over by the British Agent and would feel even more keenly the loss of his former status and privileges as Nawab of Bengal, Bihar and Orissa, he settled for the time being at Somerset House, Warden Road, Breach Kandy, Bombay. Named after Sir Henry Somerset, a commander-in-chief in the Bombay Presidency, the building is now Sophia College, a Catholic women's college, and frequently used as a site for historical films.

Soon after Mansour Ali Khan's arrival in Bombay, he sent for Valentine Holt. He also sent for Julia, who was grieving for their infant daughter Amina, who had recently died in Murshidabad. At Somerset House she gave birth to their second child, Musa, in November 1882. The Nawab considered taking up an offer from the Shah of Persia to move to Persia where his original status would be respected, but his ageing mother begged him to return to Murshidabad. And so, at the end of 1883, he and Julia travelled east to Bengal. Rather than stay in Murshidabad, however, they lodged in the cooler and more remote town of Rajmahal, in the hills of northwest Bengal.

A few weeks before their third child, Hamid, was born on 30 January 1884, Mansour Ali Khan, now aged fifty-three, suffered a stroke and was partially paralysed. Taken back to Murshidabad and in failing health, he sent for Mowbray Walker, with whom, in March 1884, he drafted a formal letter expressing his final wishes. In it, he named his oldest son Hassan, Mowbray Walker and James O'Beirne as guardians of his younger children. He desired that his 'English sons' should be schooled in England and that they should receive a good Muslim education. He left his private property to Julia. He signed a deed of trust of £18,000 to James O'Beirne, indicating that he might, if he so wished, provide Sarah with £250 a year, her father £120 a year, and Emma Hallett (Moshin) £100 a year, as well as other payments to Sarah's and Julia's brothers. In today's currency £18,000 would equate to approximately just over $1 million; £250 would be worth £16,500; £120 would be about £8,000, and £100 would be roughly equivalent to £6,600.

The deed concluded with Mansour Ali Khan's statement: 'I shall be gratified if you think fit to carry out my suggestions ... but the fund is entirely your own. You are at liberty to give money to Mohamadee Begum [Julia] if you wish.'[1] He also signed a letter directing that all his

1 *From Plassey to Pakistan*, p.110.

jewels should go to Julia for life, and after her death to his daughters by Sarah.

Mansour Ali Khan expressed his desire to be buried in Karbala, now in central Iraq, a city regarded as holy and a site of pilgrimage for Shi'i Muslims since it contains the shrine of the grandson of the Prophet Muhammad, Imam Husayn. Husayn died in battle after refusing allegiance to the Caliph Yazid, declaring, 'I will never give Yazid my hand like a man who has been humiliated, nor will I flee like a slave.' As a devout Shi'i, Mansour Ali Khan might well have had Husayn's words in mind when he chose Karbala as his last resting place rather than the traditional burial place in the family cemetery at Murshidabad. But his decision not to be buried alongside all his ancestors in Murshidabad also suggests the profound humiliation and alienation he felt, and perhaps a belief that he had failed his forefathers.

During the summer of 1884 the Nawab remained in Murshidabad, unable to move, but still able to speak. This was an anxious time for his wives, his many servants and dependents, his concubines, his children. The Nawab's wishes were not published until after he died and no doubt those who relied on the Nawab would have been concerned about their futures. What would happen to them when he died? Who would be allowed to stay on in the palace compounds? Would the British Agent acknowledge their status and rights? Sarah's children were brought to see him, but barely recognised their father lying in bed, haggard and immobile, his mumbling speech difficult to understand.

In October 1884 the ever-present menace of cholera (known in Britain as 'the Asiatic disease') developed in Murshidabad, and the Nawab became one of its victims. He fell into a coma, perhaps induced by the opiates administered to relieve the painful stomach cramps caused by cholera. His death was announced on 4 November, just six days after his fifty-fourth birthday.

Towards the end of his life Mansour Ali Khan had a fear of being buried alive. His last wishes included the very explicit stipulation that his coffin should not be closed nor his body interred until it showed visible signs of decay, and that his wife Mohamadee Begum (Julia) should be properly satisfied of the fact of his death before his interment could be permitted. It seems that, in his last days, Julia was the only person the Nawab felt he could trust. Whether she was able to fulfil that final duty is not clear. His great-great-grandson, Humayun Mirza, a descendant of the Nawab's son from his first *nikah* marriage (to Shams-i-Jahan), reports the chilling story that, when the coffin was opened soon after its arrival in Karbala so that the body could be prepared for burial, 'witnesses reported that the Nawab's hands, which had been placed across his chest at the time the coffin was sealed, were now at his side, and that there were scratch marks on the inside of the lid of the coffin'.[1]

With the Nawab's death the title of Nawab Nazim of Bengal, Bihar and Orissa also ceased to exist. Of the over 100 children he had fathered, nineteen sons and twenty daughters survived him, all with varying claims to the estate. His oldest son, Hassan, had for the past decade been in charge of affairs for the palace and estate in Murshidabad and had been given the much-diminished title Nawab of Murshidabad. Shams-i-Jahan contested both this succession and the change of title, believing that it was her son, Kurshaid Kudr, who should inherit the position of Nawab Nazim. It had been Mansour Ali Khan's will that Hassan should succeed him, and this had been agreed with the British when he abdicated in 1880, so Kurshaid Kudr's claim was denied. Unwilling to stay in Murshidabad under the rule of Hasina's son, Shams-i-Jahan moved with her son and daughters to Calcutta.

Now that their father was dead, the fate of Sarah's children had to be decided. In accordance with Mansour Ali Khan's will, Hassan determined that the two boys, Syed and Nusrat, should be sent to school in England under the guardianship of Mowbray Walker and James O'Beirne. Miriam and Vaheedoonissa, now aged thirteen and ten, had settled into life with their grandmother and the other young girls in the palace compound, and now spoke fluent Urdu. It was agreed that they should remain in Murshidabad. Sarah was not consulted. It would be more than four years before she would see her daughters again, and then only briefly.

Meanwhile Sarah waited in London for news of her children. There are no records of her residence or activities during the long four years

1 *From Plassey to Pakistan*, p.111.

of their absence. She had gone to stay with her father, stepmother, and older sister Mary in 1879, when she became aware of her husband's liaison with Julia Lewis; it is probable that she remained with them for several months. However she does not appear in the household census for that residence in April 1881, so she may then have begun living in a hotel, as she continued to do for most of her life thereafter. Indeed, apart from her younger brother George, she seems to have had little contact with her own family after 1880.

The news of the Nawab's death was reported in the English papers, so Sarah would certainly have known almost immediately that she was now a widow. She also soon discovered that no provision had been made for her, and she had no income. Following her father's death just six months earlier, she relied more than ever on her brother George's advice and support. James O'Beirne took care of the expenses for Julia and her family, drawing on the money that the Nawab had entrusted to him, but the expenses for Sarah's sons were taken from the stipend promised them in the deed agreed between their father and the British government and paid by the government to their guardian, Mowbray Walker. Together with Walker, Syed and Nusrat, Julia and her three sons arrived in Gravesend, Kent, on the SS *Manora* on 27 May 1885.

Having been defined as the Nawab's English sons in India, Syed and Nusrat now became Sarah's Indian sons in Britain. By the time he became a student at Oxford, Syed would come to accept the role of Indian prince and welcomed some of the social advantages his title offered. However, as Nusrat grew older, he increasingly found the role both false and constricting, although when he married it would offer a higher status and new opportunities for his English wife. Nusrat would go on in later life to seek escape and fulfilment in other places and professions that were far removed from the world of the Indian royal court and related English social expectations, including Jamaica, Paris, and finally, sheep farming in Australia. Apart from Syed's brief visit to Murshidabad with Sarah in 1899, neither Syed nor Nusrat would ever return to India again. Although they continued to correspond with their two sisters in Bengal, that chapter in their personal history was, as far as they were concerned, closed.

PART II

CHAPTER 8

Sarah's Fight

1885–1925

When the SS *Manora* arrived in London in May 1885, Syed, now nine years old, and Nusrat, almost eight, were met by their guardian, Mowbray Walker, and taken to live with him in Forest Hill in southeast London. Neither Walker nor James Lyster O'Beirne, who had also been appointed a guardian by the Nawab, informed Sarah that her sons were now back in England. It was Sarah's brother George who discovered that they had been dispatched from Calcutta on the *Manora*. Sarah was desperate to be with the two boys she had not seen for five years, and to have news of her daughters. She made her way to the house in Forest Hill, demanded to see her children, but was refused entry. A few days later she tried again, but again was refused. Sarah's distress and anger were used against her. When George intervened, he was told that Sarah's behaviour would upset the boys. Walker and O'Beirne were adamant that she should not have any contact with her children.

Sarah now sought George's help to obtain custody. Under English law at the time the mother automatically had custody if her children were illegitimate, but she had no rights over children born within a legitimate marriage. If Sarah claimed her marriage to the Nawab had not been a legitimate one, she might gain custody of her children; but she would not be able to claim the right to a pension or status as the widow of the Nawab of Bengal.

Sarah chose to try to regain her children. And lost. O'Beirne and Walker refused to give up custody of the boys. With George's assistance, Sarah appealed to the Court of Chancery, declaring that there had been no legal marriage between herself and the Nawab. The case was heard by Justice Chitty on 4 August 1885 and was widely reported in the British papers. Sarah's counsel, Mr Romer, argued that under English law Sarah's marriage to the Nawab was not legal, that the children were illegitimate, and that as Sarah had no criminal record she should have custody of all four children. Moreover, he claimed, the girls remaining in India were in danger of being married off, despite the fact that they were only fourteen and ten. 'There was no better case for the interference of the court,' Mr Romer contended. 'Everybody knew what a Mohammedan marriage was. It was little better than a sale and purchase of the wife, who for the rest of her life would be compelled to live in the seclusion of the *harem* or *zenana*.'[1]

In response the lawyers for O'Beirne and Walker insisted that the children were legitimate under Muslim law, that the Nawab had declared the children as his own, that the jurisdiction should be India rather than England, that the trustees were ensuring that the boys were being educated and brought up according to the wishes of 'a great potentate'. 'The trustees had been acting with the greatest care,' Mr McNaughton, QC declared for the defence:

> The requirements of Mohammedans as to the preparation and cooking of food had been most carefully carried out. The desirability of the religion was not in question, and the only fact the court had to consider was that they had been brought up in a particular religion. It would be a disastrous thing were a Mohammedan gentleman to send his children to this country, who were legitimate according to Mohammedan law, and illegitimate according to the law of this country, and to find his whole scheme of education disarranged, and his children bastardised as well.

McNaughton added that it was incomprehensible that the mother should wish to 'thus stigmatise the children'.

A week later Justice Chitty declared in favour of the defence, stating that the children were legitimate under Muslim law and tradition, and

1 *Morning Post*, 5 August 1885, p.6. v. Also *St James Gazette*, 5 August 1885, p.11.

that the wishes of the father should be respected. The boys, he thought, were being well looked after by their present guardians and were used to being in their company, whereas Sarah had been willing to let the children go to India. The fact that she had felt she could not intervene was not considered. However, he insisted that O'Beirne should promptly stop payment of any money towards Vaheedoonissa's dowry and so prevent her being betrothed at this point. He also proposed that Sarah should have reasonable access to her sons, 'reasonable access' being defined as two hours a week.

Neither the judge, nor the lawyers, nor the newspapers commented on the contradiction between the British insistence forty years previously on the Nawab's acquisition of an English education in Murshidabad during his boyhood and the present concern that his sons should receive a Muslim education in England. Some papers expressed sympathy for Sarah's plight, depicting her as a 'woman in a humble sphere', who had been told 'she would be Begum of Bengal[1],' but others were quick to censure. 'The judgement delivered by Mr Chitty is not to be regretted,' *The Globe*'s reporter wrote, 'if it has the effect of bringing home to the minds of European women the horrors of marriage with non-Christian Orientals. Such unions, although perhaps not very numerous, are becoming far too common.'[2]

With George's assistance Sarah went to the Supreme Court to appeal against Justice Chitty's decision. She again claimed that, when she married the Nawab in May 1870, she had not been aware that he had a wife (or wives) still living in India, and therefore the marriage was not a legitimate one. Her appeal was heard in October 1885 and again her case was dismissed, unanimously, by the Lords Justices Baggallay, Bowen and Fry on the grounds that she had 'assented to the children remaining in India with their father' and that it was in the interests of the children to remain with their appointed guardians 'having regard to the nature of their birth, the religion in which they had been brought up, and the mode of life which had been adopted for them[3].' Clearly

1 *Sunderland Daily Echo and Shipping News,* 5 August 1885, p.3.

2 *The Globe,* 12 August 1885, p.1.

3 *Evening Standard,* 29 October 1885, p.2.

the fact that their mother was an Englishwoman and a Christian and thus her children were half European by 'the nature of their birth' was of no significance in the eyes of these guardians of the law. In England, the Nawab's children would always be seen as necessarily Indian, just as African Americans of mixed race (even if only 1/32nd African) would always be classified as 'black' or 'coloured' on their birth certificates. Throughout their lives Sarah and her children would insist on construing their identities in more fluid and complex terms.

Whether Sarah and her lawyers truly believed that Vaheedoonissa was about to be betrothed, or were playing on British assumptions about child marriages and harems in India in order to strengthen the case for custody, is not clear. The fact is that, although they remained in Murshidabad, neither Miriam nor Vaheedoonissa ever married. At the age of eighteen Miriam refused a proposed marriage with a prince of Oudh, expressing the wish to remain single. That wish was respected.

Thus, in October 1885, it would appear that Sarah had been defeated: in a desperate gamble to regain the custody of her children, she had staked her status as a legitimate wife of the Nawab of Bengal, Bihar and Orissa, together with her claim to a dowry and substantial pension, and she had lost almost everything. Despite the judge's ruling, the British government was reluctant to acknowledge her right to a pension befiting her title as Nawab Begum; nor was it willing to grant her the £10,000 dowry the Nawab had promised in the 1875 indenture. She was allowed only the small stipend of £150 a year (equivalent now to about £11,000) that O'Beirne had recommended the India Office should give her. Her two daughters must remain in Murshidabad; her two little sons must remain under the control of guardians who were antagonistic to her. She was permitted to see them for no more than two hours a week, and then within the constraint of supervision by Walker and O'Beirne.

Meanwhile, Syed and Nusrat were gradually adjusting to their new life in London. Although the sun continued to shine that summer and the skies were blue, the boys shivered in the slight breeze outside and at night when they went to bed. Their guardian's house was damp and chilly and strangely quiet. Mr Walker took them to buy some English clothes to replace their cotton tunics and leggings, but even with their new jackets and trousers and socks they felt cold. It was also difficult to get used to their hard leather English shoes that creaked and rubbed when they walked.

Sometimes they went to nearby Mayow Park where they could throw a ball to one another or watch other boys playing tag or cricket, or running with iron hoops, which clattered along the paths. Although Syed and Nusrat had had almost daily English lessons in Murshidabad, they found the speech of these other children difficult to follow and very different from the formal sentences they had been taught to enunciate.

The boys missed their sisters and asked Mr Walker when they would see them again. Perhaps trying to fill the gap left by the absence of Miriam and Vaheedoonissa, Mr Walker took them to a little girl's tea party in a relative's house. His well-intended gesture was not a success. Nusrat later recalled that occasion and his dismay when they were offered ham sandwiches:

> Pig! Those pretty little fair-haired girls had offered me pig! Surely they knew it was a direct insult! Surely they realised that I could not sit at the same table with them and eat pig! How angry the great Queen would be if she knew how her loyal subjects were insulted.
>
> But I made no sign, of course. I am sure an impassive face gave no sign of the tumult in my heart.[1]

In his own house Mr Walker had hired a Muslim cook who went out each day to buy halal meat for their meals and cooked curries that Mr Walker also liked. The cook would knock on the boys' bedroom door early so that they could say the morning prayer together. Syed and Nusrat liked to watch the cook preparing the food in the kitchen. He would chat to them in Urdu and sometimes give them morsels to taste.

---

1 The Nawabzada Nusrat Ali Mirza of Murshidabad, 'Mecca,' *Daily Mail* (London, England) 1 June 1921, p.6. Nusrat went on in this article to note that 'subsequent years at school and varsity taught me toleration even for bacon and roast pork.'

It was warm in the kitchen, and the smells made them feel at home.

In August 1885 Mr Walker took them to see their mother for the first time since their departure for India almost five years previously. On their way to her house, Syed tried to remember what Sarah looked like, summoning up vague memories of her blue eyes and long blonde hair. Nusrat had seen some black-and-white photographs she had sent to Murshidabad, but it was hard to connect those images with anyone related to him. They knew this meeting with their mother should be an important occasion, but they were uncertain how to behave. They hoped their mother would not burst into tears.

But Sarah did. The two boys stood awkwardly as their mother tearfully held and kissed them, exclaiming at how much they had grown, how tall they were. Nusrat had been just a baby, not even three, when she last saw him. And the girls? Syed assured her that Miriam and Vaheedoonissa were well, and sent their love. Yes, they had all been well looked after in Murshidabad. Their older brothers Hassan and Subah Sahib also sent their love. The visit would have felt all too brief for Sarah, but for the boys, I imagine, the two hours seemed long.

In late August the boys, now aged ten and eight, were provided with more new outfits – long socks which covered their short woollen trousers just below the knee, boots, tight jackets, caps and ties. Then they were taken to Ashbourne House Preparatory School in Harrow. Here they would be boarding, returning to Mr Walker's house in the holidays. The other boys looked at them curiously, and some of them mimicked their accents and made them say their names over and over again. After a while they settled for naming Syed as Nawab Senior; Nusrat became Nawab Junior.

At first they found the schoolmasters difficult to understand, but it was a relief to discover that their tutors in Murshidabad had given them an adequate grounding in reading, writing and mathematics. Fortunately both boys were good at sports; they had often played cricket and other games with their older brothers and cousins in Bengal. Here in Ashbourne House they were soon among the first picked for the intramural cricket and rugby teams; the praise when they scored well or bowled someone out was very satisfying.

Nevertheless it took a long time to get used to the cold dormitories, the plain and regimented rows of beds, the heavy, tasteless food, the reluctance of the other boys to wash before meals or at all. Now they began to look forward to their weekly visit with their mother when they would be plied with cake and sweets and could sit with her by her coal fire.

For Sarah those two-hour visits were the focus of each week, two hours that were both cherished and painful. Her boys were becoming more confident, more English, more talkative in her presence, but then they were gone, and for the rest of the week she was alone. And she grieved for Miriam and Vaheedoonissa, now aged fourteen and eleven. There were occasional brief letters from the girls, sent with a covering note from her stepson Nawab Hassan assuring her that they were well, but the letters said nothing about what they were doing, who their friends were, what they were learning, how they really were. She tried to visualise them as they must be now, but could only summon up their little faces when they were much younger, playing at Pymmes Park or calling out to her at Bedford Square.

During those five long years since Sarah had been forced to leave Bedford Square – so callously betrayed by her husband, by Julia, and by the duplicitous Mr O'Beirne – Sarah had struggled against despair. At first it had been a relief to be with her father and sister Mary, away from the humiliation of seeing Julia and Mansour Ali Khan together. She had hoped, indeed believed, the separation would be only temporary. Then there was the terrible discovery that the children had been taken to India and that Julia had gone with them. For ten years she had been the Nawab's beloved *Sarah jan*, his faithful wife, the mother of his six children; now she felt her whole being as a wife and a mother had been obliterated. Sarah sometimes felt that her sister and her stepmother were not as sympathetic as they could be, that they had expected something like this would happen all along.

In the same year that the Nawab passed away, Sarah had experienced a second loss in her father's death, in June 1884. Only her younger brother George remained loyal to Sarah, vehemently angry on her behalf and determined to pursue every legal avenue to bring back the children and her rights as wife of the Nawab.

George had always been closer to Sarah than her other brothers and sisters. No doubt Sarah had encouraged the Nawab to pay for George's further training and to employ him as his secretary. After Sarah and the Nawab had parted, he found employment sometimes as a prosecuting solicitor and more often as a duty solicitor for defendants charged in the London area. In the newspapers his name appears in reports of cases involving forged coins and cheques. One report told how he managed to get charges of immoral conduct involving adultery dismissed in the case of a Mr Sewen Bastendorf by showing that conflicting identifications of the supposed adulterer were based chiefly on the length of his beard.

In 1882, George acted for the defence in the case of Charles Evans, accused of stealing a dog owned by Annie Besant, the theosophist, political activist and, in later years, President of the India National Congress. The case was reported in the *Morning Post*:

> Mrs Besant was the first witness, who declined to be sworn, and was allowed to make an affirmation. In answer to Mr Kelly, she stated that she lost the dog from her residence in Mortimer Street, St John's Wood, on 7 February. On 2 March she received a visit from a man, and in consequence of the conversation which took place between them she went to London Fields, and on receiving her dog handed [Evans] £15.[1]

Despite Annie Besant's refusal to be sworn, and George's attempt to defend Evans, the jury accepted her version of the event and returned a verdict of guilty. Annie Besant had suffered the same experience four months previously when a Mr Jones stole her dog and similarly demanded £15 for its return, an amount equivalent to almost £1,000 today.

George's legal knowledge and contacts enabled him to assist his sister in her attempts to regain custody of the children. These attempts had failed, because the judge refused to accept her claim that her children were illegitimate. Now Sarah was determined to assert her rights and status as a legitimate wife of the Nawab. She resented bitterly the fact that Julia had

1 *Morning Post*, 22 November 1882, p.3.

not only maintained custody of her [Julia's] three boys, but had also been awarded a considerably higher stipend, and was, in Sarah's view, wrongly parading under the title of Nawab Mohamadee Begum. With George's help Sarah embarked on a series of attempts to obtain the pension and dowry she believed she was entitled to as the Nawab's widow.

In this battle she was opposed by James Lyster O'Beirne who, because he had negotiated with them the terms for the Nawab's abdication and was also the Nawab's executor, had gained the trust of the Foreign Office personnel. O'Beirne took Julia's side, promoting her interests and those of her three boys. It was he who had suggested an annual stipend of £300 for Julia, but a mere £150 for Sarah, as compassionate allowances granted *ad misericordia* by the government, not as an entitlement – sums equivalent today to £22,000 and £11,000. Under Sharia law as a *nikah* wife, Sarah should automatically have received a pension equivalent to that of the Nawab's three other *nikah* wives, and no doubt the Nawab assumed this would happen. After repeated appeals, Sarah's stipend was increased to £250 (today c. £16,000) a year, but she got nowhere with her claim for the £10,000 dowry (today over £700,000) promised on her marriage and in the Nawab's 1875 deed setting out provision for his dependents. The India Office continued to question whether she could have been considered married to the Nawab on an equivalent basis to his *nikah* wives in India. O'Beirne encouraged such questioning by implying that Sarah had merely 'lived with His Highness as his wife'. He also suggested that the Nawab suspected Sarah of infidelity, that she had become impossible to live with, that she had left her children willingly, and that this was the reason for the Nawab's then forming a relationship with Julia. When a government official sent her a letter addressed to 'Mrs Sarah Vennell', Sarah was furious. George sent a sharp note to the India Office and received an apology.

Mowbray Walker's sudden death in June 1887 brought an unexpected change in the situation. Sarah again applied for the custody of the boys. This time she was supported by the two remaining guardians, O'Beirne and Nawab Hassan, her oldest stepson. O'Beirne no longer wished to burden himself with responsibility for the boys in England, and Nawab Hassan had always been sympathetic to Sarah. Given the death of Walker and the eagerness of O'Beirne to be relieved of the boys, Justice Chitty was now willing to award the custody to Sarah.

George and Sarah had become aware of the £18,000 entrusted to O'Beirne by the Nawab, and went to court in pursuit of some of that money, as well as the promised dowry. They were not successful but, now informed of O'Beirne's financial gains, the India Office became less confident in O'Beirne's credibility. They sought further evidence of Sarah's status from the Nawab's sons who had been in London at the time of the marriage, and received confirmation that Sarah was certainly their father's *nikah* wife under Shi'i Muslim law.

Finally, in July 1888, the British government formally recognised the marriage and Sarah's status as a widow of the Nawab Nazim. They sought the opinion of experts regarding Sarah's position under Indian and British law. The experts declared that, under Indian and Shi'i Muslim law, Sarah certainly should have the same status as the Nawab's three surviving *nikah* wives. And although under British law the marriage could not be recognised, neither should the relationship be regarded as an immoral one.

A response to a political despatch dated September 1887 pointed out that the government had gained a profit of more than £110,000 (today more than £7 million) per annum from the Nizamut Fund as a result of the 1880 agreement with the Nawab. It further suggested that the government could avoid criticism by treating 'with liberality all reasonable claims made in connection with the Fund'.[1] As a result of this response, the government agreed that Sarah's stipend should be raised to £480 a year (equivalent to around £40,000 today), the amount that the Nawab had given her up until the time of his death. However, the government was adamant in its refusal to hand over the £10,000 dowry, despite the same despatch affirming that Sarah was indeed entitled to that dowry according to the declaration and indentures made in 1875 and 1880. For these British officials, the thought of an English woman 'of mean extraction' being regarded as the Nawab's widow was bad enough; for her to benefit from this status to such an extent was unconscionable. Nevertheless, Sarah's finances were far less straitened,

1 Political Despatch No.65, IOR/L/PS/13/180.

and she now received an additional £900 a year (equivalent to nearly £75,000 today) to provide for the support and education of her sons until they came of age.

In spite of the snobbishly dismissive views expressed by government officials, Sarah was determined to pursue her status as the widow of the Nawab of Bengal. Indeed, now that her husband was no longer there she was much freer to do so. Whereas before the Nawab's departure from England there is no mention of her in any newspapers, now her name frequently appears. Nawab Sarah Bengal often heads the lists of upper-class people staying at prestigious hotels and resorts. One of her favoured hotels was the Metropole in Brighton, the largest hotel outside London. Commenting on visitors to Brighton, an item in the 21 September 1889 issue of the *Sporting Gazette* notes that 'Prince Synd Ullee Meerza, Prince Noosrub Ullee Meerza [sic], Anne Lady Synge, and H.H. the Nawab Sarah Begum of Bengal have attracted much attention while driving along the King's road.'

Sarah's status also allowed her to be seen as a patron of worthy causes. In July 1889 *The Queen*, a magazine which focused on 'high society' and socialites, reported that 'Her Highness the Nawab Sarah Begum of Bengal' had opened a branch of the Gordon Memorial Day Nursery for Little Children. This particular branch was situated in the East End, just across the river from Rotherhithe where Sarah had been born thirty-seven years previously. Following the death of General Charles George Gordon in the siege of Khartoum in 1885, the nursery was one of many Gordon Memorial institutions founded to educate and care for orphaned or destitute boys, a cause that General Gordon had cherished. Here it is interesting to note that Sarah used her status to help improve the lives of children who shared, perhaps in more extreme ways, the experience of her siblings' and her own childhood.

Although Sarah had finally gained custody of her sons, and official recognition of her status as the Nawab's wife, her daughters Miriam and Vaheedoonissa were still in Murshidabad. Receiving only vague responses to her suggestions that her girls return to England, Sarah decided to go to India herself. She embarked aboard the SS *Chusan* sailing from London to Calcutta on 17 October 1889. The passenger list indicates that she travelled alone on what must have been for her a daunting venture, since she had never left England before. At the Murshidabad Palace she would have been made welcome by her stepson Nawab Hassan, who had continued to correspond with her and assure her of her daughters' wellbeing.

We do not know why Miriam and Vaheedoonissa did not return to England. After almost ten years' separation, the meeting between mother and daughters, now aged eighteen and fifteen, cannot have been easy. The girls had become completely accustomed to life in their grandmother's palace in Murshidabad. It was Urdu that most readily came to them when they sought the words to greet their mother and talk about their feelings and their everyday world. In Murshidabad, among the other young women and with their grandmother, they felt safe and loved; England and English had become alien. Sarah perhaps realised that her daughters could not feel at home in London. She would also have seen that they were well cared for, indeed cherished, and may have received assurances that they would not be forced to marry.

Nevertheless, Sarah must have been heartbroken as she left Murshidabad, after what was probably a visit of just a few weeks, and returned to England without them (records of her return journey do not survive). She would see them just one more time, ten years later, when she again visited Bengal, this time together with her oldest son, Syed, in 1899. Nusrat did not accompany his mother and brother to India on this occasion. Indeed, after his return to England in 1885, he never visited India, despite his affection for his sisters, especially Vaheedoonissa, to whom he later sent some of his paintings. His childhood experience of being taken away and then returned to an alien world may have been so traumatic that he could not easily contemplate making the journey again.

In 1890 Sarah rented a house at 36 Mecklenburgh Square (next door to the house where Virginia Woolf stayed in 1939). There she lived with with her sons (recorded in the 1891 census by an odd transcription of their full names, 'Prince Synd Ullu Mazza' and 'Prince Nossut Ullu Mazza') and two servants. From there Syed and Nusrat, having gained entry to the King's College School and now aged fourteen and twelve, could walk down Gray's Inn Road, past the Inns of Court where their Uncle George shared chambers, to reach school in time for classes which began at 9.30 each morning. Situated on the Strand – in the basement of the College where Felix Seddon, their father's tutor, had been Professor of Oriental languages in the 1830s – the King's College School took pride in its strong record for obtaining entry for its students to Oxford and Cambridge. Syed and Nusrat were enrolled in both the Mathematical Division and the Classical Division, 'intended to prepare pupils for the Universities, for the Learned Professions, for the Public Service Competitive Examinations'. The Curriculum included Greek, Latin, history, French, English literature and 'freehand drawing'.[1]

Here, as at Ashbourne House School, the boys were familiarly known as Nawab Senior and Nawab Junior, easily pronounced abbreviations of their actual titles as the Nawabzidas Syed and Nusrat Ali Mirza. Syed proved a capable pupil, awarded the prizes for general literature and mathematics in his first and second years at the King's College School. After their first two years, the boys appear to have concentrated on sporting rather than academic success. Syed became captain of the school cricket eleven and the rugby fifteen in 1893; Nusrat succeeded him as captain of the rugby team in 1894. Sports were played on fields leased by the school near Wormwood Scrubs, which could be reached by the District Railway. Both boys received frequent mentions in the school magazine for their achievements in rugby and athletics.

Nevertheless, their sporting activities did not prevent Syed and Nusrat from gaining entrance to Oxford University. Syed was awarded a place at Brasenose College in 1894, and Nusrat went to study at Merton College in 1895. Once again Sarah was on her own, although the boys spent most of their holidays with her.

Then came a terrible blow; after a long and painful illness George died from lung and liver cancer in February 1895. He was only thirty-nine years old, and he did not die a rich man. Although George had a lover with whom he had a daughter, Sarah was named as the beneficiary for his estate of £396.4s.3d, equivalent to approximately £48,000 today.

1 Frank Miles and Graeme Cranch, *A History of the Kings College School: The First 150 Year's* (King's College School, 1979), pp.32–34.

George had been Sarah's beloved young brother, her closest friend and supporter throughout her marriage and during the bitter aftermath. As she wrote later to the India Office, George's intention to further pursue Sarah's case for a larger pension and the promised dowry had been prevented by his illness and death. Sarah did not feel she could continue this particular battle on her own.

Now Sarah moved away from Central London to Upper Norwood, an area considered more salubrious because of its height and distance from London's smog. She rented a house in the Avenue, a pleasant tree-lined street, near the church of St Aubyn's. But during the holidays she and her sons also spent weeks away, staying at hotels in fashionable resorts such as Bath and Brighton.

Syed and Nusrat seemed to have entered fully into the social life of undergraduates at Oxford. Neither of them planned to take the honours degree; in fact, like many upper-class Englishmen at that time, neither of them actually completed the pass degree before leaving Oxford in 1898, despite having spent three years or more (with some interruptions) in college. At university they were able to shed their Indian labels as Nawab Senior and Junior and adopt a more English identity. A fellow student named C. Eley remembered Syed as one 'than whom there was not a more loyal or enthusiastic son of BNC [Brasenose College]... To his contemporaries he was "The Prince" and nothing pleased him more than to entertain old members of the college.'

Syed's tutor, Dr F.W. Bussell (Principal of Brasenose and a man noted for his matchless eccentricity), noted that 'he was an excellent fellow and very popular, always called "Prince".' Bussell also reported that 'it was rumoured that the male members of his Sunnite Muslim family slept with a naked scimitar under the pillow'. Syed's family, as noted previously, were Shi'i rather than Sunni, and sleeping with scimitars would seem to have been an unlikely habit, whether in or out of college. His popularity and involvement with numerous college activities did not prevent Syed from becoming the victim of orientalist fantasies on the part of his Oxford companions.

Syed's non-academic activities included membership of the rugby and cricket teams, the Oxford University Dramatic Society (he was

Syed Ali Mirza (right) with members of the Phoenix Club, Oxford

in the cast for *The Taming of the Shrew*), the Octagon Dining Club, the Phoenix Common Room, and the Vampyres (a lunching club for cricketers 'who cared more about enjoying than winning'). He also joined the Masonic Lodge in Oxford, proposed by Dr Bussell and 'Brother Eley' in February 1896, advancing to the second and third degree of the Brotherhood in 1898. Membership of the Freemasons no doubt added to his valuable social contacts, and it was perhaps one of the few organisations of a social and vaguely spiritual nature that was open to Muslims, who were accepted because they fulfilled the requirement of believing in a single Supreme Being.

Like the majority of undergraduates during his first two years at Brasenose, Syed had a room in the college. His was situated on the third floor, just above his more academically inclined classmate, John Buchan, the novelist and future Governor-General of Canada. Syed spent little time in his rooms studying, however. In March 1896, the Brasenose College Minute Book records that 'it was decided that Prince Syed Ullee Meerza having failed to pass his examinations in a book substituted for Holy Scripture, and having been previously warned for idleness, should not be allowed to reside during the Summer Term, until he should have come up for his examination'.[1] This interruption may have encouraged Syed to give more attention to his studies, if only so that he could continue to enjoy life at Oxford. He returned in Michaelmas term 1896 having passed his scripture exam, and then achieved passes in classics and elements of political economy.

Nusrat's record at Merton College was not as conspicuous. He appears to have been less confident, but no more studious, than his older brother. Like Syed, Nusrat struggled to pass the scripture exam, and in June 1899 he was threatened with being sent down the following term. That same month, Nusrat and three other young men were refused leave to stay on in college for the next few days 'having wantonly broken a lamp in the Quadrangle at 2 a.m. on June 18'.[2] The following year Nusrat was still struggling to pass his exams, was gated in February for seven nights for 'knocking in after midnight', and was threatened with being sent down for a term if he and his companion in ignominy, a Mr N. Young, 'fail[ed] to keep five roll calls in each week for the rest of the term'.[3]

In the Brasenose College archives there is a photograph album that belonged to Syed. Among the photographs including him in the rugby and cricket teams, the Octagon and Vampyre clubs, the Masons at Apollo Lodge, there is a group photograph of the men in costumes for a fancy-dress ball. Many of the men are dressed as women, others as Arabs, bushrangers or Turks. Dr Bussell sits in their midst apparelled as a judge. And on the far right at the very end of the row is Prince Syed Ullee Meerza, dressed as an Indian prince.

At this stage in their lives Syed and Nusrat apparently enjoyed their roles as princes, as the sons of the Nawab of Bengal. Their titles gave them a certain status, and made them interesting. But there was also a tinge of irony in their attitudes towards those titles, a slight distancing. For Syed, the actor, the perpetual bachelor, his royal status allowed him to be sociable, to be both prince and patron. His identity allowed him

1 *Brasenose College Minute Book*, 1896.
2 *Merton College Minute Book*, 1899.
3 *Ibid.*, 23 May 1900.

to be even more loyal to his college, and he would go on to be loyal to England during the First World War, serving as a Special Constable. For Nusrat, however, the role of Indian prince became increasingly uncomfortable, and he would eventually seek to escape it.

By the turn of the century, both Syed and Nusrat had left Oxford and set up shared lodgings at 30 Whitehall Court, a grand neo-Gothic apartment building overlooking the Thames Embankment and just a short walk from Westminster. Among their neighbours was Lord Minto, who would in 1905 become Viceroy of India. They joined in the activities of wealthy English gentlemen at that time; Syed's presence in Scotland during the shooting and fishing seasons is noted in 1903 and 1904. I was intrigued to discover from one newspaper item that in 1904 Syed was fishing in the River Dee in the small town of Aboyne, Aberdeenshire. Aboyne was also the hometown of my father, Ian Innes, who would have been ten years old at the time, and also a keen fisherman.

Like other wealthy Englishmen the brothers also travelled abroad, Syed to Chile in 1898 and Nusrat to the Caribbean in 1905. Syed had visited India with his mother in 1899, but neither Syed nor Nusrat ever returned to India again. One close connection had been lost when their older stepbrother, Nawab Hassan, died on Christmas Day 1906, aged sixty; he was succeeded by their nephew, Hassan's oldest son, Wasif Ali Mirza, who had been born the same year as Syed. But their sisters still lived in Murshidabad, and Vaheedoonissa certainly maintained contact with them, so their failure to make another visit to India is difficult to explain.

It is possible that they were discouraged because of the considerable political turmoil in Bengal during 1905 and for several years afterwards, caused by Viceroy Lord Curzon's decision to partition Bengal. Curzon claimed that dividing the Bengal Presidency, which included Bihar and Orissa, and which had a population of nearly 80 million at the time, would make it easier to administer. The resulting division created a mainly Muslim province named East Bengal, and a mainly Hindu state, with a minority of Bengalis, named Bengal. Both Hindus and Muslims opposed the partition, and there were boycotts of British goods as well as violent protests throughout India, together with a strengthening of movements calling for Indian independence. The partition was eventually reversed in 1911.

Since her sons now had their own residence, Sarah decided she no longer needed the house in Upper Norwood, which was expensive to rent and maintain. Almost fifty years old, a widow without family duties, she chose, like many other women in her situation, to spend the rest of her life in hotels. Her doctor had advised her to leave London for health reasons. She spent some months in Cannes, but returned to England to be joined by her sons each summer in Bath or Brighton. Having once served others in a hotel, it may have given her an added pleasure now to be waited on and looked after. No doubt she noted whether or not the hotel maids had been properly trained. And she was insistent on her status as the Nawab of Bengal's widow, always registering as Nawab Sarah Begum of Bengal.

However, Sarah's financial situation became increasingly difficult. Due to inflation her pension of £480 a year was no longer adequate for residence in the better hotels, having diminished in value from the equivalent in the twenty-first century of £40,000 to about £30,000. Neither of her sons felt they were in a position to help her financially. From the Wellington Hotel in Tunbridge Wells Sarah wrote in April 1910 to Sir Richmond Ritchie, Under-Secretary of State for India, pleading her case for an increase in her stipend so that she could follow her doctor's advice to live abroad for reasons of health and so that she could 'live in a way befitting the widow of the Nawab Nazim of Bengal'.[1] Her request was refused. Attitudes towards 'lower-class' Englishwomen making alliances with Indian noblemen had not much changed over the previous forty years, and indeed had perhaps become more ingrained.

Sarah now moved to various less expensive hotels in Folkestone, Margate and other parts of southeast England. Although her elder son accepted some responsibility for her welfare and care, she seems to have become increasingly isolated. Following the death of her father in 1884 there is no evidence that she saw any of her siblings apart from George, who then passed away in 1895. After Nusrat's marriage, it seems she saw very little of him either. In 1924 she became terminally ill with

1 Letter dated 15 April 1910. IOR/LS/P/13/180, p.85.

cancer, and Syed wrote to the India Office seeking financial assistance so that she could receive the palliative nursing care her doctor said was necessary. The India Office now agreed a one-off sum of £250 (today equivalent to £10,000), and Sarah was placed in a nursing home in Cromwell Road, Kensington, London. She died there on 1 September 1925. Just six people attended the Christian funeral service in St John's Church, Putney Hill. She left her entire estate, amounting to £1,489 11s (today about £60,000) to Syed. There is no mention in her will of Nusrat, her two grandchildren, or any of her siblings.

Sarah's life had been a difficult and often unhappy one. Three years before her death, her daughter-in-law, Elsie, with whom she was not on close terms, published a short piece in the *Daily Mail*, titled 'Lonely Hotel Women'. 'Few people are more to be pitied than elderly, lonely, hotel women,' Elsie wrote. She went on to speculate on their mistaken expectations of a gay and varied life, moving from place to place, making new friends, enjoying the music. But, 'it is just here that the lonely woman makes the saddest mistake in her life,' Elsie continued, detailing the 'monotony of hotel food', 'the deadly sameness of the ever changing faces'. In Elsie's view women who live in hotels inevitably become discontented, bored, prone to nervous diseases, lacking in purpose and soul, because a hotel can never be a home.[1]

Elsie's judgement on Sarah's life is a harsh one, marked by a rather unpitying claim to pity. It disregards Sarah's courage and determination in her battle for her children, her refusal to accept the judgement of others concerning her status in a world that condemned marriages that crossed racial and class boundaries. Sarah did not ask for pity, she asked for what she believed were her rights. Her insistence on acknowledgement of her title as Nawab Sarah Begum was not merely a claim to aristocratic status; given the scepticism and attitudes of British officials and others towards her marriage to the Nawab, it was of the utmost importance to Sarah that she should be regarded as a respectable widow. She had remained a Christian, and she had insisted that her marriage be a

1 'Lonely Hotel Women,' by Elizabeth Marc. Published in *The Daily News*, W.A., 22 May 1922. Originally published in the *Daily Mail*, March 1922. (Elsie published under the name Elizabeth Marc.)

permanent one. It was not, as the India Office lawyers finally conceded, 'a mere immoral contract for cohabitation'. Unlike Julia she had refused to convert to Islam as a means of retaining her relationship with the Nawab when he took another wife. It was doubtless Syed who ensured that her funeral and the notice of her death in the English newspapers honoured that desire for respectability and her adherence to an identity as a moral Christian woman:

> NAWAB SARAH BEGUM
>
> The funeral of Nawab Sarah Begum, widow of his Highness Synd Munsoor Ali, last Nawab Nazim of Bengal, Behar, and Orissa, who died on Tuesday in a London nursing home, took place yesterday at Putney Vale Cemetery. The deceased was 72, and had been ill a considerable time. The first part of the service was held at St John's Church, Putney Hill, and the Rev. F. B. Wood officiated. There were some beautiful flowers. The mourners numbered half a dozen, and the proceedings were of the simplest character.

CHAPTER 9

Royal Bohemians

1907–1914

When Elsie Algar was in her early twenties, she travelled from London to Jamaica to visit her eldest sister, Eve, whose husband was principal of the Mico teachers' college in Kingston. One evening during the voyage she was seated at table next to a tall, dark-haired man. 'I hear there is an Indian prince travelling with us,' Elsie said, seeking to make conversation with the stranger. 'I can confirm that is true,' he replied, 'for I am that Indian prince.'

And that, according to the story Elsie's daughter Myriam relayed to me, was how Elsie Algar and Nusrat Ali Mirza met. Like many of her mother's anecdotes it was a good story, featuring romance, humour, and delight in the unexpected consequences of a chance encounter. But like so many of her mother's versions of the past, it was also a story that had minimal correspondence with the facts. By the time Elsie and Nusrat Ali Mirza sailed to Jamaica in December 1908, they had been husband and wife for nearly a year and a half.

Born on 13 November 1882, Elsie was the youngest of three sisters whose parents, Harry and Eliza Algar, were schoolteachers in the Kentish village of St Mary Cray, thirteen miles south of central London. Two of their children, both boys, had died in their infancy, and Elsie believed her being female was a disappointment to her father. It was nevertheless the case that Elsie was always closer to her father than to her mother.

Among the many questionable family stories that I investigated while writing this book was Elsie's claim that her father's surname referred to his descent from an illegitimate son of Horatio Nelson, Lord Trafalgar. Her father had indeed been born out of wedlock to Sarah

Elsie Algar, age fifteen

Algar, the first of her eleven children, in Suffolk in May 1843, two and a half years before she married Henry Barber, but there is no evidence of a connection to Nelson. Her mother, Eliza Campbell, was born in Kent, the daughter of Robert Campbell and Ann Penn. She too was provided with an illustrious ancestry in later years, and was supposedly a descendant of William Penn. Her daughter possessed a carved shoe-shaped stone inkwell said to have been given to William Penn by Native Americans. Only in later years did I begin to consider that perhaps an inkwell was not a plausible artefact for indigenous people to have produced in 1683.

Elsie's parents had begun their teaching careers educating young naval recruits in Sussex and then Cornwall. However, the 1870 Elementary Education Act benefited the whole family, requiring the establishment of thousands of new schools and giving Harry the opportunity to move from Cornwall to Kent and take up a position as headmaster of the local primary school in St Mary Cray. Later he became head of the school district. The family was provided with a fine new house on the edge of the village, with a large garden. All three of his daughters, Evangeline (b. 1870), Winifred Helen (b. 1878) and Elsie, attended this school, and went on to become scholars at the Bromley High School, founded in 1883 under the auspices of the Girls' Public Day School Company which sought to provide girls of all classes with a high standard of academic education. Here they were fortunate to become pupils during the reign of the founding headmistress, Mary Louisa Heppel, a strong woman who made certain that the girls were not limited, as in many other schools, by an emphasis on the domestic sciences. She also ensured that her girls could participate in sports and gym lessons, an unusually progressive stance in this period. The curriculum included mathematics, chemistry, history, geography, French, German, English, art and music.

The Bromley High School magazine for 1903, the year after Elsie graduated, features her as the school's star tennis player 'whose net play was very effective and often won applause'.[1] Elsie was also awarded the school prize for chemistry. Indeed, Bromley High School had some illustrious pupils. Elsie's tennis partner was Dorothy Brock, who was later awarded an OBE and eventually a damehood for her services to education, and with whom Elsie remained friends throughout her life. Another close friend was May Tweedy, later Lady Mellanby, a distinguished medical researcher specialising in the cause of dental disease. Later Elsie would look back on her years at Bromley High School as among the happiest in her life.

Like many of their classmates at Bromley High School the three sisters eventually found themselves working as educators, one of the rapidly developing careers for women that were now far more accessible than they had been. Theirs was a generation that also saw the expanding British Empire as a domain offering increased opportunity for self-fulfilment in terms of status, work, identity and adventure. Evangeline, the oldest sister, generally known as Eve, trained and taught in her father's school district. It was here she met Alexander McFarlane, whose father, a plumber, had emigrated south with his family from Glasgow and settled in St Mary Cray where he found work in the newly opened paper mill. Although Alexander had become headmaster of St John's High School

1 *Bromley High School Magazine*, No. 7 (May 1903).

for Boys in Friern Barnet (now the North London International School) from 1885 till 1888, Eve's father regarded Alexander's income and experience as inadequate when in 1889 Alexander first asked for Eve's hand in marriage. Alexander then took up a post as a teacher in the Boys' High School in Allahabad, India, for four years. On his return, he and Eve were at last able to marry on 1 December 1894. Their son Maynard Leslie Deedes McFarlane was born just over thirty-six weeks later on 14 August 1895.

Alexander taught for four more years in London. Eve suffered from asthma, so when the post of principal of the Mico teacher's college in the Crown Colony of Jamaica was advertised, they decided to move to the Caribbean in the hope that the climate there would be better for her health. But the post also offered a considerable advance in status and salary for Alexander, as well as a challenge and a vocation for which the years in Allahabad had provided a good foundation. And so they sailed to Jamaica in late 1898 with their small son.

Alexander McFarlane's tenure as principal of Mico was regarded as a particularly successful one for the college and its pupils. Following the earthquake that destroyed much of Kingston in 1907, Alexander oversaw the building of the new college. He introduced agriculture and hygiene as important elements in the training of teachers who would work in rural areas, and he also wrote at least two text books. One of the college's trustees noted that he was unstinting in the time he gave to dealing with individual student difficulties, whether academic, personal or financial.

The second sister, christened Winifred Helen but known by family and friends as Helen, was born in 1877. Helen was said to be the brightest and most beautiful of the Algar sisters and was particularly admired by Elsie. On leaving school she also trained as a teacher before deciding to follow her sister's family to Jamaica in November 1898. Perhaps with encouragement and assistance from Eve and Alexander she obtained a position as second mistress in the prestigious Wolmer's Girls' School in Kingston. There she met William Buttenshaw, who had graduated from the newly created agricultural science degree at Aberdeen University a year before. One of William's duties was to give a series of lectures on agriculture to trainee teachers at the Mico college where he worked closely with Helen's brother-in-law, Alexander McFarlane. Various reports in the local papers indicate that William was a lively and successful teacher. He was a young, handsome and attractive bachelor when Helen met him, probably on one of his visits to the McFarlane's home in Kingston. In 1900 they became engaged and, to the dismay of the Wolmer School governors, Helen submitted her resignation on 8 January 1901. As in Britain, women in the British Crown Colonies were not allowed to continue as teachers after marriage.

Helen and William were married in the parish church of St Andrew's, one of the wealthier areas of Kingston, on 16 April 1901. Their married life together was intermittent and brief, however. William was often away from home visiting rural areas and lecturing on agricultural methods. In a community where it was not socially acceptable for white women to venture out on their own, Helen no doubt found life as a non-employed married woman in the West Indies dull. And so just two years later, when William was posted to Barbados, Helen decided to take 'home leave'. In July 1903 Helen travelled with him in the Royal Mail Steamer *Para* as far as Barbados, but instead of disembarking there continued to London. However, Helen and William remained married; Helen returned to Barbados for long visits, and William also came to London when he could. When Helen was on a return visit from Barbados in 1905, one of the passengers who joined the ship at Kingston was Nusrat Ali Mirza. Perhaps Elsie appropriated a story Helen told about meeting a prince on a voyage when she also appropriated the prince himself.

I have a cameo locket that once belonged to my Great Aunt Helen. It contains a photograph of William, a man of about thirty, with regular features, a strong jaw and abundant brown hair. He is unsmiling – as people tended to be in photographs of that period. It was taken in a studio in Hythe, Kent, I assume on a visit to England and probably a holiday with Helen on the Kent coast before his departure for Calcutta, to 'take up a lucrative appointment under the India Office'.[1]

In London, Helen began to establish a career as a journalist under the name Helen Macdonald. She was a regular contributor to *Home*

---

1 *Jamaica Gleaner*, 5 October 1907.

Chat, a magazine aimed at women seeking to be upwardly mobile. It featured news about royalty in Britain and Europe, fashions that women could sew for themselves, recipes for inexpensive meals, and articles on jobs or professions that women could enter, mainly teaching and clerical, as long as they remained unmarried. Married women could continue in retail jobs, in clothing stores for example. Journalism was also considered an acceptable career for women, whether married or unmarried, especially if they could work from home. *Home Chat* supported votes for women, with cover pages featuring Christabel Pankhurst and Charlotte Despard. Helen co-edited *Home Chat*, and wrote articles and several weekly columns specialising in questions of etiquette and social propriety. She also published much longer feature articles on subjects as diverse as the gambling scene in Monte Carlo, prospects for women in Canada, 'Love and how to Keep It', and 'the pudding lady' who offered a cooking school for poor families in St Pancras.

After completing her studies at Bromley High, Elsie rejected school teaching as a career and instead chose to become a governess. An avid reader of fiction, and a great admirer ofThackeray and the Brontës, Elsie often read and reread *Vanity Fair*; it was perhaps such reading, as well as a desire to be a part of a more prestigious world, that encouraged her choice. Her daughter Myriam in later life compared Elsie to Thackeray's governess character Becky Sharp, and indeed she shared Becky Sharp's qualities of charm, intelligence, impatience with Victorian attitudes, and determination to escape her modest origins. But Elsie was less calculating than Becky; she was a romantic rather than a realist.

Elsie's first position was with the family of E. B. Pretyman, a Conservative MP, and here she proved herself a competent governess for the Pretymans' three young boys and two girls. Pretyman also gave her secretarial work to do.[1] It was a position that allowed her to gain an acquaintance with a wider world of politics and upper-class society, as Pretyman was Civil Lord of the Admiralty, and his wife, Lady Beatrice, was the daughter of the Fourth Earl of Bradford. In later years, Elsie's reminiscences of her life during this period would inflate

1 Letter from E. Pretyman to the India Office., IQR/L/PS/13/182

her employment with Pretyman into undertaking secretarial work for Winston Churchill, and political campaigning.

The two sisters enjoyed living in London. When she could get time off from her duties, Elsie sometimes accompanied Helen to social events or was a guest at one of Helen's gatherings in her London flat in Davies Street, Berkeley Square. It was on one of these occasions that she met Nusrat. Elsie later told her daughter that Nusrat had been one of Helen's many admirers, but tiring of his attentions Helen had encouraged his relationship with her younger sister.

What drew Elsie and Nusrat to one another? Although she lacked her petite sister's beauty and status as a journalist, Elsie was an attractive woman, with striking blue eyes and a strong, rather theatrical personality. She was ambitious and adventurous, and she would have liked to emulate Helen's charm and success. She was more than ready to end her employment as a governess. Nusrat was a glamorous figure – an Indian prince, a man of comparatively substantial means, and he belonged to 'society'. Moreover he was handsome and amiable, had spent three years at Oxford (albeit without graduating), was an amateur musician and artist, and had travelled abroad. He was different from the men Elsie's sisters had married, men who had advanced from working-class origins and dedicated themselves to their careers, men like her father.

Elsie Algar and Prince Nusrat Ali Mirza were married in London on 1 August 1907. Like the marriage between Sarah and the Nawab, it was a small and unpretentious ceremony; but unlike their parents' weddings, it was a secular occasion. This wedding took place in the St George Hanover Square Register Office, attended by Helen, as well as Nusrat's mother Nawab Sarah Begum and his older brother Syed. Harry and Eliza Algar were not present. It may be they had misgivings about their daughter marrying a Muslim of Indian descent, or perhaps Elsie wished to include only that upper-class society she was now literally espousing.

Nusrat brought to the marriage an annual pension of 10,000 rupees (at that time equivalent to about £660, comparable to around £52,000 per annum now) administered by the India Office. This was not a vast fortune, but it was certainly a considerable advance on Elsie's wage during the previous four years as a governess. The average annual wage

'Tyn-y-groes',
Sketch by Nusrat, 1907

for a governess at this time, in addition to accommodation and board, was about £25, equivalent today to about £2,000. There was also a marriage settlement, witnessed by Helen, a trust fund assigned to Elsie amounting to £4,500 (almost £400,000 pounds now), which would have been part of Nusrat's inheritance. Nusrat was then thirty years old, and their marriage certificate indicates that Elsie had given her age as twenty-one, although her birth and baptismal records indicate she would have been twenty-four.

Now formally named as Prince and Princess Meerza, the couple spent their honeymoon walking, riding and fishing in North Wales. They stayed near the small town of Dolgellau at the prestigious Tyn-y-Groes Hotel, which was a favourite retreat of William Gladstone and other grandees.

Nusrat made sketches in pencil and watercolour depicting the trees, streams, waterfalls and hills near Tyn-y-Groes. Elsie pasted some of these sketches into the large album which accompanied her on all her travels and which also contained photographs of the family and pets, and the places they visited and lived. A blank space in the album for these years notes that one of these watercolours had been sent in 1907 to Vaheedoonissa, indicating that Nusrat made efforts to remain in contact with his sister.

The honeymoon came to an abrupt end in mid-September. News reached the newlyweds of the death in India of William Buttenshaw, Helen's husband. William had arrived in Calcutta from London only three weeks previously, so his death on 9 September 1907 from heart failure came as a shock.

Elsie was less convinced than Nusrat that Helen would be so very deeply distressed by William's death. Nevertheless, on Nusrat's insistence they returned to London to be near Helen, and took up residence there in a flat in Ashley Gardens, a fashionable apartment building in Westminster. Helen now concentrated more single-mindedly on her career as a journalist, travelling in Europe, writing about Paris and other Continental scenes. In London Nusrat resumed many of the activities he had enjoyed before his marriage, playing bridge at the Union Club to which he and his older brother Syed both belonged, and also playing golf. Although both brothers remained nominally Muslims, they no longer adhered to prohibitions against eating pork or drinking alcohol. Nor did they attend the only mosque in the London area at that time, the Shah Jahan Mosque, built in 1889 in Oriental Road, Woking. They continued to share the lives and interests of other wealthy and aristocratic gentlemen in Britain.

Elsie also took up drawing and painting and bridge. Life as a lady of leisure, and her status as the wife of a prince, was certainly preferable to her former more subservient and arduous role as a governess, but she was beginning to feel restless. Nusrat had given enticing accounts of his short time in Jamaica, and Eve had for several years been encouraging Elsie to visit. Moreover, the British government was encouraging its citizens to see the West Indian colonies as part of an attractive and thriving global market, with opportunities for investment and new careers. Governed directly from Britain as a Crown Colony, Jamaica was viewed as one of the more promising areas for development, despite the deep gulf between the wealthy white and coloured upper classes and the majority black population, which had no say in political affairs. News of the devastation wrought by the earthquake in January 1907 had for some time put an end to thoughts of such a visit, but then Eve wrote to say that Kingston was again a functioning city, and their new house in the grounds of Mico College was ready to receive guests.

Elsie and Nusrat sailed from Bristol on the *Port Royal* on 28 November 1908. They travelled First Class, and are listed as His Highness Prince Meerza and Her Highness Princess Meerza. First-class passengers were not expected to indicate an occupation. The passenger lists at that time required that travellers be identified under one of six columns – English, Scottish, Welsh, Irish, British Colonial, or Alien. Both Elsie and Nusrat are marked under the column for nationality as English. The majority of the thirty passengers on the *Port Royal* were listed as English, but two were listed as British Colonial, the pianist Harold Nation and the baritone Carlton Bryan, members of the Native Choir from Jamaica. They had been touring Britain for the past two years and had appeared at the Colonial Products Exhibition in Liverpool in 1906. Stormy weather delayed the *Port Royal* for several days; it was 14 December when the ship steamed into the wide expanse of Kingston Harbour.

Writing in 1909, the Jamaican journalist and novelist Herbert de Lisser describes the harbour and town of Kingston as Elsie and Nusrat would first have glimpsed it. 'The harbour is like a great lagoon,' he notes, 'very still and quiet … a magnificent sheet of water fringed with mangrove plants and cocoa-nut palms.'[1] The city huddled between the water and the mountains, and 'for every house there seem a dozen trees'. Evidence of the earthquake remained, for beside the harbour many buildings were still in ruins, but King Street, the main commercial and shopping street, had been entirely rebuilt. It was a wide street; up and down ran electric trams, alongside more leisurely horse cabs and mule carts. Colonnades provided shade for shoppers and strollers. In contrast to the poverty that afflicted subsistence and dispossessed farmers in rural areas of Jamaica, Kingston seemed a thriving modern city.

Elsie and Nusrat were met at the port by Eve and Alexander

1 Henry De Lisser, *In Jamaica and Cuba* (Jamaica Times: Kingston, 1910).

McFarlane, and conveyed by hackney carriage up King Street to Kelvin Lodge in the grounds of Mico College, where the McFarlanes lived with their three-year-old daughter Audrey and several servants. Their fourteen-year-old son Maynard was at school 'back home' in England. Now having lived for over a decade in Kingston, Eve and Alexander had become accustomed to a world where white people were a tiny minority, where the temperature rarely dropped below 85 degrees Fahrenheit, where the larger houses were surrounded with wide verandas, and where purple, orange and bright-pink bougainvillea spread over every garden wall. But for Elsie and Nusrat the contrast between England and this new world they were encountering must have been striking – and added to their sense of adventure. For Nusrat there were reminders of his childhood years in Murshidabad: the mango trees, especially, and the pungent smell of their sweet, juicy, yellow fruits dropping on the streets and lawns; he had not tasted mangoes since his return to England twenty years ago. Occasionally he might be startled to hear an Urdu word or phrase from a passerby, and turning would see two Indians talking. Although dressed like other Jamaicans, these people, shipped as 'Coolies' to the Caribbean after 1833 to replace the emancipated slaves as cheap indentured labour, brought unexpected echoes of the servants in his father's houses and the workers in the rice fields surrounding Murshidabad.

The local paper, the *Daily Gleaner*, noted their arrival and later reported their presence at several official events. Nusrat and Elsie were royalty, a rarer commodity in Jamaica than in England, and Elsie relished her status as Princess Meerza. She and her sister attended the Mico College sports day on 8 May 1909. Nusrat seems to have stayed away. The *Gleaner* headline for that day reads, 'Athletic Contests at Mico College: Distribution of Prizes by Princess Meerza', and the reporter goes on to tell his readers: 'The prizes were distributed by HH Princess Meerza at the conclusion of the sports, and the Reverend W. L. Griffiths in a short but most happy speech conveyed the very hearty thanks of the company to Her Highness for the kindly interest shown by her in the sports, and for the most generous additions she had made to the prizes.'[1] The contrast between the publicity given to the couple's stay during this period and Nusrat's lone trip to Jamaica as a tourist in 1905 is striking: no mention of that visit or its purpose appears in the Jamaican papers, and Nusrat must have preferred remaining relatively anonymous.

After some weeks staying with Eve and Alexander in Kelvin Lodge, Elsie and Nusrat rented Cherry Gardens Great House, an elegant colonial mansion with a large garden, looking out over the town and harbour on one side and towards the ever-misty blue mountains on the other. It had once been owned by George Gordon, one of the leaders of the Morant Bay Rebellion, a mass protest in which black and coloured Jamaicans demanded rights to vote and alleviation of the extreme economic inequality between white planters and black labourers. Gordon was executed along with 500 other protestors at the order of Governor Eyre in 1865. Now it was one of the most prestigious houses in Kingston. There the couple entertained the few fellow Britons of sufficient standing, including Governor Sydney Olivier, whose Fabian Socialist ideals may have been more attractive to Alexander McFarlane than to Elsie and Nusrat.

Although the British in Jamaica had adapted their houses to suit the climate, social rituals and norms remained as in the old country. British friends and relatives would enjoy afternoon tea, tennis, and dinners together in their houses, waited on by Jamaican servants. While the Governor's parties at King's House or his country estate at Fort George included 'coloured' writers and artists such as Herbert de Lisser, elsewhere there was little mixing with members of other cultures or races unless they were employees or tradesmen. Here an exception might be made for Alexander McFarlane. His student teachers were all Jamaicans of African descent, and he seems to have genuinely treated them as having the same potential as white students.

There were other diversions on the island. There is a photograph of Elsie riding sidesaddle. There were excursions to Montego Bay, to the mountains, and to the great wide Rio Cobre River, where Nusrat made sketches. Before their departure he donated one of his landscape

1 *Gleaner*, 15 May 1909, p.4.

Elsie and Syed, March 1910

paintings to the Jamaica Institute, a gift welcomed by Sir Sydney Olivier, who lamented the lack of Caribbean landscape artists. It is now held in the National of Gallery of Jamaica.

Elsie also continued drawing and painting in this period. One picture was a portrait in oils of her brother-in-law, presented to Mico College after the main building, Buxton Hall, was reopened in 1909. The Hall, along with many other College buildings, had been destroyed in the earthquake, and Alexander had supervised its reconstruction. The portrait was hung in the entrance to Buxton Hall. Sadly a fire ravaged the building two weeks later, and although the Hall was again rebuilt under Alexander McFarlane's close supervision, it seems that Elsie's portrait was destroyed.

And there was the birth of their baby son. The 22 October 1909 edition of *The Gleaner* carries the following announcement:

> THE STORK VISITS
>
> A son was born yesterday afternoon to Prince and Princess Alee Meerza [sic], of India, who are staying in Jamaica on a short visit to Mr and Mrs A. B. McFarlane.

This son was named Syed Ullee Meerza, after his grandfather and uncle.

For Eve and Helen and their husbands Jamaica offered opportunity for professional work, an improvement in status and lifestyle and, in Eve's case, better health. As had William Buttenshaw, Alexander McFarlane dedicated himself to improving the conditions, educational, social and economic, of the island, and he rarely took time to relax. For Elsie and Nusrat, however, Jamaica offered a change of scene. They went as visitors, tourists; working for a living was not on their agenda. Moreover, the cost of living well in Jamaica was lower than it was in London; in Kingston they could afford to live and present themselves as aristocrats. They could also spend time drawing and painting scenes that seemed more romantic than those of London and the Home Counties.

But however prestigious their status in Jamaica – indeed because of their prestige as royalty – their social life and activities were restricted. Elsie and Nusrat were becoming restless, and Nusrat never felt particularly at ease with the role of Indian prince. He was keen to focus on his painting, and Elsie had also become increasingly interested in developing her skills as an artist. Nor did Jamaica seem the ideal environment for their new infant son to gain an education. The hurricane that swept eastern Jamaica on 11 November 1909, causing the loss of at least thirty lives and major flooding, made the less tempestuous climate of Western Europe seem more appealing. Moreover Jamaica felt cut off from the cultural currents and events that were making news in other parts of the world. Why not go to Paris and study art? There too the cost of living was lower than in London, and Paris was an enticing cultural scene in 1910.

The Gleaner reported the family's departure from Jamaica on 11 February 1910, after a stay of almost fourteen months, with the following headline: 'An Indian Prince Born in Jamaica'. A photograph of Nusrat holding his son is captioned 'Prince Meerza and the Infant Prince'. The paper goes on to note that their Highnesses Prince and Princess Meerza had originally came on a visit for three months, 'but were so delighted with the island that they prolonged their stay'. The report concludes with the information that Prince Meerza is 'the son of the late Nawab Nazim of Bengal, Bihar, and Orissa, and is the direct descendant of thirty-eight kings. He traces his descendants back to 600.' Presumably this report quotes Nusrat or Elsie, probably the latter. Despite the reference to the seventh century when Muhammad was born, the report avoids mention of the Murshidabad family's claimed descent from the Prophet.

And so Elsie and Nusrat said farewell to Jamaica and, after a short stay with Elsie's parents in Somerset, embarked on a new life as artists in bohemian Paris. They were, however, comparatively wealthy bohemians, who could afford to rent a comfortable three-storey house, the Villa Mathilde, in the Avenue des Chalets in Saint-Cloud.

Located on the Seine's left bank on the outskirts of Paris, Saint-Cloud had become something of an artist's colony during the late nineteenth and early twentieth century. Saint-Cloud was where Edvard Munch had lived briefly from 1889 to 1890, where the American artist Janet Scudder owned a villa and peopled her garden with sculpted figures, and where the musicians Charles Gounod and Maurice Ravel had spent their later years. Paintings by artists such as Théodore Rousseau, Monet, Sisley and Renoir depicted the river at Saint-Cloud and the formal gardens, fountains and woods of the Parc de Saint-Cloud, a large *domaine* commissioned in the seventeenth century by the brother of Louis XIV.

Those first years in Paris were happy and fulfilling ones for Elsie and Nusrat. It was the period Elsie would frequently recall in conversations with her grandchildren many years later, whereas the times spent in Jamaica and England were rarely mentioned. They entertained friends at the Villa Mathilde, and Elsie took pride in her developing skills as a cook. Nusrat enjoyed fixing up and decorating the house, which had been in poor repair when they first leased it. Numerous studio photographs of little Syed, often dressed in oriental costume, show him to have been an attractive and cheerful toddler. He was beginning to speak both French and English, and he could join in the French songs his nurse and Elsie sang to him. 'Il était une bergère' was one of those songs. The song and the little book that contained it still lingers in my memory from the times we sang it around the piano at my grandmother's house forty years later. There were family outings to the Bois de Boulogne and to the zoo in the Jardin des Plantes where the animals had been rehoused after the great flood that submerged much of Paris in 1910. It was here that, according to family legend, Nusrat thought he recognised one of the elephants from his childhood days in Murshidabad; he commanded it to kneel, and it did so.

Moreover, Parisian society enabled an escape from the world of Elsie's parents and a 'mid-Victorian outlook' which she later described as one which 'with its prudery and hypocrisy ... I find particularly noxious'.[1] Here people seemed less concerned about classifications in terms of race and class, at least as far as the English and Americans were concerned. In Paris Nusrat found his aristocratic Indian heritage less burdensome and less constricting than in England or Jamaica; he was just one of many titled noblemen with foreign names who inhabited Paris in the early twentieth century. He and Elsie envisaged remaining in France for several years, and Nusrat began planning to set up and investing in a business, probably involving the import and sale of artworks and artefacts.

Nusrat and Elsie soon became a part of the cosmopolitan society that characterised Paris during those pre-First World War years. They were an elegant couple, Nusrat distinguished by his expensively tailored suits and felt trilby hat, although he wore a top hat for formal occasions and the theatre. With his blue eyes, olive skin and English clothes, only his name made Nusrat seem a little different from the other English gentlemen who frequented Paris as tourists and residents. There could not have been a greater contrast with his father's 'exotically' turbaned appearance and distinctly Muslim culture which so fascinated reporters during his visit to Paris forty years previously. Although Elsie followed the Parisian fashion of doing her hair in the pompadour style, piled high

1 EAM, Letter to V. Steffansson, 8 November 1927.

on her head and topped with a chignon, she did not follow the craze in Paris for oriental clothing, choosing instead long tight-waisted dresses with a high neck.

While his nurse wheeled little Syed around the Parc de Saint-Cloud in his pram, Elsie and Nusrat attended art classes, diligently drawing life models, still-life compositions, sketching portraits. Recalling her own experience more than a decade later, Elsie published a short story, 'The Modern Idea', describing the trials of a young English couple seeking to become artists in Paris. In the studio of their teacher, 'no humiliation is spared and no mercy is shown'; they are 'mercilessly teased by the other students' and are 'patently ignorant of even the elements of drawing'. The story goes on to describe the daily routine, both strenuous and exuberant, of the fictional couple:

> Eight o'clock each morning found them in the studio in paint-daubed overalls, joining in a lively criticism of the model's pose. There followed desperately hard work, strenuous effort that would presently come under the fire on the visiting professors' devastating criticism. And then, at noon, a rush to the tiny *café* – (Heavens! how hungry one was!) – where a clamorous crowd of students fought for food, and where, while waiting, one drew caricatures of everyone else upon the table cloth, insulted total strangers with impunity, and ravenously devoured the excellent *plats*.[1]

Although Nusrat and Elsie tried hard to master the arts of portrait and life drawing, it was landscape painting they preferred, in both oils and watercolours. They went to exhibitions and became acquainted with other artists. One of these was the renowned and by then elderly painter Emile Renard, Professeur de l'Ecole des Beaux-Arts, whose exhibition Nusrat and Elsie attended in 1911. Elsie treasured a black-and-white print of his, 'Le déjeuner des Orphelines', inscribed 'Hommage respectueuse à Madame la princesse Meerza' and signed Emile Renard. It is also probable that Elsie and Nusrat attended some of his classes along with

1 Elizabeth Marc, *Home Magazine,* February 1925, p.462.

the American painter and sculptor Amanda Austin, and other students from America, Poland, Russia and Italy. They became close friends with the German-born artist Erna Hoppe Kinross, who had a house in Giverny near where her friend and mentor Claude Monet lived.

Unlike Erna, Elsie and Nusrat achieved little recognition as artists during their four years in Paris. According to his daughter, Nusrat did have an oil painting accepted for one exhibition, but the details were vague and I have not been able to find any trace of it, nor indeed of any of his oil paintings apart from the small landscape I now possess and the landscape he donated to the Jamaica Institute. However, the couple must have attended many exhibitions during their Paris years, and especially those including works by their friend Erna, whose pictures appeared frequently alongside paintings by Miró, Mondrian and Monet. From Saint-Cloud Elsie and Nusrat could travel to Paris by the tram which ran to the Louvre, or they could take the steamer which followed the Seine to the city centre.

Fluent French speakers, they enjoyed the society of a wide group of Parisians and expatriates. These were the years following the signing of the *Entente Cordiale* and the determination to strengthen British and French relations in a context of an alliance against Germany.

In March 1911 the French journal *L'Intransigeant* reported that Prince and Princess Meerza were among those who took part in a debate leading to the formation of a committee to form a 'ligue anglo-française'. The list of people contributing to the debate is in itself indicative of the heady cosmopolitan world Elsie and Nusrat now enjoyed. They included Jane Dieulafoy, an archaeologist, journalist and novelist, singled out in French society because she had cut her hair short and preferred to wear men's clothing; although this was unlawful in France at the time, she had been given special *permission de la travestissement* by the prefect of police. She was a devoted wife to the archaeologist Marcel Dieulafoy. There was Maurice de Waleffe, a Belgian journalist who came to Paris in 1897 and founded the midday newspaper *Paris-Midi*. Other writers included the successful playwright and novelist George LeComte, and Maurice Gignoux, a special correspondent for *Le Figaro,* who as 'Saint-Charamand' was co-founder with Albert-Birot of the art journal *La Poétique*. There was also Henri Fescourt, who would become a pioneering film director, producing his first film in 1912.

Another close friend who was almost certainly a supporter of the *ligue anglo-française* was the journalist and historian Charles Dawbarn, the Paris correspondent for the English *Pall Mall Gazette* and the *Observer*. Charles Dawbarn was one of several men with whom Elsie formed an intense although, she insisted, entirely platonic relationship. In 1915 he dedicated his First World War book *France at Bay* to Princess Nusrat Ali Mirza, as a public token of his esteem. His illustrated book *France and the French* served as a guide to understanding Paris and French culture and politics from a fairly conservative point of view. He commended French imperial practice in Africa as an example that 'even England' could learn from, but regretted the power of the trade unions, and the volatility of 'the Gallic temperament' which, faced with 'a real or imaginary grievance, is certain to boil over and require force to suppress it'.[1] For him the essence of the French character lay in the intent 'to make the most of the present world, to catch the last ray of the sun, to utilise every moment as an opportunity for life and, perhaps, for love, for the two words are almost interchangeable in this fascinating country, where intellectual existence presents the variety of the kaleidescope'.[2]

Despite being impressed with 'the forward march of feminine achievement in France', Dawbarn was not a supporter of feminists, fearing their influence would lead not only to a loss of 'feminine charm' but also to 'the growing effeminacy of the male'.[3] That Elsie was no feminist may have been one of her attractions, her manifest enjoyment of French culture and society another. Dawbarn's summary of the achievement of French women may well also express his admiration for Elsie: 'In France the woman has succeeded in the astonishing feat of capturing man by her natural charms and yet in imposing herself upon the world by her intellectuality and capacity.'[4]

---

1 Charles Dawbarn, *France and the French* (London: Methuen, 1911) p.167 and 207.

2 *Ibid*. pp.1–2.

3 Charles Dawbarn, 'The French Woman and the Vote,' *Fortnightly Review* (August 1911), p.329.

4 *Ibid*., p. 335.

Her involvement in and enjoyment of Parisian life did not prevent Elsie from contriving ways to enhance her family's status and future in England. During the first week of January 1912 the papers were preoccupied with King George V's tour of India with Queen Mary. In particular, there were detailed reports of the lavish reception given for the King and Queen in Calcutta. Nusrat's nephew, Wasif Ali Mirza, had succeeded to the title Nawab of Murshidabad, after his father, Hassan's, death in 1906; he had laid on a spectacular replica of the procession which Nusrat's great-grandfather, the Nawab Nazim Ali Jah, had arranged 100 years previously for the Viceroy of India. According to the papers, the present Nawab provided 'twenty-seven elephants, twenty camels, scores of horses, and warriors with axes, swords, lances, and matchlocks, fakirs, musicians, and hundreds of sepoys, all dressed in the costumes of Medieval India'.[1]

Here was a relative with impressive status and royal contacts, a relative worthy of cultivation. On 12 January Elsie wrote to her former employer, Mr Pretyman, to seek his intercession with the India Office. It was a personal letter which she probably did not show Nusrat before it was sent. Elsie explained that she was very anxious to clarify her husband's correct title and status, so that he could then be presented at court and pay his respects to the king. This, she declared, was something Nusrat and his brother should have done when they came of age. But 'owing solely to the indolence which is characteristic of the family' they had, she said, failed to maintain contact with their relatives in India in order to ascertain their correct titles.[2] Elsie feared that her husband's seeming indifference might have offended his nephew in India, and perhaps even the royal family in England. She hoped the India Office might assist her in restoring relations with the family in India. She added that the birth of her son and the forthcoming arrival of a second child now made the establishment of her husband's status urgent.

As so often in her communications with India Office and other officials, Elsie was being disingenuous. Wasif Ali Mirza had been a student at Oxford at the same time as Nusrat and Syed, and although

1 *Homeward Mail from India, China, and the East,* 6 January 1912, p.4.

2 Letter to E Pretyman, IOR/L/PS/13.

he was in a different college (Trinity), it is very unlikely that they were not aware of one another's presence and did not meet occasionally, especially as Wasif was, like his uncles, a keen sportsman. In 1902, he represented Bengal at the coronation of Edward VII, and again at the coronation of George V in 1911. Nusrat and Syed must have known that their nephew was in England on these occasions, and Elsie's album contains a substantial newspaper cutting dating from 1911 featuring the Indian royalty, including Wasif Ali Mirza, attending the coronation. As a child I remember leafing through a book in my parents' library titled *A Mind's Reproduction*, which contained short poems and meditations composed by Nawab Wasif Ali Mirza; published in 1934, it had been sent to Nusrat. Although it may have been Vaheedoonissa who sent the book, its presence in our home in Australia suggests a continuing relationship between Nusrat and his nephew.

However, Wasif Ali Mirza differed from his grandfather, the Nawab of Bengal, in his willingness to take an active part in local government meetings. Whereas Mansour Ali Khan had resisted Frederick Layard's suggestion that he become a member of the local Government Council, Wasif Ali Mirza was a member of the Bengal Legislative Council and a patron of the Calcutta Historical Society. He later became the founder and president of the Hindu-Muslim Unity Association and was influential in bringing about the 1911 reversal of the partition of Bengal.

Elsie's concern about her husband's title and status was superseded temporarily one month later when the family suffered a devastating family tragedy. On 11 February 1912, while speaking to a fellow journalist on the telephone, Helen shot herself through the heart. Her father came from his home in Somerset to London to identify the body. The coroner accepted the possibility that while talking on the phone she might have been toying with the revolver that she kept in her study and accidentally pulled the trigger. Her maid had heard Helen talking, then the shot, followed by Helen's call for help. Helen was by now a well-known journalist and the story of her death was widely reported in Britain, New York, Australia and New Zealand.

Although the coroner's and newspaper reports provide no evidence for this, Elsie always believed that Helen had committed suicide, and that the journalist she was speaking to was a lover who refused to leave his wife for her sake. There is no information that the journalist Edward Roe, who testified at the inquest, was Helen's lover, or that Helen might have previously threatened suicide. Elsie may have had such evidence; her version of Helen's death does undoubtedly provide a more dramatic and romantic story than the official verdict of accidental death.

For Elsie, Helen's death and the manner of it was deeply distressing. She had always been closer to Helen than Eve, admiring her social charm and sophistication, and her success as a journalist, as well as her rejection of 'Victorian' values. When Elsie emigrated to Australia fifteen years later, she took with her some of Helen's clothes – her shoes, her parasol, her shawl, a dress and some of her jewels, including the cameo locket I now possess. Helen was tiny, at least six inches shorter than Elsie, and wore size-two shoes, several sizes smaller than Elsie's shoes. These were not clothes that Elsie could wear; they were simply something of Helen's that she could not bear to part with. More than forty years later when I was thirteen and needed an outfit for a fancy dress competition at my boarding school, Elsie lent me Helen's shoes, shawl, fan and parasol. At the time I wore size 1 shoes and was no more than 4ft 7in tall, but Helen's shoes fitted me perfectly. Only later did I consider how extraordinary it was that my grandmother had brought Helen's clothes with her when the family emigrated to Australia, and kept them for so many years after Helen's death.

Nusrat and Elsie attended the funeral in London and then returned to France. However, as the birth of their second child was imminent, they came back in early June to England to stay with Elsie's parents near Weston-super-Mare. On 20 June 1912, Elsie gave birth to a daughter, who was given the names Myriam Sarah after Nusrat's mother and sisters. It was an agonising breach birth, and Elsie took some time to recover from it, from the effects of Helen's death, and from post-natal depression. Nevertheless, Elsie and Nusrat ensured that the status of the baby and its parents, as well as the connection with the present Nawab of Murshidabad, was made evident in the announcement of Myriam's birth:

> Society. Princess Nusrat Ali Mirza, who for some little time past has been staying in the West England, gave birth yesterday to a baby daughter. The infant is a grandchild of the Nawab of Bengal, Behar and Orissa, and cousin of Sir Wasif Ali Mirza, Nawab of Murshidabad.[1]

Together with their two little children and the children's nurse, Nusrat and Elsie returned to Paris in September to resume their art studies. In Paris everyone was talking about the theft of the 'Mona Lisa' from the Louvre and the arrest of the proto-Surrealist writer Guillaume Apollinaire as the main suspect. Others suspected that the culprit was Picasso. The painting was returned later that year when Vincenzo Peruggia, a decorator who had been working part-time in the Louvre, was caught attempting to sell it in Florence. In October they joined the crowds flocking to the Boulevard Haussmann to admire the newly furbished Galeries Lafayette with their sweeping Art-Nouveau staircase and great glass and steel dome.

June 1913 brought another sad family loss when news came of Eve's death from tuberculosis in Jamaica. Now Elsie was the only surviving sister. Although Eve's son, Maynard, was now eighteen and fairly independent, her daughter, Audrey, was only eight years old. It was characteristic of her strong sense of family responsibility that Elsie offered to take Audrey into her own family. Audrey's father was suffering from depression and overwork, so was glad to accept the offer from Elsie and Nusrat, and Audrey became a part of the Mirza household.

The family made frequent visits back to London and to Elsie's parents in Somerset. In May 1914, there was a special visit to London, for Nusrat was at last to be presented at court, indeed, twice – first on 25 May and again, along with a number of Indian princes, on 5 June. The Fourth Court, held on 4 June, had been disrupted by a suffragette who had gained entry; before she was hastily removed from the scene she asked the King when he would stop torturing women prisoners. On the occasion of Nusrat's presentation the next day, 'the Queen wore

1 *The Globe,* 21 June 1912.

her diamond crown in the centre of which blazed the famous Koh-i-Noor'.[1] *The Birmingham Daily Post* reported the event:

> The King and Queen held in Buckingham Palace last night the fifth and last Court of the season. There was a brilliant gathering in the State rooms. The suffragette incident the previous evening was not allowed to interfere in the slightest degree with the arrangements which were an exact counterpart to those for Thursday's court. In addition to their Majesties, there were eight members of the Royal family present, and others attending included a party of gorgeously-apparelled Indian princes.[2]

A photograph of Nusrat in court dress appeared in *The Times,* identifying him as 'The Nawabzada Misrat [sic] Ali Mirza of Murshidabad who attended court on 5 June. The Prince is the son of His Highness the late Nawab Nazim of Bengal, Behar, and Orissa and is the Uncle of the present Nawab of Murshidabad.' Erna Hoppe Kinross later painted a portrait of Nusrat in his princely costume. Elsie thought the portrait made Nusrat look weak, and left it with the Kinross family when she emigrated. Now the portrait hangs in my study, having been willed to me by Erna's son, Rupert. I see Nusrat's expression not as weak, but patiently resigned. For Elsie however, resignation was a weakness; it was not a virtue she either admired or practised.

Elsie and Nusrat's expanding family and now officially acknowledged status in England did not affect their plans to remain in France and seek a life there. Like many others they neither foresaw nor believed that the troubles in Eastern Europe might affect Paris. As their friend the Belgian journalist Maurice de Waleffe wrote, 'In Paris no one saw the war coming. No one wanted it, no one thought of it'.[3] But the worst happened: following the assassination of Archduke Ferdinand and his wife on 28 June 1914, Germany joined forces in July with the Austria-Hungary Empire against Serbia. On 2 August Germany declared war

1 'Ladies News-Letter', *Derby Daily Telegraph* (13 June 1914), p.3.
2 *Birmingham Daily Post,* 6 June 1914, p.8.
3 *Quand Paris était un Paradis,* p.243.

on France. At once the French government organised its defenses and the Villa Mathilde, high on a hill above the Seine, was one of the many buildings requisitioned by the government to be demolished and replaced by gun emplacements.

Together with Syed, Myriam, Audrey and the servants, Elsie and Nusrat were forced to leave in haste. The trains and cross-Channel boats were full as thousands left Paris; transportation was extremely expensive. They left behind much of their furniture and almost all the paintings and sketches they had completed and accumulated in the Villa Mathilde. Nusrat later calculated that the retreat had cost him over £350 – today equivalent to £25,000 – in the worth of furniture and goods the couple had been forced to leave behind, as well as the investments in Nusrat's projected Parisian business enterprise that he was forced to abandon. They also left behind the dream of becoming artists for, like the young couple in Elsie's story, they had come to realise that they were neither sufficiently talented nor dedicated to make art their vocation. The Parisian idyll was over.

CHAPTER 10

Weathering the War

1914–1919

After their hurried retreat from Paris, Nusrat and Elsie found a temporary home with Elsie's parents. Harry and Eliza Algar were living in Norton, a tiny hamlet three miles north of the popular seaside resort of Weston-super-Mare, bordering the Bristol Channel. Their small cottage could not contain the sudden influx of three more adults and three children, as Elsie and Nusrat came together with five-year-old Syed, two-year-old Myriam, nine-year-old Audrey McFarlane, and the children's nurse, Lucy Drury – who now joined the family with recommendations from several aristocratic families. Myriam called her Pursie, and soon that was the name used by everyone in the family, of which she became a key member.

Opposite the cottage was a large rambling farmhouse, Norton Beauchamp. It was in a dilapidated state, and had not been lived in for some years, but it was available for a low rent. Here was the kind of challenge Nusrat enjoyed tackling. He had made changes to the Villa Mathilde to make it comfortable; Norton Beauchamp would require substantially more basic repairs. Once the owner of the farmhouse had assured him that there were no plans to sell, and that he could regard the tenancy as more or less permanent, Nusrat set to work. Within a few months the family was able to move in, although living conditions remained fairly primitive. A visitor to the family, Elsie's nephew – Audrey's brother, Maynard – recalls how, at this time, the house had no telephone, no electricity, and only the most basic water storage system. Every evening Nusrat had to spend twenty minutes working the pump lever in order to fill the water tank.

Elsie's niece Audrey had now been living with the family for over a year following her mother's death in June 1913. Her brother, Maynard McFarlane, had ben a frequent visitor to his grandparents in Kewstoke while he was in boarding school in England from 1908 till 1913, and in June 1914 had just completed his first year of study at McGill University in Montreal, Canada. He was now nineteen, and in July 1914 he had returned to England for a family reunion with his father and Audrey in Somerset (his father was on brief leave from Jamaica). When war was declared he applied for a regular army commission and, owing to his previous experience in Officer Training Corps at school and university, was commissioned as a second lieutenant to the Middlesex Regiment known as the 'Duke of Cambridge's Own'.

Maynard was involved in active fighting with his battalion in France, alongside large contingents from the Indian Army, the Canadian Army and also the Gordon Highlanders, with whom my father, Ian Troup, was enlisted. Just before his regiment became engaged in the Battle of Neuve Chapelle, which began on 10 March 1915, Maynard transferred to aviation to become an observer with the Royal Flying Corps. In his family memoir, Maynard remarks that his transfer undoubtedly saved his life. The officer who took his place, Thomas Craven, was killed, as were more than a thousand men in his 1,200-strong regiment. In that battle also, more than 4,700 Indian soldiers died. They were taking part in the Indian Army's first engagement of the war. A memorial for them now stands on the edge of the small village of Neuve Chapelle.

Maynard was severely injured in April 1915 when his plane, an Avro 504, crashed on landing after a sortie near Hill 60, just south of Ypres. After emergency treatment at a hospital in France, he was repatriated to the Harold Fink Memorial Hospital in London, and finally spent some time recuperating with Elsie, Nusrat and his relatives in Norton Beauchamp. Since his thigh had been badly damaged he did not fly again, but remained attached to the Royal Flying Corps. He was posted to Aircraft Repair and other staff posts in England and later again in France, near Amiens. On his leaves he visited Norton Beauchamp and was eventually assigned his own lodgings in the coach house. Maynard retained affectionate memories of the Mirza family, and wrote to

Elsie frequently throughout her life. Their world contrasted with his father's rather cheerless home in Jamaica where, following Eve's death, Alexander McFarlane had gradually succumbed to depression. In 1919 he was institutionalised following an attempted suicide and his erroneous belief that he had committed some grievous crime. He took his own life in 1921.

In September 1914, Nusrat was thirty-seven and his brother Syed was almost thirty-nine. The uppermost age at the time for military recruitment was thirty-eight. Throughout the war and afterwards Nusrat's brother Syed served as an Assistant Commander in the Special Constabulary in London, for which he was later awarded an MBE. His role was to train the volunteer Special Constables in his locality, to reinforce the regular police whose ranks had been diminished by enlistment in the army, to ensure that blackouts were observed, to patrol the streets night and day, and to be involved in plans to counter any invasion.

There is no evidence that Nusrat put himself forward for active service. Like many other men of his age and older he helped with agricultural work on the nearby farm, gathering in the hay in the autumn, growing vegetables and fruit in their own large garden, breeding poultry and rabbits.

In a memoir written after his retirement in the 1950s, Maynard remembered Nusrat as a charming, easy-going man, who played the piano and the banjo. The three children, Audrey, Syed and Myriam, all loved music, and the family often gathered around the piano to sing as he played. Audrey later became an accomplished cellist. Nusrat was particularly fond of Chopin, whose nocturnes and waltzes he played with such feeling that little Myriam would burst into tears and have to be taken from the room. For his children Nusrat carved small wooden animals and other toys, and amused them with sketches of the dogs and pony. He enjoyed entertaining guests with humorous anecdotes, but irritated Elsie by laughing so much at his own stories that no one could hear the punchline. Elsie was a good storyteller, with a gift for impersonation and a fine sense of timing. The two of them addressed each other affectionately as Elsie and Noossie. Nusrat also played golf and was one of the more successful members of the local club and team.

The family's life in Somerset during the First World War seems to have been almost idyllic. Elsie's album contains photographs of the three children playing in the hay in the fields and building sandcastles on the beach by Sand Bay, about a mile from the house. In other photographs the whole family is piled into an open carriage, setting off down the tree-lined Kewstoke Road to Weston-super-Mare, where there was the excitement of a donkey ride on the sands, or a Punch and Judy show on the Great Pier, or perhaps a short trip along the esplanade in one of the new electric trams. In the absence of the men who had been recruited for the war, some of the trams were actually driven by women, causing much talk and shaking of heads. At one end of the beach, they could see soldiers digging trenches as training before being posted to France.

The photographs show Syed in a sailor suit and cap, Myriam in a frilly dress and bonnet, Audrey in stockings, long-sleeved dress and wide straw hat. The pony waits patiently, the dog impatiently. There is another photograph of a group including Elsie and Nusrat, Erna and Charles Kinross, having tea on the lawn, tennis rackets set aside. It was perhaps on one of these visits that Erna painted the portrait of Nusrat in court dress. In these photographs the sun is always shining; one does not detect the fierce winds that often attacked the coast, the high tides that flung themselves against the sea walls, the large and dangerous expanses of mud flats left when the tides receded. Nor are there shadows cast by the war across the channel, except for three photographs of Maynard and a companion in uniform. A note beneath one of these photographs identifies it as 'Maynard and Clark after staying up all night', and notes that 'Clark was killed the next day in action'. Maynard's companion was possibly Thomas Henry Clarke, also a member of the Middlesex regiment, who was killed in France on 13 March 1915.

Now that her husband had been received at Court and formally acknowledged as a member of Indian royalty, Elsie enjoyed her new situation as lady of the manor. As previously in Jamaica, she performed roles that marked her status. She became a patron and vice-president of the Weston-super-Mare Fanciers' Association, which focused on excellence in poultry, pigeon and rabbit breeding. The records show that she opened their first show in 1919 and handed out the prizes. Her speech stressed the importance of the growing industry in breeding poultry and rabbits not only to provide food for the country at a time of scarcity, but also to capture future markets.

Elsie was also occupied with activities at home. Syed and Audrey needed schooling, but Elsie did not want them to go to the small local school and mingle with the children of farmworkers and tradesmen. Since she had once been a governess, there was no need to hire one; she could teach the children all the basic skills. The garden and orchard also became Elsie's domain. She had some of the trees cleared and planted more. Archways and trellises were constructed, with roses, honeysuckle and clematis climbing over them. A tennis court was put in. Then, when walls had been built around the perimeter, Elsie bought several pairs of peacocks to strut around and flaunt their brilliant tails. The neighbours, and perhaps also her parents, complained about their raucous calls, but Elsie was determined to keep these accessories that she deemed appropriate for an oriental prince and princess.

There was also plenty of time for visits to Bristol and Bath to shop, or to entertain friends for tea. On these occasions the children could be left with their grandparents in the house opposite Norton Beauchamp. However, Nusrat's income was not sufficient to cover all the expenses the improvements to the house and their lifestyle incurred. There was the additional expense of sending Audrey to the Abbey School in the Malvern Hills, which she attended from 1918–20, and later Bromley School in Kent – Elsie's former school. They sold their car and one of their best horses, along with the brougham and harness, but still expenditure exceeded income. It was while they were living in Somerset that Elsie began to follow her sister Helen's example and supplement their income with her writing. The *Daily Mail* reached a relatively wide readership with its human-interest stories, serials, features and competitions. It welcomed contributions from freelance journalists. Both Elsie and Nusrat shared that paper's support for the British Empire, and so it was the *Daily Mail* that first published Elsie's journalism. Like Helen, she made a feature of emphasising a woman's point of view.

Using the pen name Elizabeth Marc, Elsie wrote a series of articles in 1918 and 1919 reflecting on how women would use their newly acquired power to vote, on how women longed for security in the aftermath of the war, on the desirability of women having careers of their own. Several of her contributions were written in the voice of the 'plain woman', Mrs Brown, who laments the loss of her two sons in the war, and hopes that her remaining son might be given his 'own little bit of land' if Prime Minister David Lloyd George could restrain the landed aristocrats who made up the majority government during the Wartime Coalition.

Communications with family in Murshidabad had been difficult during the war. It was a shock for Nusrat to learn, when at last a letter from Vaheedoonissa reached him in early 1919, that their older sister Miriam had died the year before, on 14 January 1918. She would have been forty-six when she died, possibly from cancer. Perhaps her death and the renewed contact with Vaheedoonissa brought back for Nusrat memories of his childhood in India, as well as a desire to identify with his Muslim heritage. Now he published several articles in the *Daily Mail*. One vividly written piece, 'Magic I Have Seen', published in February 1919, recalled his witnessing 'the Indian rope trick' for the first time as a child in his father's court in Murshidabad:

> On that occasion I was very little and I viewed it from behind the shutters of my grandmother's apartments. The boy went up the rope, and then – oh, horror! – he came down in pieces! I clasped my sister around the knees and, terror-stricken, we counted the bits! They were all there, however, and a moment or two after out popped the boy, smiling and whole, from under the conjuror's cloth.[1]

An earlier, more serious contribution by Nusrat warned of the danger of religious conflict in India and the need for the British government to show support for 'Mahommedans' as well as Hindus. Englishmen, he wrote, should remember that 'Britain is the greatest Mahommedan

1 'Magic I Have Seen', *Daily Mail,* 19 February 1919, p.4.

Elizabeth Marc (Elsie), 1922

Nusrat Ali Mirza, c. 1920

Power in the world and that the opinions, the susceptibilities, and even the ideals of Islam should be consulted in matters concerning it'. At this time, British 'possessions' with large Muslim populations included India, Egypt, the Sudan, Iraq, Yemen, Palestine, Malaysia, Tanganyika, Zanzibar, Nigeria and Somaliland.

Like his father, Nusrat identified himself firmly as a Muslim, and also as a supporter of the British Empire, which he hoped would safeguard the interests of Muslims in the Indian subcontinent. Like his nephew, the Nawab Wasif Ali Mirza, and most other Indian royal families, he also shared the view that India was right to offer all possible support to Britain during the First World War, including over a million troops. Britain was particularly anxious to secure the loyalty of Muslim Indian rulers to oppose the Muslim Turks who had sided with Germany. In turn, like the Nawab of Bengal in his support for Britain during the 'Mutiny', these Indian rulers hoped to gain recognition, further power and privileges in return for their support during the war.

A later article by Nusrat, published in June 1921, expressed his distress at the casual disregard and disrespect on the part of the English for Islam. The occasion for this article arose from a dispute over whether a musical comedy should be called 'Mecca', 'the name of our Holy City'. In reply to those who claimed that no one would have protested if that title had been used, he declared, 'Mahommedans do not as a rule protest. One of the greatest dangers – for England – is the silence of Islam. Mohammedans are proud, sensitive, and they are fatalists.' And 'although they may accept a slight in silence,' he continued, 'it is hard for Englishmen to realise how bitter and dangerous such a silence may be!'[1]

A letter written in 1920 by William Robinson to Antony Hirzel, a prospective trustee for the India Office-managed pension fund (which distributed quarterly payments to Nusrat and his brother Syed), gives a revealing glimpse into how the two brothers and Elsie appeared, from a distance and from an assumed height, to members of the British establishment. Robinson's letter also suggests the breezy ignorance and dismissal of Nusrat's character, religion and status that Nusrat (and his brother) usually suffered in silence:

1 'Mecca', *Daily Mail,* 1 June 1921, p.6.

> Syud Ullee [sic] is not married, Mr Teesdale tells me. He lives in London, does nothing, has not much good or harm in him, and is generally hard up. Noosrut Ullee is married and lives in the country. He has children. His wife, an Englishwoman, is a rather superior lady, Mr Teesdale says, and manages him well.[1]

This letter, dated 8 January 1920, was more than a little unfair to Syed, who was at the time continuing to serve as a Special Constable, as he had done with distinction throughout the war. It also reveals a lack of information about the family circumstances at that time. Just a few weeks after this letter was written, the family's relatively carefree Somerset way of life came to an abrupt end. Norton Beauchamp together with the surrounding farmland had been put up for sale. Thanks to the many repairs and improvements Nusrat had made, as well as the steep rise in post-war prices, the farm house had now risen in value from the £700 it was worth in 1914 to £7,000 (in today's currency an increase from about £41,000 to £200,000) a price that Nusrat and Elsie could not possibly meet given the diminishing value of the rupee. Nusrat's annual 10,000 rupees pension was then worth approximately £660 per annum (that is, about £20,000 today). So the family was forced to find a new home. It was an unwelcome disturbance for Nusrat and Elsie; for the children it meant the loss not only of the home they were to remember nostalgically, but also the nurse who had been their companion. Myriam, then seven years old, especially missed Pursie, and to the end of her life kept the book her beloved nurse had given her at their parting – *A Little Princess* by Frances Hodgson Burnett.

Where could they find a new home, affordable but large enough to accommodate Elsie, Nusrat, the three children, Elsie's parents who were now quite frail, and one or more servants? A house, moreover, which might be seen as a suitable dwelling for a prince and princess? Weston-super-Mare had become a popular resort where house prices were relatively high. In 1919, post-war inflation had caused all prices to rise rapidly, so that the buying power of Nusrat's annual pension was lower than it had ever been.

1 Letter from W Robinson to A Hirzel, 8 January 1920. IOR/L/PS/13/ 182.

Elsie had prized the relative isolation and surrounding space they had enjoyed in Norton Beauchamp, the wooded walks and the view across to the hills in the distance. She and Nusrat remembered the rugged mountains and wide coastal bays of North Wales near Tyn-y-Groes where they had spent their honeymoon twelve years before. There was a large house for rent at a reasonable price on a hill above the small town of Dolgellau, ten miles south of Tyn-y-Groes. It was in poor condition, but it had ten rooms, and five acres of land. Moreover it was next to a golf course. This was Pen-y-Coed Hall. Elsie was delighted with the great staircase that dominated the entrance hall, the intricately carved fireplace in the downstairs reception, the spacious upstairs front rooms with a view across the town below to the misty mountain range dominated by Cader Idris. The wide upstairs landings on either side of the main staircase separated the two front rooms, each accompanied by two smaller rooms and a bathroom, thus creating distinct apartments for the two families.

Once again, Nusrat set to work on repairs. All their belongings, including Nusrat's piano and the chairs, bedsteads and pictures that had furnished Harry and Eliza Algar's house, were transported from Somerset. The expense was considerable. Elsie and Nusrat hoped that they might be able to top up their income by farming the five acres, 'their own little bit of land', and so they bought some sheep, pigs and hens. But apart from the hens' eggs, they gained little profit from their animals during the first two years. Somehow they needed to find more money. The necessity to increase their income was exacerbated by the realisation that Syed, now aged ten, was no longer interested in the lessons Elsie was providing for him; indeed he was becoming defiantly uncooperative. The school in Dolgellau was not, in Elsie's view, a viable alternative; he should go to a good preparatory school and then an elite public school, preferably Harrow.

Nusrat's dwindling pension and the cost of their move to Dolgellau left no money for school fees. The kind of preparatory school they sought might not be one of the most expensive, but the boarding fee of over £100 a year, together with extras such as uniforms and sports equipment, was beyond their means. Elsie was determined to find the necessary money.

CHAPTER 11

Writing for a Living

1920–1925

When it became clear that Nusrat's allowance was not going to increase, Elsie took matters into her own hands. After the First World War employment opportunities for married women were limited, but now Elsie took her sister Helen as a role model. Perhaps she could emulate Helen and earn not just a little extra 'pin money', but a substantial income through journalism? A downstairs room in Pen-y-Coed Hall with an elaborately carved fireplace became her study and library, and she set to work writing up some of the stories she had created to entertain her children.

In early 1920 Elsie offered some preliminary pieces to *Home Chat*, the magazine Helen had co-edited. The 14 February 1920 issue carried Elsie's two earliest works of fiction for children: the first of a weekly series called 'The Adventures of Conrad the Cock', included in the children's section of the magazine; and a short one-page article on 'Reading without Tears'. Both pieces were published under the name Elizabeth Marc, the name Elsie would continue to use for most of her publications.

Episodes from 'The Adventures of Conrad the Cock' – interspersed with children's stories by other writers, including the frequent appearance of 'Epaminondas, the quaint nigger boy' [sic] by Sara Cone Bryant – appeared almost every week throughout the year 1920, concluding with a final episode on 1 January 1921. While 'Conrad the Cock' illustrates an appeal to childish innocence and sentimentality typical of the period, the Epaminondas stories reveal the casual racism that was all too characteristic of that time.

For adult readers of *Home Chat*, Elizabeth Marc also continued to publish a series of commentaries on everyday social and personal problems. Like Helen, she created dialogues between fictional persona to discuss issues; but whereas Helen's more mature commentator was a woman named Aunt Mary, Elsie's is a man, an older brother named Peter who checks his younger sister's faults and foibles. One of Peter's earliest appearances is titled 'Peter on Fibs and Facts', in the 3 July 1920 issue of *Home Chat*. Here Peter gently teases his sister for her tendency to exaggerate facts and her desire to appear grander and wealthier than she is. With his easy-going humour and resistance to pretentiousness the character of Peter seems rather like Nusrat, and this little dialogue suggests that Elsie was at times more self-aware than some of her later statements and actions suggest.

Throughout 1920, 1921 and 1922, Elsie's children's stories and adult commentaries appear regularly in *Home Chat* alongside stories by O. Henry, pages of recipes, fashions, gossip about royalty and 'society', debates and articles about how to make marriage work. There is a short pause in Elsie's weekly contributions between March and May 1921. It was during this period that Elsie's father, Harry, died, on 5 April after a brief illness. The death certificate gives the cause of death as stomach cancer and heart failure. Nusrat was with Harry at his death, and Harry's wife Eliza must also have been present. After her husband's death, Eliza continued to live with Elsie, Nusrat and the children at Pen-y-Coed.

Elsie's second children's story for *Home Chat*, 'Timothy Tinkles: the Adventures of a Small Black Kitten', began as a serial in July, 1921, followed quickly by 'The Tale of Tosh and Tim' that October. Peter and his sister continue to gently reprove one another for worrying too much, for concern about not being understood, for being discouraged too easily. 'Peter on Pluck' has Peter chivvying his sister for giving up on her painting, and encouraging her to take it up again. In addition to the serials, there are separate children's stories by Elizabeth Marc, one of which, 'Myriam's Easter Egg', uses her daughter's name.

By mid-1921, Elizabeth Marc had become a well-known author, and her articles were being quoted in other publications. She also published short pieces on domestic life under the name of Mary Hickford (a pseudonym presumably intended as a humorous allusion to the popular American film actress Mary Pickford, known especially for her *ingenue* roles). Some excerpts from Elsie's contributions under both names to the *Daily Mail* are picked up and commented on with heavy-handed male humour in the *Sporting Times,*[1] which found her series on 'the girl of today' a particular source of amusement:

> Elizabeth Marc says the girl of to-day has learnt to play the game as the boys play it, and to be a sport.
>
> Quite right, Elizabeth, and unless we are much mistaken she enjoys it just as much as the boys do. [30 April, 1921]

The 'girl of to-day' appears again in August:

> Elizabeth Marc thinks that the girl of to-day is simply in tune with her generation. 'She is as much a wartime product,' says Elizabeth, 'as is the high-income tax.'
>
> Yes, maybe, but most of us find her 'form' far more interesting. [20 August 1921]

Elizabeth Marc's reference to the high post-war income tax, which by 1918 had risen to an average of 30 per cent of income, is a reminder of the connection between her writing and the need for a higher income. In 1919 Nusrat had written to the India Office to claim that his pension should not be subject to taxes, a claim dismissed by the government. He also requested an increase to his pension so that he could support his wife and the three children for whom he was now responsible. He was granted a supplement of £250 a year, so that now his total stipend amounted to approximately £900, reduced by tax to £600. In today's currency, his net annual income was now the equivalent of about £17,500.

By 1921 Elsie's earnings from her writing were sufficient to cover

1 *The Sporting Times,* 13 August 1921, p.1.

Syed's fees at a preparatory school in Malvern Hills. Probably on Nusrat's insistence, his son did not go to school under his given names. To avoid any embarrassment his Indian name and status might incur, Syed now became known as Savile Mostyn. Why Mostyn? One association may have been with Helen's fictional character Daphne Mostyn, who was instructed by her Aunt Mary on the complexities of social etiquette. Another association making the name attractive to Elsie may have been with the village of Mostyn near Llandudno fifty miles north of Dolgellau, the seat of the wealthy and aristocratic Mostyn family.

Two years later, Savile progressed, as his parents had wished, to Harrow. This was the school that Byron, Trollope, Stanley Baldwin, Winston Churchill and Nusrat's headmaster at Ashbourne School had attended. It was also the school where Jawaharlal Nehru, a leader of India's independence movement and the future first Prime Minister of India, received some of his education (1905–7); this was unlikely to have influenced either Elsie or Nusrat, since they did not support the Nehru family's nationalist politics.

Meanwhile, in October 1922 Audrey had begun her studies for a degree in household and social sciences at King's College for Women, attending lectures in the Strand building where her uncles Syed and Nusrat had been pupils thirty years previously. However, she soon felt these studies were too restrictive and wanted to change to medicine. Although Audrey had done well in the relevant examinations, the Dean discouraged her from taking this step, saying that it was not a career easily accommodated by women, especially those without an independent income. The Dean encouraged her to study psychology instead. Despite Elsie's considerable misgivings about this direction – misgivings arising from what she referred to as the history of 'insanity' in Audrey's family (that is, the suicides of Audrey's father in 1921 and perhaps of her Aunt Helen in 1912) – Audrey did go on to study psychology successfully at University College London.

Audrey's brother Maynard had been discharged from the Army in mid-1919, and had married Margaret Armistead that same year. He was unable to offer much help towards funding his sisters' studies, and so the majority of the financial burden fell to Nusrat and Elsie, who were now her legal guardians. Elsie wrote numerous letters on Audrey's behalf in pursuit of possible scholarships, and about accommodation and future studies. She also sought assurance from the Dean that if she (Elsie) made 'the tremendous effort necessary for sending Audrey to King's College, she [would] when she leaves have an absolute certain means of livelihood, either here or in the colonies'.[1] In response the Dean reassured Elsie that 'unless the country goes bankrupt, or some other equally serious menace threatens, there is a practically certain means of livelihood in this country, after taking the course'.[2]

While Elsie spent long hours writing in her study or travelling to London to deliver her latest piece and discuss future possibilities with her editors, Nusrat took care of the pigs and sheep and kept their five acres secure and neat. He joined the Dolgellau golf club, which adjoined their property, and soon became one of the club's several vice presidents. Myriam often trailed after him as he played golf; with her brother away and her mother preoccupied with her writing, she was frequently lonely and bored. Although there was the very reputable Dr William's School for Girls just a few minutes' walk down the hill from Pen-y-Coed, her mother was adamant that she should not attend a local school. (Interestingly Pen-y-Coed later became a boarding house for the same school.) Elsie took time off from her busy writing schedule to give her daughter lessons; Nusrat also did some more informal teaching. Sometimes Myriam and her father would go for a long walk with their two English collies, Arran and Yarrow, along the track past the golf course and down the hill to the towering grey ruins of Cymer Abbey, or along Precipice Walk bordering the steep slopes of Cader Idris. And sometimes they would go riding together, Myriam on her pony Pat, and Nusrat on Bess, his bay hack.

In 1922, Elsie's reputation as a children's author received a considerable boost when Hutchinson & Co. agreed to publish in book form the three stories that had been serialised in *Home Chat*. In addition to prominently featuring the author as Princess Nusrat (with Elizabeth

1 Letter Princess Nusrat Ali Mirza to the Dean, King's College for Women, 31 January 1922, King's College Archive.

2 Letter from the Dean to Princess Ali Mirza, 1 February 1922, King's College Archive.

Marc added in smaller print), the books were adorned with attractive dust jackets and colour plate illustrations by Christian M. Ade. They received flattering reviews such as this one in the *Aberdeen Press and Journal*:

> FOR THE TINIES. Volumes for the Nursery Bookshelf. Princess Nusrat (Elizabeth Marc) is a name to be conjured with in the list of writers who make nurseryland ring with peals of merry laughter from childish hearts. She does not write down to her young readers, but talks with a simple charm intelligible to all who have mastered their ABC. Above all, she is possessed of a genuine fund of humour, spontaneous and unforced. Three of her delightful little studies of bird, animal, and child life are represented in Messrs Hutchinson's Christmas lists, gracefully illustrated, and published at half-a-crown the volume.[1]

There was also a longer fourth book, not previously serialised, *Doris and David All Alone*, illustrated by Charles Robinson. For Elsie this was a real coup, as Charles Robinson (brother of William Heath Robinson), was well known for his illustrations for Robert Louis Stevenson's *A Child's Garden of Verses* (1885) and Frances Hodgson Burnett's *The Secret Garden* (1911), both immensely popular books for children.

All four of Elsie's books received favourable reviews, but *Doris and David All Alone*, together with its illustrations, was especially singled out. 'This book breathes childhood rapture, childhood dismay, breathes, indeed, all the feelings of childhood,' declared a reviewer for the *Pall Mall Gazette*.[2] 'Princess Nusrat, in all her magazine stories and books, shows a deep insight into the child's mind,' the *Sheffield Independent*'s reviewer wrote, before singling out *Doris and David All Alone* for special praise:

> The adventures of Doris and David will delight all her child readers. What jolly times the pair have! They make the acquaintance of a

1 *Aberdeen Press and Journal*, 23 November 1922, p.5.

2 *Pall Mall Gazette*, 8 December 1922, p.7.

> dog stealer, and then a Punch and Judy man. They then camp on the cliffs of Dover, drop into the sea and are rescued and taken to France. Then they get on a sailing vessel as stowaways and a lad named Ginger helps, and shares their adventures on a tropic island, inhabited by savages. They really do have some wonderful times before they are rescued and meet their father.[1]

Many episodes in this book draw on Elsie's own memories, evoking the smell of the hop fields that surrounded St Mary Cray, and the East London accents and idioms of the hop-pickers who travelled down to Kent each summer. There is a vivid description of a tropical storm that engulfs the steamer where the children hide, a storm and a steamer like the one Elsie and Nusrat experienced en route to Jamaica. And the tropical island with its banana trees, coconut palms and waterfalls is occasionally reminiscent of rural parts of Jamaica. The 'savages' referred to in the review, however, come from that imaginary realm created by European writers and their readers, and featured in popular books such as Rider Haggard's *King Solomon's Mines* (1885), J. M. Barrie's *Peter and Wendy* (1911, based on his 1904 play *Peter Pan*), Helen Bannerman's *The Story of Little Black Sambo* (1899) about an Indian child, and Hugh Lofting's *The Story of Doctor Dolittle* (1920), in which the Doctor bleaches an African so that he can marry the white princess with whom he is in love. Doris and David are sure that that the natives they encounter are all cannibals, and the author does not completely disabuse the reader, although she does make play with the Robinson Crusoe narrative. Doris rescues one 'savage' from death, and determines to call him 'Man Wednesday Morning', but in contrast to Defoe's more submissive Man Friday, he insists on her calling him by his own name, Ionano, a pointedly un-English name.

Elsie's publishers, Hutchinson & Co, enthusiastically publicised her books, giving prominence to her title, and issuing press releases. For them, clearly, promoting the combination of royalty and an oriental name was an effective way to arouse interest and boost sales. It was at this time that they had her photographed at the prestigious Bassano Studio in London.

---

1 *Sheffield Independent,* 16 November 1922, p.6.

For her adult readers Elsie continued to publish under the name of Elizabeth Marc. Her commentaries on love and marriage, contemporary children and women appear in the *Daily Mail*, and were often re-published in Australian and Canadian papers. One such article, 'Should Parents Obey?' laments 'modern educational methods' which encourage 'the child of 1922' to do what she likes and go where she likes 'without considering the anxiety of those at home'. Elsie appears to have been especially irritated with children of her own sex here, adding that 'the tendency to take the law into their own hands is particularly marked among the girls of the period'.[1] Perhaps this article draws on Elsie's exasperation with Myriam at this time, after she had been late home after going for a ride to Barmouth harbour, or wandering around the town of Dolgellau while her parents were preoccupied with writing or golf? Was Myriam inspired by the enthusiasm of the very self-sufficient girls in Elsie's stories, who explored the world around them?

In 1923, Elsie began to develop a new specialism: the Arctic. She read the anthropologist Vilhjalmur Stefansson's account of the four years he spent living in and exploring the Arctic, *My Life with the Eskimo*. The book and its author fascinated her. Stefansson was certainly an extraordinary character. Born William Stephenson in 1879 in Manitoba, Canada, to Icelandic parents, he changed his name to Vilhjalmur Stefansson in adulthood. For his first expedition in 1906, he travelled to Herschel Island in the Arctic Circle with the Danish explorer Ejnar Mikkelsen, where he became interested in the lives and history of the blue-eyed 'Copper Inuit' people who lived there. He returned to Herschel Island in 1908, where he remained living among the Inuit for four years, learning their language and customs, and forming a secret liaison with an Inuit woman named Pannigabluk, with whom he had a son. Between 1913 and 1918 Stefansson co-led a Canadian arctic expedition, funded by the Canadian government. It was a tragic voyage, resulting in the loss of eleven of the twenty-two crew members due to starvation, illness and suicide. Despite this disaster, Stefansson was not discouraged and in 1921 he sponsored an expedition for four

1 'Should Parents Obey?,' *The Daily News* (Perth, WA: 15 June 1922), p.3. republished from the *Daily Mail* (n.d. given).

young men to colonise Wrangel Island north of Siberia, which was where the eleven survivors of the expedition ship the *Karluk* had lived from March to September 1914. Stefansson planned to claim the island for Canada or Britain, and to form an exploration company based on the island.

This trip also ended in disaster. The four men were inexperienced and not adequately equipped. All perished on the island or in an attempt to get help from Siberia across the frozen Chukchi Sea. The only survivor was an Inuit woman, Ada Blackjack, whom the men had hired as a seamstress in Nome, Alaska. She was rescued in 1923 after two years on Wrangel Island. The details of how this expedition ended had not yet reached the ears of the general public in early 1923.

Soon after she'd read Stefansson's book, Elsie wrote several short stories based on his anecdotes. Typical of these stories is 'The Sunday Taboo', which was published in *Pearson's Magazine*. It tells the tragic fate of a young couple who become lost in a blizzard on a Sunday and are left to die because missionaries have instilled in the minds of Eskimos the belief that the gods will punish them if anyone does any kind of work on a Sunday.

On 23 May 1923, numerous newspapers announced the arrival of Vilhjalmur Stefansson in London. Elsie promptly wrote to him a formal letter presenting the compliments of Princess Nusrat Ali Mirza, congratulating him on his 'astounding feats of courage and endurance', and inviting him to visit Pen-y-Coed, if he could 'endure the boredom of a small country house'.[1] Stefansson politely declined the invitation.

Another longer and less formal letter from Elsie followed, protesting her admiration and desire to make his work better known to a wider public, and asking if she might send him her story 'The Sunday Taboo' so that he could see that she did not use his books merely as a background, but took 'the information in them as a most precious trust and present[ed] them, in popular form, to England'.[2] She acknowledged her 'astounding impertinence', as she realised the stories 'teem with the inevitable errors of second hand effort'. But, she wrote, 'you – under

1 Letter from EAM to Vilhalmur Stefansson, 29 May 1923.

2 Letter from EAM to Stefansson, 4 June 1923.

diverse names, are always the hero. You are always the superman who goes empty handed to the North.'

For Stefansson's benefit, Elsie had now acquired a new but entirely fictional set of ancestors, 'men who were whalers and seafarers', many of whom 'went North and did not return. I suppose their spirits call', she wrote. In later years she would talk about listening to her father, now transformed from teacher to sea captain, telling tales of their adventures at sea.

She again invited Stefansson to visit and he again declined, but promised to send Elsie a copy of his most recent book, *The Friendly Arctic*. In return he received a nine-page letter from Elsie offering to send him four of her Arctic stories and mentioning her children's book *With Pucker to the Arctic* due out later that year, which drew on her frequent re-readings of *My Life with the Eskimo*. Once again Elsie acknowledged her enormous admiration for Stefansson, describing herself as a woman 'with few enthusiasms, a woman far beyond the age of hero worship' (she was now forty years old), a woman who had 'fallen completely under the spell of one man's personality', and thus a woman uniquely suited to be 'the proper mouthpiece – the voice crying in the wilderness'.

The same letter reveals Elsie's awareness of her technique as a popular-genre author, writing not for literary people 'but for the millions. One rejoices, of course, in having so wide a pulpit,' she insisted:

> But there are certain rules that must be strictly followed. There must be a love element: the heroine must be good and beautiful – and beautiful to the English understanding. It is not hard to make the hero as he is always you and the villain must be beyond the pale! Hence you must allow me a certain latitude otherwise I could not be 'popular'. My 'Blond' Eskimo heroine is always very beautiful![1]

Like Stefansson himself and his readers, Elsie was intrigued by the groups of light-haired Inuits, or Eskimos, that Stefansson and other

1 EAM letter 11 June 1923.

explorers encountered in the Arctic. Stefansson himself preferred the term 'Copper Inuits', but the newspaper reporters made the description 'Blond Eskimos' popular. One theory, favoured by Stefansson, was that this group of Eskimos were descended from Viking explorers. Elsie's letter betrays a complex attitude to her own writing. She is eager for Stefansson's approval, while also confessing that her writing is blatantly commercial in its appeal to popular English preconceptions about beauty, simple oppositions between good and evil, and interest in the most exotic of the exotic – 'Blond' rather than dark Arctic peoples. At no time did she include Indian people in her fiction, although she did not hesitate to advertise the connection of her husband and her children to Indian royalty.

Aware that her letters might be becoming too frequent and importunate, Elsie promised at the end of her long missive not to write again. But she did. She sent a card on 15 June, and another long letter on 18 June. At last a dinner date at the Savoy was made for 21 June, with telegrams to and from Dolgellau to confirm.

What was Elsie to wear for the meeting with her heroic Arctic explorer? She chose an Arctic fur stole and wrote to let Stefansson know how he could recognise her: 'I shall wear an orange dress with a very long white fox fur. Five foot 6", greying hair.'[1]

Following their meetings, for dinner on the 21st and lunch on 22 June, Elsie's letters became more businesslike and less effusive. She now signed her name as Elizabeth, or E. A. M., instead of Elizabeth Ali Mirza of Murshidabad, although she continued to address Stefansson as 'Cher Ami'. Stefansson had read some of her stories and suggested extensive corrections and 'tonings down'. Elsie subsequently published, after Stefansson had seen and edited it, an article summarising his claims in *The Friendly Arctic: The Story of Five Years in Polar Regions*, that the Arctic should be seen not as a barren waste hostile to human habitation but as a source of minerals and oil; an area that could sustain large herds of reindeer and cattle, and thereby supply food for populations south of the North Pole. Her article was in turn summarised in several British, Canadian and Australian papers.

1 EAM letter, 20 June 1923.

Stefansson did eventually take up the invitation to visit the Prince and Princess (as he always referred to them), at Pen-y-Coed, where he met the children. He also dined with Nusrat and his brother Syed in the Union Club, and again with Nusrat and Elsie at his own London flat in September. This last dinner followed the discovery, widely reported in the press, that the Wrangel Island expedition had resulted in the deaths of all four of the young men involved. Stefansson was blamed by many for having sent such ill-equipped young men to Wrangel, and the discovery also brought to an end Stefansson's hopes of persuading the British government to annex Wrangel Island and form, among other things, an airbase for flights across the Arctic.[1] Elsie was outraged that he was blamed for the disaster. She wrote to Stefansson to express her grief at reading the news and emphasised her unstinting support for him.

With Stefansson's departure from England in October, the correspondence became less frequent, although it persisted sporadically for many years. Meanwhile Elsie continued to write children's books, adult fiction, and journalism related to the Arctic. *With Pucker to the Arctic* (1925) took Jerry and his sister Phyllis, aged twelve and ten, on a series of breathtaking adventures and escapes from swirling seas, rivers and icebergs. It also includes details about polar bears and how to catch them. The story features Pucker, a very tough and resilient Boy Scout, who at first appears as a young orphan boy of lower-class background. In true Dickensian mode, however, Pucker turns out to be not lower-class at all but the cousin of the two children and the son of the true landowner of the country estate on which Phyllis and Jerry live. The novel ends with a bow to Stefansson, as Pucker plans to become an explorer when he grows up – a great explorer – 'like Stefansson and Scott'.

More polar bears and icebergs are encountered in *Lost in the Arctic* (1926), a novel aimed at young teenagers and with a preface that commended to Elizabeth Marc's readers the works of Stefansson and other Arctic explorers. *Lost in the Arctic* was dedicated to her children, now identified as 'Myriam and Savile Mostyn'.[2]

---

1 London: Macmillan, 1921.

2 *With Pucker to the Arctic* (London: Thomas Nelson, 1923), p.264.

1923 had been a year of great excitement and fulfilment for Elsie: she had met and befriended her great hero Stefansson; she had found a special role and theme, beyond money-making, for her writing, which was now earning about £750 a year; Nusrat had persuaded the India Office and his pension trustees to give him a lump sum to buy Pen-y-Coed, the house all the family loved; and Savile/Syed had managed to pass the entrance exam for Harrow.

The following year, however, brought anxiety and depression. Life in Dolgellau with Nusrat seemed dull and unrewarding. Both Elsie's mother, Eliza, and Myriam were seriously ill for several weeks, and Elsie herself feared that she had breast cancer. Then it became clear that Savile hated Harrow. His teachers noted that he was increasingly inattentive and disruptive during lessons. The school suggested he should be removed.

Elsie sought help from different sources; she became interested in Unitarianism and Spiritualism, and she underwent psychoanalysis with Hugh Crichton-Miller, at that time one of the most prestigious psychiatrists in England and the founder of the Tavistock Clinic. There is no record of the psychoanalytic sessions, sessions that would profoundly affect the lives of the whole family.

Himself the victim of a domineering mother, according to his biographers, Hugh Crichton-Miller believed strongly in the importance of separating boys from their mothers after the age of eight. Elsie did not question the view that Savile's inability or unwillingness to succeed at Harrow was all her fault, or nearly all her fault, for she felt that Nusrat should have been a stronger male presence. 'Every schoolmaster of experience,' Crichton-Miller wrote:

> … recognises that a mother's influence in the life of her son in this period [the Father Phase from eight to twelve] may become not only hampering, but detrimental. There is a real danger that by her mere domination in this sphere, she may paralyse his development … During this period the mother must at all costs stand aside.[1]

1 Hugh Crichton-Miller, *The New Psychology and the Parent* (London: Jarrolds

Myriam, age 12

Crichton-Miller was a strong advocate of both the Boy Scouts and the English public school system as arenas for limiting the mother's harmful influence. He believed that public schools provided the exemplary model for a boy's development, from his protected status as a fag in the lower school, till age twelve, then his emulation or hero-worship of older boys as he advances to the middle school, and then his assumption of responsibility as a prefect in his final years. The linking of power and responsibility at this stage was, in Crichton-Miller's view:

> … the great genius of our public school system, and of our Anglo-Saxon temperament … And it is largely, I believe, because the British nation has sacrificed the comfort of hundreds of small boys to the character development of these powerful young adolescents, that it has attained to a certain success in the administration and protection of primitive races.[1]

Publishers, 1923), pp.75–76.

1 Hugh Crichton-Miller, *The New Psychology and the Parent* (London: Jarrolds

Elsie also accepted, and later in her daughter's presence reiterated, the view that she herself had been 'damaged' because she was the last of three daughters, disappointing her parents' longing for a son. Crichton-Miller had written of the 'danger of allowing a girl to grow up with the impression that she was unwanted, because there were already several daughters in the family and a boy had been hoped for. Such an idea may do a lasting injury to the mind of the growing girl.'[1]

Meanwhile, Myriam, now eleven years old, had also been deposited in a boarding school, St Helen's in Northwood. The reason for Elsie's choice of St Helen's for her daughter is not known, but it may have been influenced by the school's admiration for adventurers. Two of the houses were named after Antarctic explorers – Captain Robert Falcon Scott and Sir Ernest Shackleton, and a third was named after the Himalayan explorer Brigadier-General Charles Bruce. The distress of both mother and daughter at the parting is revealed in a memory Myriam passed on over seventy years later: she was dropped abruptly at the school in midterm (early 1924) without any uniform or other school equipment. Once left inside the main building, she looked through the window and watched with dismay as her mother ran away very quickly up the path towards the school gates.

Since she had always been home-schooled, Myriam did not find it easy to adjust to the regime and social life of a boarding school. Moreover, she had to remember that her name was now Myriam Mostyn, not Myriam Ali Mirza, for her the beginning of a lifelong fissure between her English and her semi-Indian identity. Nevertheless, she concentrated on her lessons and showed herself an able pupil. At the end of her third year she was awarded Robert Louis Stevenson's novel *Catriona*, a sequel to *Kidnapped*, as a prize for 'General Good Work'.

Sometimes her Uncle Syed visited and took her out for tea, or to a film. One silent film she saw was *A Tale of Two Cities*, in which the chaotic scenes of the French revolution seemed to go on endlessly, with the captions failing to make much sense of them. Myriam preferred films like *Little Annie Rooney*, starring thirty-three-year-old Mary

---

Publishers, 1923)., pp.71–2.

1 *The New Psychology and the Parent*, p.94.

Pickford as a young Irish orphan fighting with other New York street urchins. But the film Myriam and her Uncle Syed enjoyed most was Charlie Chaplin's *The Gold Rush*. Although the outings were a welcome break from her school routine, Myriam remembered them as rather awkward occasions on which neither she nor her Uncle Syed quite knew what to say to each other.

By the summer of 1924 it was clear that Savile could not and would not continue at Harrow. He wanted to become a farmer, and so his parents agreed that he could take a year out from school, stay with one of Elsie's relatives in Kent, and work on their farm. This was a temporary measure, however; a more radical and long-term solution had to be found. The solution settled upon for Savile was Australia.

Elsie's hero Stefansson had toured Australia between May and September 1924, and declared it a promising area for settlement, reckoning that much more of the sparsely settled non-coastal areas could be made productive. In an past issue of the magazine *Nineteenth Century and After* (where Elsie had published her essay in support of Stefansson's views on the 'Friendly Arctic'), an Australian author, Frederic Eggleston, had touted the rich resources of his country and the need to redistribute populations from the crowded metropolis to the scarcely populated colonies 'to allow less expensive exploitation of those resources'.[1] The coastal belts of Australia with their healthier climate were – according to Eggleston, who was speaking very much in line with Australian government policy – 'well-fitted to be a home for the British people':

> The race has been maintained pure. Social life and political institutions being inspired by British traditions the surplus population of Great Britain can be placed there with a minimum of disturbance ... Pastoral life is the ideal for the type of the English country gentlemen, is easily learnt, and is not exacting.[2]

And so the decision was made: Nusrat would accompany Savile to

1 *Nineteenth Century and After,* Vol. XCIII (January–June 1923), pp.453.
2 *Nineteenth Century and After,* Vol. XCIII (January–June 1923), pp.453–464.

Australia, where they would spend some time studying agriculture and then buy a farm. Elsie and Myriam would follow in two years or so, by which time the farm should have been bought and established. The intervening time would allow Savile to be away from his mother, become more independent of her influence as Elsie's psychoanalyst had recommended, and spend more time with his father. Australia would make men of them both. They could apply for assisted passage, a scheme that was introduced in 1925 enabling any British person who was accompanied by a child under nineteen to travel to Australia for £11, the equivalent of £450 today. The sale of Pen-y-Coed would provide the funds for the farm, and animals to stock it. Nusrat hoped it would be a chance to make a new start and escape the burden of his ancestry, which he believed had prevented him from pursuing a worthwhile career in Britain.

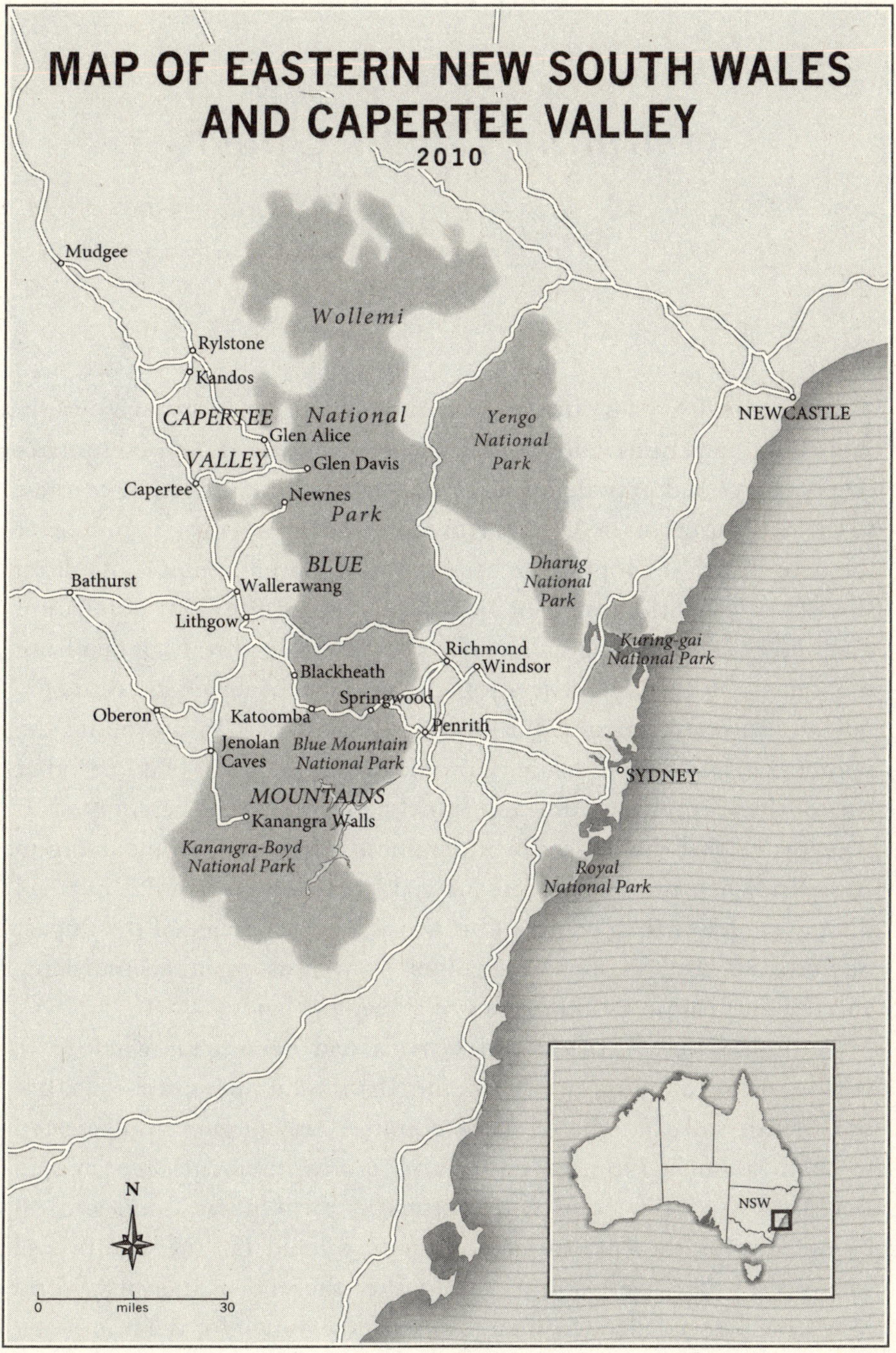
MAP OF EASTERN NEW SOUTH WALES
AND CAPERTEE VALLEY
2010
Mudgee
Wollemi
Rylstone
Kandos
CAPERTEE
National
Glen Alice
VALLEY
Glen Davis
Capertee
Newnes
Park
Yengo
National
Park
NEWCASTLE
BLUE
Bathurst
Wallerawang
Lithgow
Dharug
National
Park
Kuring-gai
National Park
Richmond
Windsor
Blackheath
Springwood
Oberon
Katoomba
Penrith
Jenolan
Caves
Blue Mountain
National Park
SYDNEY
MOUNTAINS
Kanangra Walls
Kanangra-Boyd
National Park
Royal
National Park
N
0
miles
30
NSW

CHAPTER 12

Farming Down Under

1925–1927

In the early 1920s the Australian government was vigorously encouraging immigration by British-born people to fill the continent's empty spaces and provide labour for its growing industries. In contrast to the population of the United Kingdom, which was over 42 million at the time, Australia's population in 1921 was just over 6 million, of whom almost three-quarters were of British or Irish origin. This population total did not include the indigenous peoples, who were excluded from the census. When the Federation of Australia occurred in 1901, the new constitution contained a provision that stated: 'In reckoning the numbers of the people of the Commonwealth, or of a State or other part of the Commonwealth, aboriginal natives shall not be counted.' It is estimated that there were over a million indigenous people living in Australia when the first settlers arrived from Britain in 1788; by 1925 there were fewer than 90,000. This was as a consequence of the impact of European diseases such as smallpox, as well as organised massacres, and the occupation by Europeans of aboriginal lands.

Australia, New Zealand and Canada had been acknowledged as self-governing dominions within the British Empire since 1907, but the British still thought of these countries as colonies and referred to them as such. From as early as 1906 advertisements appeared in British newspapers, along with posters in the Underground and on buses featuring the opportunities Australia offered, but the volume and intensity of the advertising increased after the end of the First World War. One poster called for 'men for the land, women for the home' and offered guaranteed employment. Another huge poster in the Strand in

London promised 'a hearty welcome, a generous return for your energy and enterprise', and 'a climate that is the healthiest in the world'.

Faced with the problem of a large population, diminished resources, and growing unemployment following the end of the war, the British government saw resettlement of some of its citizens as a useful solution. Moreover an increase in the number of Britons in the colonies would make them more secure against other would-be empire builders, particularly the Japanese in the case of Australia. The Empire Settlement Act (1922) established close cooperation between the British and colonial governments for the redistribution of people from Britain to the colonies. Under this act Britain promised to cover up to half the cost of resettlement.

But not all immigrants were welcome in Australia. Shortly after the Australian states came together to form the Federation of Australia in 1901, the new federal government passed an Immigration Restriction Act prohibiting non-European immigration to Australia, an act generally known as the 'White Australia Policy', which remained in force for over sixty years. This act was specifically intended to prevent 'Asiatics' such as Chinese and Indian 'coolies' from entering the country and competing with white settlers for jobs, but it was underpinned by a more general racism and extended to cover all non-Europeans.

Speaking in favour of the Immigration Restriction Act in 1901, Alfred Deakin, Australia's second Prime Minister, declared:

> A united race means not only that its members can intermarry and associate without degradation on either side, but implies one inspired by the same ideals, and an aspiration towards the same ideals, of a people possessing the same general cast of character, tone of thought, the same constitutional training and traditions – a people qualified to live under this constitution, the broadest and most liberal perhaps the world has yet seen reduced to writing; a people qualified to use without abusing it, and to develop themselves under it to the full height and extent of their capacity.

Australian defenders of the policy often cited the conflicts between

Indians and whites in the South African Province of Natal as proof that Indians and Europeans could not coexist. During the second half of the nineteenth century, the Province of Natal had brought many people from the Indian subcontinent to work in the sugarcane fields. Most of the Indians who came over to work decided to settle there, and by the end of the century outnumbered the white settlers. In 1894, when he was living in Durban, Mahatma Gandhi helped found the National Indian Congress to fight discrimination against Indians in South Africa, and led a series of non-violent protests to demand equal rights with Europeans, including freedom of movement and voting rights. Gandhi and hundreds of other Indian protestors were imprisoned and beaten during these protests, and it was not until 1914 that apartheid laws against Indians were partially lifted.

Defenders of the 'white-only' immigration policy for Australia promulgated Natal as an example of 'inevitable' conflict between Europeans and Asians, and also successfully advocated Natal's practice of using a dictation test as a means of excluding 'undesirable immigrants'. At the Inter-Colonial Conference in March 1896 delegates from five countries resolved that their parliaments should amend the specifically anti-Chinese laws and apply them to all coloured races. Joseph Chamberlain, in line with Queen Victoria's pledge not to distinguish among British subjects on the basis of race, origin, language or creed, asked delegates to find an 'inoffensive' way of administering their immigration policies. Australia followed the example of Natal's Immigration Restriction Act of 1897, which required literacy in any European language, later amended to include 'any prescribed language', meaning any language the applicant would not understand. A similar tactic was used to prevent African Americans from voting in the southern states of America.

When, at the Versailles Peace Conference in 1919, Japanese delegates sought to include a clause in the covenant guaranteeing equal treatment of all races, Australian Prime Minister William Hughes indicated that such a clause would be unacceptable to Australia. 'The people of other nations do not realise that the whole existence of this democracy depends upon our maintenance of the great principle of a White Australia,' proclaimed West Australian Senator Drake-Brockman in 1920.[1]

Fully aware of the discrimination against 'Asiatics', Elsie wrote to the Australian High Commission in London pleading that an exception might be made in Nusrat's case and that of his children. His mother was English, she pointed out, and he and his children were all fair and blue-eyed. 'This is a Persian family,' Elsie claimed, quite falsely. 'Therefore the Prince is not what is termed an Eurasian. Anthropologists class Persians as European and not "coloured" and the Prince looks like an ordinary English country gentleman, very fair skin, blue eyes.'[2] Although many North-Indian ruling families claimed descent from Persian ancestors and Persian was the dominant court language until 1857, Mir Jafar, Mansour Ali Khan's ancestor, was actually of Iraqi descent. Elsie went on to mention that her husband had been educated at Harrow and Oxford, passing over the facts that it was only a preparatory school he had attended in the suburb of Harrow, that his later schooling had been as a day pupil at the less prestigious King's College School, and that he had not completed his Oxford degree.

Along with her letter, Elsie enclosed photographs of Nusrat and Savile, and explained that a doctor had advised that Savile should be taken away from school at Harrow and allowed to take up farming. 'Now,' Elsie wrote, 'the question arises – shall this boy farm in England or the Dominions?'

> We feel it would be best to start again in a new country. A farmer, in England, cannot be followed about by a title. We would like all to take the name of Mostyn and leave the complications of the title behind. We cannot get away from it in England. There are too many Oxford and Harrow friends.

The family would not be a burden on the state, since the Prince, according to Elsie, had an income of £1,000 a year; she earned from her writing about £750 a year (a joint income of around £75,000 in today's money); and they would have about £5,000 or £6,000 in

---

1 Commonwealth Parliamentary Debates, 1920, p.4863. Cited by Willard, p. 211.

2 Letter from EAM to Australia House, Feb.2, 1925. IOR/L/PS11/162/825.

capital (presumably from the sale of Pen-y-Coed, equivalent to around £300,000 today). Her clinching point was that father and son were 'both good horsemen'.

The case was referred to the Home and Territories department in Australia, with attention drawn to the statements about income and capital. It was also noted that the father and son 'appear to be European'.[1] An Australian official in Melbourne commented that 'the father might be regarded as half caste, but in view of his general circumstances, upbringing, British wife and children born in England, the case appears to be one for special consideration'. Admittance was approved on 30 March 1925.

As soon as approval for immigration status was granted, Nusrat applied for passports to be issued in their new names – Norman Allan Mostyn and Savile Allan Mostyn. Writing to the India Office he explained his reasons for emigrating and emphasised the necessity for concealing his identity as an 'Asiatic'. His letter indicates that he and Elsie had discussed how best to explain the decision to emigrate in a way that would not involve her psychoanalyst's view that she had too much influence over Savile at this stage in his development.

Nusrat's letter also placed emphasis on wishing to escape the burden of his title. This does indeed connect with earlier episodes in his life – for example his discreet visit to Jamaica in 1905 when his presence went almost unreported, his desire to remain in Paris and set up a business there where the attitudes of Imperial Britain were less dominant, the decision to give his children English names when they went to school. In his letter of explanation to the India Office officials, Nusrat wrote:

> When I left Oxford I had every intention of taking up a useful career, but I found my way blocked in every direction on account of the title, and I was very anxious that my son should not be so hampered, and so I sent him to Harrow under the name of Mostyn and my little girl goes to school under the same name ... [My] boy is extremely anxious to take up farming in Australia. But he is only fifteen and a half and we cannot contemplate

1 Letter from Australia House to The Secretary, Prime Minister's Department, 13 Feb. 1925.

> letting him go off alone; yet we feel it would really be by far the best thing for both the children to emigrate to a new country and leaving the title and all its associations behind, start life there as ordinary citizens.
>
> I therefore approached the Government of Australia and put all the facts before them, explaining that we would all like to emigrate to Australia if they could see their way to make an exception in their Asiatic Restriction Law, and saying that my wife and I would go as Mr and Mrs Mostyn and we will drop the Eastern name. I have just received a cable from the Government of Australia to say that they will be pleased to receive us as settlers.
>
> I therefore propose to go out with the boy as soon as possible; probably next month. My wife will sell up the house here and follow with my daughter in two or three years time; the little girl must not leave school yet.
>
> The difficulty is that I must now take the name of N.A. Mostyn and I have given the Government of Australia a very solemn assurance not to let my real name transpire in any transaction with lawyers and bankers over there, for they very rightly urged that they were making an exception in my case and I must not cause them any embarrassment. I must ask you therefore to be kind enough to make some arrangement as to the payment of my income.[1]

This meant that his pension sent every three months to Australia should be made out to Norman Allan Mostyn. One India Office official privately expressed doubt 'whether he will succeed in concealing his identity'. He also wondered whether they should be 'concerned to make sure that he is not deserting his wife'.[2] Despite these suspicions that as an Asian Muslim, Nusrat would be unlikely to 'pass' as an Englishman, and might not be a faithful husband to his English wife, the India Office agreed to transfer his pension to Barclay's Bank in Australia under his new name.

---

1 NAM letter to India Office, 1 April 1925. IOR/L/PS/13/1809.

2 Memorandum, Secretary of State Office, 4 April 1925. IOR/L/PS/13/1809.

Nusrat now applied to Australia House for assisted passage for himself and Savile. When this was refused, he booked a third-class cabin, costing about £45 for the two of them, equivalent today to about £1800, on the SS *Osterley*, sailing from London on 30 May 1925. He told one of the trustees for his pension fund, William Robinson, that, although Australia House had refused any monetary assistance, he had been promised 'all the necessary introductions' when they arrived in Sydney. 'I am now very glad,' Nusrat added, 'that I am not getting an "assisted passage" as I now find this is given to the rather lower class of settler, the farm labourer class and I should have found myself in quite a false position on my arrival out there.'[1]

Once everything had been arranged, Nusrat and Savile had just one month to pack and say their goodbyes, not only to their close friends and cousins, and to Elsie and Myriam, whom they would not see again for another two years, but hardest of all to Syed and Sarah. To Syed they may have spoken without much conviction of a return visit to England, or his coming to Australia. Sarah, however, was now terminally ill with cancer and in a nursing home in Cromwell Road, Kensington, London. Nusrat and his mother had seen very little of each other over the past seventeen years, first because Nusrat was abroad and then because of the mutual dislike that developed between Elsie and Sarah. Now Nusrat felt it his duty to visit, knowing that this was a final parting.

Sarah's sadness must have been deepened, perhaps embittered, by Nusrat's rejection of his title and status, a status she had fought all her life to protect. Nusrat might not be getting an assisted passage, but he would not be far removed from 'the rather lower class of settler', the class that Sarah and her siblings had belonged to before her elevation to wife of the Nawab.

On the evening of 29 May 1925, when he boarded the *Osterley*, the Nawabzada Nusrat Ali Mirza of Murshidabad became Mr Norman Allan Mostyn. That was the name on his passport, and that was how he would be identified in Australia. Now he was no longer an Indian prince, but simply one ordinary man along with nearly 1,000 other passengers, almost all travelling third class. Most were British or Irish single men and

1 Letter from NAM to W. Robinson, 1 May 1925. IOR/L/PS/13/1809.

women under the age of forty on their way to Melbourne and Sydney to find work and a new life. At first sight Norman Mostyn differed from them only because he was slightly older (he would celebrate his forty-eighth birthday three weeks later, and his hair was turning grey), and because he had an upper-class accent. Savile had adapted his accent while working on the farm in Kent, and now could mix more easily with other passengers.

Never before could father and son have spent so much time so close to one another – hour after hour lying at night in the bunk beds in their tiny cabin. I imagine them sometimes talking about what Myriam and Elsie might be doing, sometimes about what they would do when they got to Sydney, and where they would buy their farm. And sometimes perhaps they just lay silently listening to one another, breathing or turning restlessly in their narrow beds. As the ship steamed near to Suez, the cabin would have become unbearably hot and stuffy and they might have stayed on the deck leaning over the railings to watch the phosphorescent flash of fish in the dark water. It must have been a relief to stop at Aden, get off the ship for a few hours, and taste food that wasn't either salt beef or salt pork.

After a journey of thirty-eight days they docked early on the morning of 6 July at Princes Pier, Port Melbourne. Under a grey sky they caught their first glimpse of an Australian city, with its wide boulevards and hundreds of wooden bungalows hugging the sandy shore. Since the *Osterley* was stopping only briefly to offload passengers and the mail from England, they did not disembark. As they steamed out of the harbour that afternoon they could see more clearly the eucalyptus forests that thickly covered the hills above the sandstone cliffs. The air had a fresh, sharp smell.

On 9 July they finally reached Sydney and joined the line to have their passports and visas checked – perhaps a slightly anxious moment for Norman lest he be detected as Nusrat. But the customs officials were working quickly to move the long queue on, and they scarcely glanced at the father and son. Their trunks and cases were loaded into a cab that took them the short half-mile to their hotel in the city centre. It was a new experience for Norman to be addressed as 'mate' rather than 'sir', and be called a 'pommie' by the cab driver, an experience that amused Savile. After an evening meal in their hotel, they could at last sleep in comfortable full-sized beds.

During the next few days father and son explored the city. In 1925 Sydney was busy, with a population of one million. Trams rattled up and down the main streets where six-storey department shops displayed all the latest fashions from England. Theatres featured variety shows and comedies, a farewell programme starring Harry Lauder, and silent films such as *Helen's Babies*, starring Baby Peggy and Clara Bow. Norman and Savile's main business, however, was in the wide expanse of Martin Place, with its sturdy sandstone and granite banks and post office. Here they sent telegrams to Elsie announcing their safe arrival, posted longer letters, and made an appointment to see the manager of Barclay's Bank. Back at their hotel they read the local newspaper, the *Sydney Herald*, leafing through page after page of advertisements before reaching the national and international news. Many of the items were concerned with migration and Empire: complaints that too many 'juvenile migrants' were not being properly trained and cared for, a denunciation from Mr T. A. Chen in Hawaii of laws which discriminated on grounds of 'race colour', an account of the Prince of Wales attending a 'native indaba' in Southern Africa and being given 'a magnificent pair of elephant tusks, joined together with a broad band of Rhodesian gold'.

Norman's plan was to enrol them both in the Agricultural Experiment Farm School in Bathurst, 150 miles west of Sydney. This agricultural college had been established in 1895 to provide not only basic training in agricultural skills for urban immigrants, but also to experiment with new kinds of plant and animal breeds that might be more suited to the Australian environment. By 1925 it had gained a reputation for making significant trials and advances that could be used to make Australian farming more productive. A few months after Norman and Savile arrived in Sydney, the *Mudgee Guardian* reported that the Bathurst Experiment Farm [sic] was conducting trials 'to determine the most profitable type of crossbred lamb for the market; also whether hand feeding of lambs can be profitably carried out'.[1]

1 *Mudgee Guardian,* 5 November 1925, p.1. (Mudgee was a significant agricultural

Savile, 1925

Nusrat, 1925

As the minimum age for enrolment was sixteen and Savile's birthday was not until October, Norman made an appointment with the Under Secretary for the Department of Agriculture in Sydney to see whether Savile could be granted permission to begin their course in July. His request was approved. Despite knowing that students admitted in the second half of the year would not be able to attend lectures until January, and that they could only do practical work till then, it seems that Norman and Savile were anxious to start straight away. They visited Anthony Hordern's department store, and bought two sets of the Farm School's prescribed clothing and articles: 'two suits of working clothes, one suit for Sunday wear, one waterproof overcoat, two pairs of suitable boots, one pair of slippers, four sheets, three pillow-slips, and six strong bath-towels'.[1]

Their business and purchases completed, Norman and Savile took an early morning train across the Blue Mountains to Bathurst, passing small tin-roofed railway stations separated by seemingly endless forests of eucalyptus trees as the train laboured up the steep slopes, and arriving late on a bleak wintry afternoon. They stayed at a hotel near the station, and the next day explored the town, which still retained many of its historical features. Bathurst had been settled by Europeans in 1815, and was the first town and post office established on the great plains west of the Blue Mountains. A century later, it now had a population of about 12,000. The town's wide streets were lit by ornate electric lamps, and lined with two-storey shops and numerous hotels characterised by corrugated iron roofs and verandas with elaborate ironwork balustrades. Many of these buildings dated from the gold-rush years that followed the discovery of some specks of gold in nearby Summer Hill Creek in 1851. Near the towering red-brick Catholic and Anglican cathedrals in the centre of the town they were pleased to discover a library, which would allow them to borrow many of the latest novels as well as information about Australian history and agriculture.

---

centre about 150 miles northwest of Sydney.)

1 Ian Bowie, Robin McLachlan, et al, *Celebrating 100 Harvests: A Centenary History of the Bathurst Agricultural Research Station, 1895–1995* (Bathurst, NSW: NSW Agriculture, 1995), pp.77–78.

Students were required to live on the experimental farm, so Norman and Savile were given a room in the student's quarters where they unpacked their belongings. Besides the clothes they had bought and the few photographs and books they had brought with them, there was little to unpack. Norman placed his Qu'ran carefully in a bottom drawer of their small cupboard, along with his and Savile's passports and official papers.

The next morning, Norman and Savile began their duties on the farm. During their first weeks they were chiefly tasked with helping to bring the cows in, and rising at dawn to milk them. The paddocks were white with frost, and a bitter wind blew across the plains. Over the following weeks and months they would be assigned to different areas, rounding up and checking the sheep, exercising the horses and, in September and October, working in the vegetable gardens and learning to prune and graft in the orchards. Their fellow students were a mixed group, mainly comprising young men from Britain and Australians who had fought during the war, but also others who were less typical. Robin McLachlan, in his history of the experimental farm, remarked that among the atypical post-war students were ex-officers of high rank, young men from noble English families, and one former Russian prince. Another unusual student noted by McLachlan was Norman, who had managed to pass incognito through the Bathurst agricultural college during the late twenties. It was only on the occasion of his death, when his photo was published in Sydney newspapers, that some members of the staff realised that one of their former students had been an Indian prince.

Despite the India Office's doubts that he could do so, Norman had indeed succeeded in concealing his identity as an 'Asiatic' and a prince, at least for the time he spent at the experimental farm. It must have been a challenge for him, a forty-eight-year-old man, used to a comfortable upper-class life and a certain amount of esteem.

For his fellow students and the staff at the college, it was Norman's class and quintessential 'Englishness' that distinguished him among his peers. He was evidently better educated than most of his classmates, and he seemed to his tutors 'the best type of Englishman, a very fine gentleman with a fine personality'.[1] But he was also something of a mystery. Apart from telling staff that he had travelled in the tropics, he revealed little about his past and, in characteristically Australian manner, his silence was respected.

Norman and Savile remained at the experimental farm for twelve months, attending lectures during the first half of 1926 as well as learning the practical techniques of ploughing and harvesting, and management of cattle and sheep. Although the course was intended to take two years, after the first year they were impatient to embark on managing their own property. Elsie had also telegraphed in March to let them know that she had sold Pen-y-Coed and its contents and so the necessary money was available. She too was impatient to set out for a new life.

Sheep farming seemed to be the most viable and practical enterprise, for Australian wool was in demand. To keep 1,000 sheep and some cattle, and have orchards, pastures and hayfields, they would need a property of at least fifteen-hundred acres. Real estate agents in Bathurst were advertising numerous farms in the surrounding areas; among them was 'Myalla', located in the Capertee Valley about sixty miles north-east of Bathurst and 120 miles northwest of Sydney. It was advertised as having 1,500 acres of safe grazing land, available water, and a four-room house. At 35 shillings an acre (equivalent to about £70 today) the price seemed reasonable.

In the second-hand car they had bought in Bathurst, Norman and Savile drove the winding, muddy road from Bathurst to Glen Alice in the Capertee Valley; a canyon wider than the Grand Canyon in Arizona, USA. The last twenty miles of their journey took them up and down a steep road, into a wide valley surrounded by ancient craggy mountains. Every two or thee miles there was a small track leading away into the fields and, in the distance, the glint of a corrugated-iron-roofed house near a windmill. A real estate agent from Rylstone, the nearest little town twenty-five miles away, was waiting for them beside the track that led to Myalla, whose name was roughly stencilled on the tin mailbox that stood beside the gate at the entrance.

They followed the estate agent's car, and there was the house, a small

1 Bowie and McLachlan, Chapter 5.

Myalla, 1927

bungalow, built some fifty years previously, its sturdy sandstone walls half hidden by verandas. The iron roof had once been painted a dark red. Behind it were some rusting sheds. On every side of the house the fields, green after the winter rain, stretched towards the mountains, blue and hazy in the distance. Above them the sky seemed enormous, stacked with great clouds. This was to be their new home. Nusrat would now be listed on local electoral and post office directories as Norman Allan Mostyn, Esq, Grazier, thus identifying him as the owner of a large Australian sheep and cattle farm.

Norman set about the task of making a family house habitable. Before Elsie and Myriam arrived there was much to do. The rotten planks on the floors and verandas had to be replaced, the walls stripped of the ancient newspapers that covered them, and repapered, the gutters cleared, windows and shutters inserted. Elsie would also need an additional room built for her to write in. This room Norman built onto the back of the house with windows facing away from the road and the sheds, looking out towards the trees and mountains in the west. He and Savile made a fence to surround the house, and planted trees, bushes and bougainvillea in the beginnings of a garden.

So much needed to be done: there were the everyday tasks of finding and chopping wood for the kitchen stove, bringing in and milking their two cows, feeding the horses, arranging supplies of hay, and the more domestic chores such as cooking and cleaning. There were also fences to be repaired and fields to be cleared of thistles and other weeds before sheep, horses and ploughs could be bought. It soon became apparent that the property had not been the bargain they had first thought. Savile remained optimistic; he loved working with the farm machinery, dismantling and mending it when it broke down.

Together father and son would ride out when it was cool in the morning to check the sheep and cattle. When dingoes attacked and killed some of their sheep, Savile swore, but he believed they could simply move the sheep to paddocks closer to the house. Norman, however, became increasingly anxious: there was very little money left to repair the fences and buy more hay; if it did not rain soon they would not have enough grass or water to feed all the sheep and cattle. Visiting farmers forecast a long, dry summer ahead. There was a plague of grasshoppers; the air was thick with their wings and the ground in the paddocks seemed to move as the grasshoppers devoured every tiny blade of green grass. Then, suddenly, a great flock of ibis appeared in pursuit of the grasshoppers, stalking steadily with their long legs and beaks. Norman had not seen ibis since he was a child in Murshidabad. Here, the birds were a good omen.

Occasionally men from the neighbouring farms would call in, first to make their acquaintance with the newcomers, and then to offer laconic pieces of advice along with pessimistic forecasts for the future, and stories about floods, droughts and plagues in the past. There were also half-admiring stories of the 'Lady Bushranger' Mrs Elizabeth Jessie Hickman's latest exploits: how she had tricked the Rylstone police and made off just a few months before with some prime bullocks from a property five miles away. Jessie Hickman was notorious as the leader of a cattle-rustling gang in the area. In 1928 it was reported in the local paper, the *Mudgee Guardian*, that the police had caught up with her 'dressed in men's clothes' in a paddock in Glen Alice, whereupon she became 'obstreperous, struggled and kicked, and tried to hit Constable Smith with a pitchfork'.

One grazier in the area was a Mr Saville who had a small son called Norman, a coincidence of names that amused them all. Like Myalla, most of the surrounding farms had aboriginal names, such as Umbiella and Warrangee, but nobody knew what the names meant and there were now no aborigines who could enlighten them, since almost all the indigenous people had been killed or driven out of the area during the previous century. Some of the advice that the Mostyns received was helpful, but it also made Norman and Savile feel that their year spent at the experimental farm had not been particularly useful. Perhaps they had been unwise to leave with only half the course completed.

As the summer approached, the grass began to brown and the water in the dam shrank to a muddy puddle. The fields shimmered in the heat, and the animals crowded under the trees in the paddocks. On Christmas Day it was over 90 degrees Fahrenheit in the shade. One of their neighbours invited them to come for Christmas dinner, but it was not easy to enjoy the roast chicken and steaming pudding in the sweltering dining room, whose windows had been closed to keep out the flies that swarmed around people and food. For Norman and Savile, the occasion must have been a stark contrast to their last Christmas in Dolgellau two years before, when they welcomed the open fire in the library as they all sat round it to open their presents.

Just before Christmas Elsie had sent a telegram to let them know that she and Myriam had their tickets, and would be leaving England at the end of January. Norman was becoming increasingly apprehensive about how Elsie would react to their new world, but there was no going back.

CHAPTER 13

Divided Families

1927–1941

On 28 January 1927 Elsie, now forty-four, and Myriam, fourteen, travelled from London to Liverpool to board the SS *Ceramic*, one of the largest and most comfortable of the passenger liners that sailed from London to Australia. Unlike Norman and Savile, they travelled first class and had separate cabins. Following the sale of Pen-y-Coed and most of its contents, Elsie had arranged for her seventy-eight-year-old mother, Eliza Algar, to be cared for in a nursing home in Dolgellau, where she stayed until her death the following year.

Among the possessions Elsie could not bear to leave behind were the family's two English collie dogs, Arran and Yarrow. She also packed some of Helen's clothes and jewels and Nusrat's court dress and sword. Numerous trunks contained Elsie's books, papers and manuscripts, as well as clothes for herself and Myriam. Elsie also organised the shipping of her most cherished glassware and china and some elegant furniture with which the journalist Charles Dawbarn, her former admirer, had equipped the flat he had provided for her in London before his death in 1925.

Two months before her departure, Elsie had written to Vilhjalmur Stefansson telling him that 'the Prince', as she always called her husband when corresponding with others, and Savile had bought 'a sheep farm in New South Wales 80 miles from anywhere – and need a Cook – General– me!!'[1] She enclosed copies of three of her adult 'Arctic stories' and said she would send separately her recently published children's book, *Lost in the Arctic*, which had a preface recommending to her readers

1 EAM Letter to VS, 22 November 1926.

all of Stefansson's published works. She had taken only ten days to write it, Elsie told him. 'That does not necessarily mean bad work,' she added. 'I write best when pressed.'

Stefansson's reply suggests a shrewd appraisal of her character:

> I am sorry about your going to Australia only so far as you may be sorry that you have to go. I liked the country very much when I was there three years ago, but am by no means certain that you will like it as well. Certainly you will have to show a good deal of adaptability and a broad willingness to believe that things very different from England or continental Europe may nevertheless be fitting in another environment and pleasant enough when you get acclimated to the manners of the people and the behavior of the weather.[1]

On board the *Ceramic*, Elsie, now officially Elizabeth Mostyn according to her passport, took to her cabin and remained there for almost the entire voyage. Myriam exercised the dogs on the deck each day that the weather permitted, but did not venture off the ship on her own at Cape Town, where many of the passengers disembarked, nor at Colombo. As they neared the equator, the two long-haired English collie dogs lay panting in the scant shade. Not for the first time, Myriam wondered how they would all adjust to Australia's climate and way of life.

Savile met them with the car when the ship docked at Sydney on 17 March. Norman had stayed at Myalla, as the car would have been quite full enough with Elsie, Myriam, Savile and the luggage. The temperature was over 100 degrees Fahrenheit that day, setting a new record for March temperatures in Sydney. Driving up George Street from the overseas quay, they were held up at a crossing, and sat sweltering as hundreds of Catholic school children marched past for the St Patrick's Day Parade. Eventually they reached the hotel where they were to spend the night and cool off a little, beneath the overhead fan.

Arrangements were made to have their furniture and belongings transported to Glen Alice, and the dogs placed in quarantine. The next

1 Letter from VS to EAM, 20 December 1926.

day Savile, Elsie and Myriam drove the car, loaded with their cases, out of Sydney and up into the mountains. All the windows were open to let in the air, but still the heat and the sharply curving road made Myriam quite queasy. She welcomed the frequent stops to allow the water in the car's radiator to cool down, and another to repair a puncture. The road was flanked by forests with tree trunks blackened by bushfires: steep ravines below, endless mountains beyond. It was a long, dusty and tiring journey. At last they reached Myalla, where Norman waited apprehensively.

Many years later, Myriam described that first day of their arrival at their new home. As they drove, Savile had described proudly all the improvements they had made to the house, and perhaps had led them to expect something a little grander than the shabby, three-bedroom bungalow that was to be their new home. Savile and Norman had now lived in Bathurst and Glen Alice for nearly two years and had grown accustomed to Australian homesteads of which Myalla was a slightly superior example. Elsie was dismayed at the contrast between Myalla, squatting amid brown, parched fields in the unrelenting heat, and Pen-y-Coed with its great sweeping staircase, its large rooms and bay windows looking out over green hills and forests. The life of a heroic pioneer in a slab hut – or an igloo – might have appealed to her imagination, but this, this house, she considered 'a sardine tin', entirely lacking in aesthetic appeal or romantic possibility. She made her feelings known.

Nevertheless, it was here that husband and wife were now reunited after twenty-two months, the time that they had agreed was needed for Savile to gain independence from his mother, and here they would stay for the foreseeable future. Their ties with England had been cut, and all their money was invested in the farm; they would have to make the best of it. Australia seemed indeed to have been the right choice for Savile, who had noticeably become a much happier and confident young man.

Both Elsie and Nusrat (for Elsie he was never Norman) had looked forward to new challenges, new experiences. For Nusrat especially, this move offered hope, perhaps his last hope, of escaping what he had found to be a hollow and restrictive status as a prince and an Indian in England. In Australia, as an ordinary man among ordinary people, he wanted to find a career and identity that had substance and which he could feel was worthwhile. As Norman Mostyn, grazier, he envisaged a new start to his family life too. In recent years, money problems, Elsie's obsession with Stefansson and her anguish over both Savile's education and Nusrat's reluctance to live up to the princely role she wished he would assume, had all created serious fissures in their relationship. In Australia, where these old problems would be eclipsed by new challenges, perhaps their marriage would find a new beginning too.

With so much weighing on it, it was unsurprising that Elsie and Norman's first night together at Myalla was a disaster. Her voice mimicking Elsie's, Myriam remembered how she and Savile were woken up that night by their mother storming out of their parents' bedroom declaring loudly and dramatically 'He's im-po-tent, he's impotent!' The dismay and confusion that fourteen-year-old Myriam felt at the time still haunted her half a century later.

Six months after arriving at Myalla, Elsie wrote to Stefansson from Australia for the first time. 'As far as the children are concerned,' she declared, 'this experiment is a complete success.' Savile had become confident and competent, and Myriam, at boarding school in Melbourne, 'threatens to be rather clever'. But, she continued,

> The whole thing has disagreed with the Prince vehemently. I imagine the change of environment and habit in his time of life (50) was too much for him. When I arrived things were just as bad as they could be and the man was absolutely intolerable. He is a little better, but very far from his old self. Very nervy and difficult to do with.[1]

Her letter went on to describe how isolated they were twenty-five miles from the nearest township, Rylstone, and how their farm was one among just four others in the huge valley. 'You are entirely right as to my reaction to this environment,' she continued. 'I love the solitude; the great blue space; the silence. The delight of sunset and sunrise and the night skies.' However, she complained that her neighbours were

1 EAM to VS, 8 November 1927.

obnoxiously 'mid-Victorian in their ideas and outlook', and that there was no one she could talk to. It was true that people living in rural areas in Australia were often socially conservative, and they had little access to or interest in the books and ideas that Elsie had encountered in Paris and London. On the other hand, many Australians were politically far from 'Victorian', and took pride in being part of a society that boasted (not always accurately) that it had left behind class and birth as criteria of worth.

For Elsie, Australia and the farm had become a place to retreat to rather than explore. Norman and Savile went out riding almost every day, across their farm or up into the mountains. Myriam joined her father and brother on their outings during the school holidays. But, eight months after her arrival, Elsie told Stefansson that she had 'no time to go out', and had 'only once, so far, ridden out to look at the property and rode a quarter of the boundary'.

In the room Norman had built for her, Elsie sat writing day after day. She would rise at dawn, to the sound of magpies warbling and currawongs calling, prepare the meals, do the housework (for the first time in her life she had no domestic servants), and then sit down at her desk, with her books and files arranged around her. Her filing cabinet was constructed of four-gallon kerosene tins cut in half and stacked one on top of the other. She continued to write stories set in the Arctic, a world far removed from Myalla, or Pen-y-Coed, or Somerset or Kent, in every imaginable way. That challenge to the imagination was what most engaged her. Elsie's research for these Arctic stories was meticulous, and was carefully anchored in the details drawn from Stefansson's books, since she had no recourse to libraries or other archives. Her albums reveal page after page of carefully drawn Inuit faces and notes about seal-fishing, igloo-making, the habits of polar bears and caribou, Inuit traditions and beliefs. Her concern for accuracy when it came to writing about the Arctic regions contrasts markedly with her colourful accounts of her own family life and history, which frequently had little basis in reality.

In the six months between May and October 1927, Elsie wrote nine 'Arctic' stories commissioned by major journals in England, for which she was paid an average of £40 apiece, the equivalent today of about £2,400. She hoped Stefansson might help her place her work in even more lucrative American journals, but she seems not have been successful in obtaining his assistance or finding American publishers. Australian journals and newspapers, however, did republish some of her essays and stories, although she never appeared in Australia's most well-regarded and politically progressive magazine of the time, *The Bulletin*. Her next letter to Stefansson, dated 25 February 1928 and written after a long, dry, summer, describes what she misses: the flowers, the familiar birds, the sound of running water. She is glad the days are short and that she is immersed in writing since 'there is not even much time for tears'. Her 'very unhappy childhood and disastrous marriage', as she now regarded it, had made her hope she may not live long, but, she added, perhaps remembering the pain caused by her sister Helen's death, 'I do not think one is ever justified in killing oneself.'[1] Less than twelve months after her arrival in Australia, Elsie had given up all hope of rescuing her marriage.

Elsie's earnings became increasingly important during the next few years when Australia was one of the many countries affected by the reverberations of the Wall Street Crash in 1929. For a while her fees and Norman's pension, both paid in sterling, held their value better than the Australian pound. The drop in demand for Australian wool and the subsequent fall in prices made it almost impossible for their sheep farm to make a profit. Moreover 1929 and 1930 were exceptionally dry years. Even though most of the kurrajong trees on the property were severely lopped to provide fodder for the sheep, many of the animals died, while those that survived were in poor condition and produced low-quality wool. Since the windmill that pumped water from the borehole was not working properly and the dams had dried, water had to be hauled from the river in a water cart drawn by their four draught horses to troughs from which the animals drank.

As the effects of the depression and drought spread, unemployment rose to over 30 per cent. Urban workers and ruined farmers wandered the country seeking a living doing odd jobs on the land and working as

1 EAM to VS, 25 February 1928.

rabbiters. Rabbits, brought to Australia with the First Fleet to provide food, and then in 1859 released into the wild by English settlers so that they could enjoy hunting them, had become a big problem for Australian farmers, destroying their crops and causing erosion. It was reckoned that sixteen rabbits could consume the food needed for one sheep. Moreover, their holes were a danger for horses and their riders. In the late 1920s it was estimated that there were about 10 billion rabbits in Australia, mostly in the regions where they could find grass. In addition to fining farmers who failed to clear their properties of rabbits, the Australian government had begun to offer bounties for dead rabbits, whose skins and carcasses could also be sold. Thus trapping and killing rabbits had become a means of livelihood for thousands of people. A skilled rabbiter could earn more than £2 a day (equivalent to £80 now) just for selling rabbit skins.

One of the people who came to the Glen Alice district in 1929 offering to get rid of the rabbits was a thirty-five-year-old Scotsman named Ian Troup. After experiencing the worst of the First World War fighting in France, where he had lost many of his comrades in the Gordon Highland Regiment, he had taken a job as a butcher for The Dairy Farm Company in Hong Kong, and then emigrated to Australia in 1921. He worked on a sheep station in New South Wales and afterwards as a stockman and boundary rider on various Queensland stations. Following the extensive flooding that overwhelmed parts of Queensland in early 1927, he took a job dealing with cattle in the Solomon Islands. There he was one of twenty-nine Europeans recruited by the Australian and British governments as military policemen to help put down a Kwaio warriors' uprising on the island of Malaita. The punitive expedition shot at least sixty Kwaio dead. The leader of the rebellion, Basiana, was tried and executed and another thirty or forty of the Kwaio warriors were imprisoned, later dying of diseases in jail.

Although Ian Troup's stay in Malaita lasted only a few months, it was long enough for him to be infected by blackwater fever and malaria, from which he suffered for the rest of his life. On his return to Australia in late 1927, he spent time and all his money seeking treatment in Sydney, and then, between bouts of malaria, earned his living travelling from place to place in New South Wales working as a rabbiter and general farm hand. Within a few months of his beginning work as a rabbiter on Myalla, Troup was hired as a stockman and given accommodation in a small hut a few hundred yards from the homestead. His previous experience working on the land proved timely. Neither Norman or Savile had acquired the familiarity with Australian conditions, seasons and climate that would allow them to grasp intuitively the essential tasks needed to set the property in order, and foresee the problems that lurked ahead. Ian Troup's knowledge was what they needed, and. he became virtual manager of the farm.

Savile, now nineteen, was beginning to find life on the isolated farm less appealing. There was little company other than his increasingly irritable parents. Soon after Ian Troup had become involved with the management of the property he decided, with his parents' encouragement, to go to Sydney and study for a science degree. Like his father and uncle at Oxford, he thoroughly enjoyed his freshman year at university, disregarding anything that might interrupt his social life, such as lectures and revision for examinations. Moreover, since he had left school at the age of fourteen, he would have had a great deal of catching up to do in order to reach first-year university level. Elsie believed he was naturally brilliant and capable of achieving anything he wished for. Whatever Savile wished for, he did not pass either his matriculation or his first-year examinations. He did succeed, however, in injuring himself in a motorcycle accident, and he returned home to recover.

Meanwhile, following a bad attack of malaria, Ian Troup had, at Elsie's insistence, moved from his small hut to the main homestead on Myalla. She looked after him during his illness, and she listened with fascination to his accounts of his experiences in Australia. Now Elsie had begun to write teenage fiction, set in the Capertee Valley. *Two in the Bush* (1929) follows the journey of a brother and sister by ship, along with their two dogs, Arran and Yarrow (to whom the book is dedicated), to Australia via Cape Town, to stay with their uncle in Glen Alice. There they learn to ride the boundaries, deal with snakebites and bushfires, help cart water to the dams, and work with sheep shearers. It is all described as a great adventure, with delight in the newness and informality of Australia and friendliness of Australians, and enthusiasm for their pioneering spirit. Published in London by Cassell and illustrated by the Cornish artist John de Walton, the novel sought to attract young British readers, and it conveys a response to Australia that is very different from the forlorn letters Elsie was writing to Stefansson. Like Elsie's other novels for children, *Two in the Bush* seems not to have been published or reviewed in Australia.

In October 1929, Elsie published *Two Men's Tale*, her only novel intended for adult readers. Written for a British audience, the book is narrated by two different men, and despite the melodramatic plot successfully ventriloquises male voices and attitudes. One of the novels that Elsie had brought with her to Australia was Joseph Conrad's *Typhoon*, and in the descriptions of storms at sea and life on board you can find Conrad's influence in *Two Men's Tale*. It is mainly set in the Arctic, with detailed descriptions of the Arctic landscape, travel with dog sleds, hunting and 'Eskimo' customs, and with frequent reference by both narrators to Stefansson's writings. However, the final section is set in the 'Hapertee Valley', a very thinly disguised Capertee Valley, and 'Silent Glen', where one of the protagonists works as a rabbiter after travelling to Australia in a Japanese ship, as Ian Troup had done. *Two Men's Tale* thus achieves the unlikely combination of Troup's experiences with those of Vilhjalmur Stefansson. In Britain the novel received mixed reviews; the *Aberdeen Press and Journal* admired the 'graphic descriptions of the desolate wastes of the Arctic and the vast spaces of Australia', but thought the plot was 'marred by exaggeration'. The *Nelson Leader* newspaper praised the device of using two male narrators, the good characterisation and the descriptions of adventure in varied locations.

By the end of 1929 it had become plain to Norman and also to Myriam that Elsie and Ian Troup were lovers. When Norman remonstrated, Elsie made it clear that she would not give up her relationship with Ian. To Myriam she declared that she only wished to save her daughter 'from a fate worse than death; if he didn't have me, he would have you'.[1] Seventeen-year-old Myriam did not at that time question this

1 *Myriam Innes, Family History*, p.4.

explanation. By early 1930, Norman had departed to live in a small flat in the Sydney seaside suburb of Manly. Apart from brief visits to Glen Alice, he would remain in Sydney for the rest of his life, existing on an income of less than £250 a year, the equivalent of £10,000 today, leaving Elsie the remaining £1,000 of his annual pension for her own expenses and those of the farm.

Norman's flat in Manly was on the seafront, facing out to Sydney harbour. From his balcony he could watch the ferries crossing the harbour to the north shore, and in the summer crowds of people disembarking to swim and sunbathe on the fine sandy beach. To Myriam he commented sardonically on the contradiction between the sunbathers' adherence to the 'White Australia' policy and their eagerness to turn brown in the sun.

Myriam had begun an arts degree at Sydney University, studying English, Latin, and oriental history covering the history and culture of Japan, China and India. On weekends, Myriam frequently stayed with her father, taking the tram from the Women's College to Circular Quay, where she boarded the Manly ferry. With its long esplanade and wooded hills Manly's seaside resort may have evoked memories of Weston-super-Mare and a time, just over a decade ago, when the family lived happily together.

But Sydney was very different place from the rural idyll of Norton Beauchamp. The city's population continued to grow rapidly, bringing Italian and Greek immigrants as well as increasing numbers of Scots, Irish and English. In June 1930, the city's population was one-and-a-quarter million, a 25 per cent increase since 1925. New redbrick bungalows crowded the headlands that protected the harbour. Following a noisy election, the socialist Labour leader Jack Lang became Premier for New South Wales, and embarked on a programme of construction to give work to the large numbers of unemployed. As Myriam crossed the harbour on the Manly ferry she could see the arches of the new Sydney Harbour Bridge reaching closer and closer to one another. The underground train system was extended and new stations built in the expanding city centre.

Compared with Glen Alice and Rylstone, the cultural offerings in

Sydney were abundant. By March 1930, when she began her studies at Sydney University, Myriam could join her father in watching a film of *The Taming of the Shrew*, or go to hear pianist Isador Goodman play Liszt at the Conservatorium, or visit the Art Gallery to see an exhibition of Margaret Preston's paintings of Australian flowers and trees. In the summer months they could sit on the balcony of Norman's flat in the evening, watching the lights on the yachts rocking in the harbour, and talk about oriental history and culture. In the winter they could listen in the evening to the wireless as it relayed commentary on the test cricket series in England, where a young batsman named Donald Bradman was scoring century after century. Perhaps Norman shared memories with Myriam of his school and university days, when he and his brother had been star cricketers.

Meanwhile, Savile had fallen in love with Eileen Stevenson, whose parents owned a property in the Capertee Valley not far from Glen Alice. They were married on 3 November 1931 with Elsie and Ian Troup as witnesses. Norman was not present. Wishing to allocate Myalla to Savile and his bride, Elsie planned and supervised the construction of a more elegant house, situated in a corner of the property on a slope at the foot of the mountains. It had wide verandas, a central sitting and dining room with leaded French windows and dark-wood panelling, a large tiled kitchen, and well-ventilated bedrooms. When the young girl narrator of *Two in the Bush* describes her aunt Eileen's home (Eileen being named after Savile's wife), she gives an exact plan of Elsie's house:

> [It] was a six-roomed bungalow, with wide verandas all round, and a sort of covered-in veranda running through the house and open at the ends; so that the whole house seemed somehow in the open air; because all the rooms gave on to this inside veranda, and if you kept your room door open you could see the trees and mountains through the open door and the ends of the veranda as well as through your window.[1]

Elsie moved to her new house, named, together with her own half of

1 *Two in the Bush by Elizabeth Marc* (London: Cassells, 1929), p.99.

Ian Troup, Tyar, 1934

the property, Tyar. Savile and Eileen now lived in the Myalla homestead, while Ian Troup managed both halves of the property, and began to make it pay. Elsie set out to make Eileen in her view a fitting wife for her son, seeking to 'improve' Eileen's accent, 'educate' her, and make her aware of what Elsie deemed the rules of social etiquette. In short, Elsie wished to encourage Eileen to become more English and less Australian. She believed this could be best achieved by removing Eileen from the influence of her own rural Australian family, whom Elsie regarded as socially inferior. Indeed, this separation of Eileen from her own family was so unrelenting that, according to Eileen's daughter, Beth, Eileen's mother was refused, on Elsie's instructions, access to see her daughter and granddaughter when they were in hospital following the baby's birth.

During the long university holidays and after the completion of her degree, Myriam worked as a farm hand alongside Ian on the properties. Elsie also encouraged her to seek help from Ian during the summer of 1932–3 when she had to re-sit and revise for her third year Latin exam. Ian had benefited from a good Scottish education at the local school in Aboyne. A romance between Ian and Myriam developed. On 18

September 1934 they were married in the local register office. Neither Elsie nor any other family members were present. Ian was then forty, and Myriam twenty-two.

During these years, relationships in the Mostyn family had become increasingly difficult and complicated. Following the birth of his daughter, Beth, in 1932 and son, Barrie, in 1934, Savile formed a liaison with their nanny, Rene Dougherty, and deserted his family. Elsie offered Tyar to Ian and Myriam, and went to live with Eileen and the two little children in the Myalla homestead. She offered to let Ian and Myriam own the Tyar half of the property, as long as Ian would also manage the rest of the property, keeping half of the profits and allotting the remainder of the profits to Savile.

Eileen and Savile's children, and especially Elsie's first grandchild, Beth, enjoyed the attention Elsie lavished on them, reading to them, telling stories, giving them pets and a little goat cart of their own, helping them with lessons sent weekly from the correspondence school in Sydney. During this period Elsie wrote her last and perhaps her best novel for teenagers, *Bush Ragamuffins,* published in London and dedicated to Elizabeth Ann Mostyn (Beth), 'the Littlest Bush Ragamuffin' and Garry, 'a Golden Collie Sheep-dog'. Like her other fiction, this novel served up an excitingly dissimilar world for British readers, a world full of adventure and possibility, where children and adults could find new strengths and experiences. For Eileen, however, deserted by her husband and confined first to Myalla and then to a small cottage nearby on the property, life was lonely and unbearably restrictive.

In 1941 Savile visited and there was an angry confrontation. Eileen, together with the children, secretly took the mail car to Rylstone to see a solicitor, before seeking refuge with her sister Mavis, who lived on a property near the small village of Geurie in central-western New South Wales. In 1945 they moved about forty miles further west to Narromine, where Eileen had taken a job caring for the two young children of Quentin Shepherd, a farmer whose wife had just died. Quentin visited the children at weekends. Eileen and Quentin were married in 1947. Neither Savile nor Elsie ever saw Eileen or the children again.

Savile married Rene Dougherty in 1960. They lived in Sydney and later moved to The Rock, a small town near Wagga Wagga in southern New South Wales, and had no children. Savile died of cancer in Wagga Hospital in 1977. Rene died in 1995.

Meanwhile Norman had also formed a relationship with a young Welsh woman, named Hilda Shoppee, eleven years his junior. Details about Hilda have been difficult to trace, since she was rarely mentioned in my family and few records exist beyond birth, death and marriage certificates, and some census records. What we can ascertain is that she had married Flight Lieutenant Lionel Shoppee in north Yorkshire in 1917. Following the death of their second child, Joan, aged five, in 1926, the couple emigrated to Australia. By coincidence they embarked on their voyage on 17 March 1927, the day Elsie and Myriam arrived in Sydney. In 1932 Hilda sued Lionel for divorce on the grounds of desertion, and was making her living by taking work as a housemaid. Both Hilda and her ex-husband claimed descent from French families even more elevated than Elsie's supposed ancestors, Horatio Nelson and William Penn; Lionel was said to be the direct descendant of Charlemagne via Hugh Capet, the first King of the Franks, while Hilda claimed descent from Napoleon Bonaparte. There is no clear evidence of either ancestral claim, but nonetheless the lineage was reported as part of their wedding announcement.

Whether Hilda was aware of Norman's aristocratic ancestry is unknown. Doubtless knowledge of that ancestry would for her have added to his attractions, but mainly one might see Norman and Hilda as two lonely people, suffering the humiliation and hurt of rejection by their spouses. They shared a love of golf and probably met at the Manly Golf Club, which had included women members almost since its foundation in 1903. Both of them had hoped that emigration to Australia might revive a troubled marriage, and both had been mistaken in that hope. In 1935 they moved from Manly to a small house further up Sydney's north shore, in Narrabeen. Here the house faced out to the great expanse of the Pacific Ocean, and the sound of water gently lapping in Manly harbour was replaced by the unceasing rush of the surf churning up and retreating from the wide, sandy beach. Norman and Hilda lived together here for the remainder of the 1930s, visited occasionally by Myriam and

Savile. After all the fret and upheaval of his earlier life, from England to India, and back to London, then to Jamaica, Paris, Somerset, Wales and, hardest of all, Glen Alice; after the impossibility of reconciling Elsie's dreams of how they should live up to his princely status with the facts of his limited income, his pleasure in a close family life, his desire to do something worthwhile; after all the conflict and worry, perhaps Norman found relief settling into quiet anonymity with Hilda, who provided comradeship and made few demands.

By the end of the decade, Elsie was living on her own in Tyar, although she remained in communication with Norman and with Savile and Myriam. She had sold half of the property, including the Myalla homestead, and given the money to Savile. With the help of an old farm hand named Herb Turner, she was managing the remaining 900 acres, which contained a few sheep and cattle. After numerous broken promises, misunderstandings and recriminations – Elsie having offered them Tyar and half the farm and then changed her mind – Myriam and Ian had moved away and bought their own sheep farm on a remote mountain top, Nulla Mountain, about fifty miles away. They were now the parents of two children. Ian named the farm Rhu-na-Mohr (Gaelic for on the bend of the hill), and planted gorse on the hillside and birch trees in the garden. Elsie persisted in writing the address as 'Rue no More' in her letters to Myriam (Ian often referred to Tyar as 'Rue some More'). Wishing, like Nusrat, to break with his past and make a new start in life, Ian had changed his name from Ian Troup to Ian Innes. Believing Elsie's version of events – that is, that Myriam had betrayed and then deserted her – Norman stopped communicating with Myriam, to her great distress.

After the end of the Second World War, Myriam and Ian sought to mend their relationship with Elsie, beginning with brief visits to Tyar at Easter and Christmas. Nevertheless, Elsie's letters to Vilhjalmur Stefansson showed that she was often desperately unhappy in later life, feeling unloved and deserted. She wrote in 1947 that she was entirely alone, owing to Savile's divorce and Ian Innes's 'spitefulness', and owing to the violent prejudice against 'pommies'. She was trying to manage the estate on her own, while her neighbours, she claimed, deliberately

Elsie in her home at Tyar, 1936

left gates open, refused to help, and caused trouble. She did not ever seem to realise that the antagonism was towards attitudes of class superiority rather than English birth *per se*. Again, in 1955, she wrote that her happiness had been ruined by 'her son's and daughter's acquisitions', leaving her 'almost incredibly alone'. She failed to mention that at this time, following Ian's death four years previously, Myriam and her two youngest grandchildren children were living with her.

None of these family troubles were allowed to surface in Elsie's public life. In an interview Elsie gave to the Australian magazine *Woman* in June 1936, she appeared in a three-page spread, featuring her 'dream home', marriage to 'her Persian prince', and memories of listening to her father's tales of 'sea adventures'. An advertisement for the interview is headed 'In her Bush Castle', and the introduction reads:

> 'Elizabeth Marc' famous to *Woman* readers for her Arctic stories is also the Princess Nusrat Ali Mirza by marriage and plain Mrs Mostyn to her neighbours. In this interview with her at her home at Myalla, Glen Alice, near Rylstone, N.S.W., she is revealed as a

> woman who has turned comparative failure into success because she did not know the meaning of the word 'can't'.[1]

In 1940 Norman was diagnosed with cancer. Hilda cared for him until Elsie discovered he was ill and began to make frequent visits. He died in Sydney's Prince Alfred Hospital on 13 January 1941, with Elsie by his side; in accordance with Muslim practice he was buried the next day. An ocean and more apart, Syed also died in 1941.

Norman's will, written in 1938, left the few jewels he had taken with him to Sydney to his granddaughters, Elizabeth Mostyn and Evelyn Innes. Everything else was left to Elsie, but in truth that was very little, for there were only a few items of basic furniture, some books, a cigarette case, and several pairs of cufflinks listed in the final inventory, with a total value estimated as eighty pounds and seventeen shillings. In falsely proclaiming a close relationship to the Shah of Persia, the notice of his death, placed by his wife and son, managed at the same time to both reveal and falsify his identity. Even after he died Norman/Nusrat was compelled to take on a fictional, inflated persona. The newspaper announcement read:

> IRAN SHAH'S COUSIN DIES IN SYDNEY
>
> SYDNEY. THURSDAY. – Prince Nusrat Ali Mirza, 63, cousin of the former Shah Ahmed of Persia (Iran) died in Royal Prince Alfred Hospital on Monday. He had lived incognito in New South Wales for 15 years as Norman Allen [sic] Mostyn.
>
> The prince, who was educated at Harrow and Oxford, married Elizabeth Marc, an English journalist. His father ruled a large hereditary principality in India, until the property was cut up during the late Prince's youth.

1 *The Sun* (Sydney, NSW), 25 June 1936, p.16.

Now, of the Nawab and Sarah's six children, only Vaheedoonissa survived. She would live another forty-seven years to witness perhaps the most tumultuous and tragic period in the Indian subcontinent's history. During the Second World War Bengal became the frontline against feared invasion by Japanese forces via Burma, and thousands of British and American troops were stationed in Calcutta. Many more thousands of Bengali troops joined British forces fighting in Europe, North Africa and South East Asia. In those years also Bengal suffered another devastating famine when up to 3 million people died of starvation at a time when the British War Cabinet was diverting rice stocks to supply its armies elsewhere.

The end of the war brought irresistible pressure for Indian independence from Indian nationalists. But by this time the two main independence organisations, the Indian National Congress and the Muslim League, envisaged different futures. Fearing discrimination against Muslims by the Hindu majority, the leader of the Muslim League, Muhammad Ali Jinnah, sought a separate homeland for Muslims, despite the belief of Mahatma Gandhi and Jawaharlal Nehru, India's most prominent nationalist activists, that Hindus, Sikhs and Muslims could live together on equal terms in a united India. Britain accepted Jinnah's claim for the desirability of a separate nation. So in 1947 a civil servant named Cyril Radcliffe was assigned the task of drawing a line through Bengal and Punjab, both of which had large Muslim as well as Hindi populations, to decide which sections of those provinces should be assigned to which country. There had been riots when Bengal was divided previously in 1905, but now the stakes were much higher and the reactions much more horrifying. Rumours spread fear and terror, leading to riots and massacres in which thousands of Muslims and Hindus were killed as the two groups attacked one another. Once Bengal had harboured different religious groups living more or less harmoniously with one another; and, like his ancestors, Vaheedonissa's nephew Nawab Wasif Ali Mirza had sought to maintain that harmony.

When the Radcliffe Line was first drawn, Murshidabad was placed in East Bengal, which would in August 1947 be renamed East Pakistan, and in 1971 become Bangladesh. On 15 August 1947, the day that India and Pakistan became independent self-governing countries, the flag of Pakistan was hoisted above the Hazarduari Palace. Two days later, Pakistan and India exchanged Khulna province, bordering on the Bay of Bengal, for the district of Murshidabad, and the flag of India flew above the Palace. Thus Vaheedoonissa and the Nawab Wasif Ali Mirza, founder of the Hindu-Muslim Unity Association ten years earlier in Bengal, were to remain citizens of India for the rest of their lives.

Many of Mansour Ali Khan's other descendants, however, chose to move to Pakistan. Among them was Vaheedoonissa's and Nusrat's great-nephew Iskander Mirza, a descendant of Mansour Ali Khan's with his first *nikah* wife, Shams-i-Jehan. Iskander Mirza was one of five Indians from royal families admitted to Sandhurst for training as Army officers, and became the first Indian to graduate from Sandhurst. He was assigned on graduation to command a Scottish battalion stationed in the North West Frontier, but the assignment at first was vetoed by those who found it unthinkable that an Indian should lead Europeans. After several months, however, the appointment was agreed, and thereafter Iskander Mirza rose rapidly from Second Lieutenant to Deputy Commissioner to Political Agent in various provinces in the Indian subcontinent. When the partition of the continent was announced he was appointed Joint Secretary for Defence, representing Pakistan's interests, and then became Secretary of Defence for newly created Pakistan. In September 1955 he was appointed Governor-General of Pakistan, and then, as a new constitution was enacted and Pakistan became a Republic, he was elected unanimously by the National Assembly first President of the new Republic in March 1956.

Despite the divisions, both within the family and the continent, Vaheedoonissa remained attached to her nephews and nieces great and small. She wrote to her brother's family in Australia with news of Iskander Mirza's achievements, and later, when he was ousted in a military coup in 1958 and forced into exile in London, she wrote in his defence. She also sent news of her nephew Wasif Ali Mirza's death in 1906, and the succession to the title of Nawab of Murshidabad by his eldest son, Waris Ali Mirza Khan Bahadur. Vaheedoonissa passed away aged ninety-three in Murshidabad in 1968 and was buried in the family cemetery near the grave of her grandmother, Rais-un Nisa Begum. With her died the only living person likely to have personal memories of Sarah Nawab Begum and Prince Mansour Ali Khan, the last Nawab Nazim of Bengal, Bihar and Orissa.

EPILOGUE

It Is Fitting That I Should Know Who I Really Am

The writing of this history began as an exploration of my own identity, an identity connected to an ancestry that seemed in my childhood at odds with being Australian. What mattered for me was discovering, in so far as I could, the truths, and the actual people, whose lives had preceded and resulted in mine. For my grandmother, it was an identity and status conferred by marriage that needed to be made definite; her ancestry could be reinvented to suit changing contexts.

In December 1941, Elsie wrote from Tyar to the Secretary of State for India thanking him for sending the money due to her and Savile following Nusrat's death. She also wished to know what her title should now be, and how she should be addressed if she 'again had the happiness and honour of attending another court function in England'. Would 'The Nawabzadi Elizabeth of Murshidabad' be appropriate? Or perhaps 'The Right Honourable Lady Elizabeth Mostyn'? The latter title, she thought, 'might be of some use in this country' (Australia).[1]

Responding briefly from a London enduring the Blitz, the aide-de-camp explained that no ruling or custom existed that could entitle her 'The Rt. Hon. Lady Elizabeth Mostyn'. As to the question of how she should be addressed if attending court, he remarked drily that 'the question of the style by which you be summoned to attend Court functions had better be left open until the occasion arises'.

Annoyed by this dismissive response, Elsie wrote back on 10 July 1942:

Although I sympathise with your desire to shelve these trivial

1 IOR/L/PS/6.

tiresome matters, especially at the present time, I must admit that your suggestion leaves me unhappy. It is true that 'Mrs Mostyn' does very well for this detestable country, but God forbid that I remain here for the rest of my days. And I think that in any case, whether I am here or in England or anywhere else, it is fitting that I should know who I really am. I think these mixed marriages most unfortunate and undesirable, but there it is. It is vitally important for me and my children that my position should not be equivocal and I must be so styled as to identify me with my proper position as the wife of the Nawabzada Nusrat Ali Mirza of Murshidabad, who was the son of H.H. the Nawaab Nazim of Bengal, Behar, and Orissa. I was presented at court as the Nawabzadi Ali Mirza of Murshidabad. Do you think the Nawabzadi Elizabeth of Murshidabad would do? I do not much want to be a Begum, and I won't be a Mrs.

So sorry to trouble you.

I am, sir,
Yours faithfully,
Elizabeth Mostyn[1]

There is no record of a response to this letter.

Elsie's demand to know 'who she really was' might perhaps be more accurately seen as a demand that others acknowledge who she would really like to be. If an English title as the 'Honourable Elizabeth Mostyn' cannot be agreed, then her title and status as the wife of an Indian aristocrat would be next best, even though she and Nusrat had previously decided that the Indian title was an obstacle for him and their children. Their disagreement about the importance of that title as an indicator of desired identity was probably the fault line that finally destroyed their marriage. For Nusrat the Nawabzada title, inviting British preconceptions about Indians, and about Indian princes, undermined the self he wished to be, a man who could measure his own worth

1 IOR/L/PS/6.

by what he made of his life – as an artist, a craftsman, a sportsman, a father, a farmer and a Muslim. An Englishman or a European could choose to be an aristocrat who also wrote, or painted, or farmed, or was even, as in Lord Henry Stanley's case, a Muslim; an Indian Prince was required to do no more than parade his status as a symbol of the jewel in the imperial crown. While Nusrat hoped to escape the confines of an identity imagined by others, Elsie clung to a series of identities she herself imagined and created to impress other people and herself.

Identities and names are also linked to place. In different modes, Jamaica, France and England had allowed Elsie to capitalise on the title of princess; in Australia's supposedly classless society, 'Mrs Mostyn does very well.' That Australia reduced her to a mere 'Mrs' was precisely what made the country 'detestable' for Elsie; that it allowed him to become a mere 'Mr' was what it made it seem desirable for Nusrat and his children. Neither Savile nor Myriam advertised their titled Indian ancestry. In Australia it was not an identity to be valued. Indeed Savile would in the 1950s change his name to Stan, a name that, despite his upper-class English accent, felt more appropriate in his career as a car salesman. Myriam and Savile found that they could be both English and Australian (though not Indian), and that among Australians they could at least blur the class boundaries that mattered so much to their mother.

Why did Elsie 'think these mixed marriages most unfortunate and undesirable'? Her claim that her husband was really Persian was no doubt made mainly for diplomatic reasons, to gain entry to Australia, but the strength and persistence of that claim suggests that she too regarded a Persian identity as grander and more desirable than an Indian one. Though it was a claim that might have been questioned in England, it could be asserted in Australia without much fear of contradiction. However, Nusrat's father at no point claimed Persian ancestry, although he was an admirer of Persian culture. For him, the status of Nawab of Bengal, Bihar and Orissa was of the highest order, and he devoted his life to regaining recognition of that status and all that it entailed in terms of wealth, rights and rituals for himself and his descendants. The British government ensured that this lifelong ambition was defeated.

Elsie did not 'much want to be a Begum'. Here she differed

completely from Nusrat's mother, Sarah, who fought for the right to be named Sarah Nawab Begum, a title which marked her identity as a respectable wife and then widow of a Muslim nobleman. For Elsie this was the kind of concern for respectability she associated with the Victorian values she found oppressive and hypocritical. Moreover she had never admired Sarah, and almost certainly deplored her family background and employment as a chambermaid. It was Elsie who misleadingly informed Myriam that Sarah had been a governess. In matters of class, Elsie's attitudes remained Victorian.

'God' did not 'forbid' that Elsie should remain in Australia for the rest of her days. She never left the country after her arrival in 1927.

In March 1964 Elsie was diagnosed with breast cancer. In her letter to her beloved granddaughter Evelyn, at that time a nurse in Henty near the Victorian border, she wrote that she did not fear death and wanted only that the doctors told her the truth. 'It is very sad when people die young – as did my sisters and Audrey,' she wrote. 'But when one has had a fair go and death is really a release from inconvenience, no one should grieve.' She believed that the soul continued in another realm: 'That is why I think *Character* is so important. *That* one takes with one.'

Elsie died that September in Rylstone's tiny hospital. In accordance with her will, her ashes were scattered over Tyar, where for good and ill she had by then lived for almost half her life.

*

The twenty-sixth of January 1991 marked my first visit to India, and my fifty-first birthday. Having checked in to my hotel in Delhi, I decided to celebrate this double event by ordering a cold beer, only to learn that no alcohol could be served that day because it was India Republic Day. That my birthday fell on both Australia Day and India Republic Day seemed wonderfully serendipitous, an endorsement of my own composite identity.

The television in my hotel room showed the commencement of the Republic Day parade and, since the hotel was not far from Connaught Square, where crowds were gathering to watch, I made my way there.

Dazed by jet lag, the crowds of people, the noise, the dust, I hesitated near a group of men, only to be hastily ushered by marshals towards the women and children seated on the ground. There was, I now realised, a clear gap of about three yards between the standing men and the seated women. A group of women smiled and beckoned to me to join them on the rug they had spread out; gratefully but less gracefully I sat with them, exchanging halting snatches of English conversation. The children looked at me curiously; one small girl approached and placed her brown arm against my pale pink one, and laughed at the strangeness of the contrast and her own daring. In an odd way that encounter seemed almost a mirror image of my first experience of colour prejudice in that school bus in Australia, but this time the child's discovery of colour difference brought fascination and delight.

Some years later I finally visited Murshidabad, together with my friend and colleague Professor Bala Kothandaraman. We hired a guide to show us the sights, ending with a visit to the Hazarduari Palace. There it was, the palace of a thousand doors, an imposing building similar in style to the National Gallery in London. We passed rooms full of guns and swords, a stuffed crocodile with gaping mouth, a cabinet displaying a plate that changed colour if the food on it was poisoned, the durbar hall with a silver throne and a huge chandelier gifted by Queen Victoria, a library filled with leather bound volumes by Aristotle, Gibbon and Scott. The library also displayed a magnificent thirteenth-century Qu'ran that had once belonged to the Caliph of Baghdad. And then we came to a gallery with a great row of ancestral portraits. Among them were two life-size portraits of my great-grandfather as a young man, one showing him standing regally in red robes, the other seated more casually and dressed in white silk. He looked remarkably handsome and elegant.

Bala, who was perhaps even more excited than I was about my Indian ancestry, told our guide about my relationship to the Nawabs of Bengal. A long discussion in Hindi ensued. 'I know your people!' the guide then exclaimed in English. 'Would you like to meet them?' I hesitated, not at all sure that 'my people' would welcome such a meeting, but Bala was determined that it should happen. And so the guide took us to the house of the '*chote nawab*' (the young nawab) Syed Reza Ali Meerza, who claimed direct descent from Mir Jafar. His resemblance to my mother was what first impressed me – although her skin was paler, I saw the same narrow face and high cheekbones, the same prominent nose and ears, even the same air of peering into the distance when speaking. I was made very welcome, invited into the house for tea, and shown photographs of other relatives. On parting, Bala asked him, 'So what is your relationship to Lyn?'

Syed Reza Ali Meerza took my hand. 'She is my sister,' he said.

The distance between myself and my Indian ancestors had suddenly narrowed. With a new sense of entitlement I returned to London to research the first chapter of their story, which would also become the story of my grandparents and parents, their journeys and mine.

MURSHIDABAD FAMILY TREE

MIR JAFIR
(1691–1765)

(then six more generations)

HUMAYUN JAH = Dhoolin Jah Begum (Rais-un-Naisa)
d.1838 d.1893

Shams-i-Jahan Begum = Julia Lewis = Shams-un-nisa Begum = Mehr Leka Begum (Hasina) = Hajiyya Begum = **SARAH VENNELL = MANSUR ALI KHAN**
d.1905 d. 1948 d.1892 d. 1858 d.1884 1852–1925 1830–1884

Syed Iskander b. 1846
[Amina, Musa, Shoaib, Hamid] b.1880–1884
Subah b.1856
[Hassan b.1846 Suleiman] b.1855
[Miriam 1871–1918 Sara b.1872 Hajira 1873–80 Vaheedoonissa 1874–1968 Syed Ali Mirza 1875–1941 **Nusrat Ali Mirza**] = **Elsie Algar**
1877–1941

[Syed Ali Mirza/Savile (Stan) Mostyn = Eileen Stevenson
1909–1973 1910–1999

Myriam Sarah Mirza/Mostyn] = Ian Troup/**Innes**
1912–2010 1894–1951

Elizabeth Barrie

Evelyn John **Lyn** David Sylvia Peter

ALGAR FAMILY TREE

Sarah Algar = Harry Barber

Harry Algar = Eliza Penn Campbell
(1843–1921) (1848–1928)

Alexander McFarlane = Evangeline (Eve)
(1860? –1920) (1870–1913)

Maynard
Audrey

Winifred Helen = W. Buttenshaw
(1877–1912) (1875–1907)

Elsie = Nusrat Ali Mirza
(1882–1964) (1877–1941)

Syed/Savile
Myriam

ACKNOWLEDGEMENTS

The ingredients for this book have taken many years to assemble and their assembly owes much to the generous assistance and encouragement of many people. More than thirty-five years ago, important genealogical details and references were provided by Morris Bierbrier, a distinguished genealogist and Egyptologist, who not only put me in touch with Julia Lewis's descendant, Keith Meerza, but also assisted my cousin, Humayun Mirza in the composition of his family history, *From Plassey to Pakistan: the Family History of Iskander Mirza, the First President of Pakistan.* Another genealogist, Anthony Adolph, recovered significant details and documents for my session with James Walvin on BBC Radio 4's 'Meet the Descendants' in July 2004. Rozina Visram's groundbreaking history, *Ayahs, Lascars and Princes*, provided a context and references, and Rozina has also steered me in the direction of the relevant India Office Files.

These details became the foundation which allowed me to check and select from the often confusing and inconsistent family history that had informed my childhood and continuing questions about my ancestry. But it was only after I had retired that I was able to set to work on the construction of this biography. In 2008 Professor Bala Kothandaraman accompanied me on a lecture tour of India, culminating in a visit to Murshidabad and my great-grandfather's palace. There I was able to see portraits of my ancestors and encounter the world of my grandfather and his siblings when they were children and about which my mother had relayed several evocative anecdotes. On a return visit in 2013, Shri Nayan Anand Chakraborty, the Superintending Archaelogist of the Hazarduari Palace Museum, kindly explained the history and significance of the building and its contents.

In Murshidabad I met cousins who were also descended from the Nawabs of Bengal and who welcomed me to their homes and showed me photographs and genealogical documents. One of the most rewarding aspects of my research has been the discovery or rediscovery of many of my cousins in Britain, Australia, India and the USA. My first cousins, Barrie Shepherd and Beth Reid, and Barrie's son Richard, have given me invaluable information, photographs, and have read and corrected sections of the book. Frances Ellison, descended from Elsie's sister Eve, has shared his grandfather Maynard's memoirs and other details about the family's life in Jamaica and Britain. Another of Eve's descendants, John Klein, kindly sent information about his grandmother Audrey's time as a student.

Almost a decade ago I was delighted to discover and meet a descendant of Sarah's brother George – Miriam Unsworth. She and her daughter-in-law, Helen Barton, had already researched details of the Vennell family, and gave me a wonderfully drawn family tree, along with other details and photographs.

A Leverhulme Emeritus Fellowship provided funding to trace records and sites where my grandparents had lived in Australia, Jamaica, Paris and Britain. In all those places I received generous time and assistance from librarians, historians and archivists. In Bathurst my most significant debt is to Dr Robin McLachlan, who not only gave me further information about the Experimental Farm, but also sent on to me copies of all the letters exchanged between Elsie and Vilhjalmur Stefansson, and read and corrected relevant sections of my draft manuscript. Without Robin's generous assistance, this book would have lacked crucial elements of my grandparents' story.

In Jamaica, Hyacinth Birch, curator of the Mico College Museum, found a portrait of my great-uncle, Alexander McFarlane, and kindly arranged a tour of the college. Mrs Winsome Hudson, at the National Library of Jamaica, gave me advice about sources of information for the first decade of the twentieth century in Jamaica, while Dr Michael Bucknor, Head of English at the University of the West Indies, as well as our driver, Steven Grant, introduced us to contemporary Jamaican food and culture. Roxanne Silent, at the National Gallery of Jamaica, managed to locate and send a photograph of my grandfather's painting of a Caribbean landscape. My thanks also to Alison Donnell and

Anthony Kelly, whose advice and emails provided helpful introductions.

In Paris, Florence Duchemin-Pelletier of the Institute of National Art History offered help and advice for my research on my grandparents' involvement in the Paris cultural scene. Archivists at the Musee d'Orsay directed me to records of exhibitions and artists in Paris during the years 1910–1914.

Tony Horry and Sue Ryall of the Weston-super-Mare Family History Society helped me find photographs and records of the relevant period and also took me to the Norton Beauchamp farmhouse where my grandparents lived and where the present owners kindly showed me around. In Dolgellau Madge and Nigel Hawkins, who had acquired Penycoed Hall and managed it as a guest house, provided great hospitality as well as records of the past, including the sales catalogue for 1926.

Helen Sumping, archivist for the Brasenose College Library, undertook several searches which, amazingly, produced my great-uncle Syed's photograph album and other details about him, all of which cast much new light on his character. Information from the King's College School archives was found for me by Sophie Bell and Diana Manipud, as well as John Klein.

Over the past decade the staff in the British Library's African and Asian Reading Room have cheerfully and expertly helped me find the relevant files and books for my research.

Many friends and colleagues have read, heard about, or listened to sections of this book at various stages in the process of its composition. They include Elleke Boehmer, Margaret Busby, Helen Carr, Arlyn Diamond, Thomas Docherty, Rod Edmond, Lucy Ellmann, Neelum Saran Gour, Abdulrazak Gurnah, Githa Hariharan, Aamer Hussain, Ruchir Joshi, Myra Joyce, Suvir Kaul, Bahriye Kemal, Mukul Kesavan, Donna Landry, Ole Laursen, Blake Morrison, Kaori Nagai, Denise DeCaires Narain, Susheila Nasta, Pramod Nayar, Mohan Rao, Ray Ryan, Bapsi Sidwha, Dennis Walder and Bill Watson. Their comments and encouragement kept me writing and rewriting. I am especially grateful to Clare Ungerson, Judith Hattaway, Janet Sayers, Jan Pahl and Sarah Carter, who formed a writing group with me so that we could discuss each other's work. Joining a *Guardian*/University of

East Anglia Masterclass on reading and writing biography allowed me to frequently rethink the nature of this biography, gave me a series of deadlines for completing sections, and provided a thoughtful and constructive group of readers. For their attentive and helpful comments I thank Liza Coutts, Diana Devlin, Carrie Dunne, Monique Goodliffe, Ted Powell, Jo Rogers, Barbara Selby, Ann Vinden, David Warren and Hephzi Yohannan. I am especially grateful to our tutor Jon Cook. His meticulous and thoughtful commentaries on almost every chapter and on the whole structure of the book, as well as his faith in the project, have been invaluable. Richard Holmes very kindly read some early chapters and gave me timely and supportive advice.

I owe a large debt to my editor at Saqi Books, Elizabeth Briggs, not only for her enthusiasm for the project but also for her careful and thoughtful reading and detailed suggestions for its improvement. Thanks for his meticulous corrections and queries to my copyeditor, Brian David.

My friends Rubina and Abdullah Iqbal have explained aspects of Islam and have tried hard to teach me to speak and read Urdu.

My greatest debt is to my immediate family, and this book is dedicated to them, their families and children. My mother's anecdotes first inspired my interest in exploring the story of her father and his parents. My brother John knew the Capertee Valley and Tyar and its history, and also first made contact with Robin McLachlan. John and Pat's daughter Kylie and her husband Jeff were able to give me further information about the area and locate the Myalla homestead. Sylvia and Peter, my youngest siblings, passed on contacts made while they researched our family history. My sister Evelyn and brother David have shared memories and confirmed dates. My daughters Robin and Rachel, and my grandchildren Melissa, Oliver, Elliot and Caitlin, have constantly reminded me of their desire to read the book sooner rather than later.

As well as reading and commenting on a draft of the book, my husband Martin Scofield has been my companion on research travels to India, Australia, Jamaica, Paris, Somerset and Wales. Seeing these places and worlds also through his eyes has widened my vision and inspired new questions.

GLOSSARY

Note: These definitions refer to usage in the nineteenth century; many will have a slightly different meaning and spelling now.

Angrezi: English, foreign.

bara: big, also older (as in older brother).

Begum: a lady, a woman of high rank, wife of a nobleman.

bivi: wife.

chhota/I: small, also younger, as in younger brother/sister.

deorhi: porch, foyer. Also used in nineteenth century to mean an adjoining room or house.

dhoolin (dulhan): a bride.

diwan: financial minister.

Eid-al-Fitr: occurs on the first day of Shawwal, the tenth lunar month in the Islamic Calendar and celebrates the end of Ramadan. The first Eid was celebrated in 624 CE by the Prophet Muhammad with his friends and family after the victory of the battle of Jang-e-Badar.

Eid-al-Adha: occurs two months and ten days after Eid-al Fitr and is one of the main days in the Hajj pilgrimage. It commemorates Abraham's obedience to God's command that he sacrifice his son Ismael, but an angel was sent to substitute a ram for Ismail. (n. The Quranic version of this story differs slightly from the Judaic and Christian versions, which name Isaac Abraham's younger son by Sarah, rather than Ismail, his older son by Hagar).

Hazarduari: a thousand (*hazar*) doors (*duari*).

Hijri: The Islamic Hijri calendar is a lunar calendar, with the years beginning in April 622 CE, when Muhammad and his followers migrated from Medina to Mecca.

Imambara (also spelled *imambarghar*): literally, a building for the Imam. Most of the mourning sessions held during Muharram to commemorate the death of Imam Hussain, the grandson of the Prophet Muhammad are held in the Imambara. The Imambara complex opposite the Hazarduari palace in Murshidabad was also designed to house pilgrims who came for the mourning festival.

lakh: one hundred thousand.

larka: boy.

larki: girl.

muharram: the first month of the Islamic year.

mutah: a wife with whom one has made a temporary rather than a permanent marriage contract.

Nawab (*navvab*): ruler, lord, monarch of a semi-autonomous princely state.

Nawabzada: son of a nawab.

Nawabzadi: daughter of a nawab, or wife of a *Nawabzada*, a princess.

nikah: marriage or marriage contract.

Nizam/ Nizamat: arrangement, government.

Ramadan (*ramzan*): ninth month of the Hijri calendar; fasting month.

rupee: official Indian currency, worth 16 annas, or 100 piasas. In 1840, one rupee was the equivalent of c. £0.40, which would today be worth c. £110.

Sahib: respectful title for a man; sir; mister.

Sahiba: respectful title for a woman; lady; Mrs.

Shia: one of the two main branches of Islam. Shias share the same basic beliefs as Sunnis, but differ from Sunnis in their view that Hussain, the grandson of the Prophet Mohammed was the hereditary leader and interpreter of Muhammed's teachings. Hussain was martyred in 680 CE.

Sunni: Sunnis represent the majority of followers of Islam (c. 85%) and believe that the Imam (or teacher of Islam) should be appointed or elected rather than inherited.

Zenana: women's apartments.

CREDITS

p57, The Nawab's Turban Jewel. Reproduced by kind permission of the V&A, London.

p59, 'Be Just and Fear Not' by Matt Morgan. The Nawab kneels with Britannia to petition Queen Victoria, his two sons standing behind him. Reproduced from *Tomahawk*, 16 April 1970.

p78, 'A Living Monument to Injustice', Vanity Fair (16 April 1870). Reproduced by kind permission of The National Portrait Gallery, London.

p95, Pymmes House, Edmonton, 1895. Home of the Nawab, 1875–1878. Reproduced by kind permission of The Francis Frith Collection.

p129, Syed Ali Mirza with members of the Phoenix Club, Oxford. From the collection at Brasenose College, Oxford.

p166, Studio Photograph of Elizabeth Marc by Bassano. Reproduced by kind permission of The National Portrait Gallery, London.

BIBLIOGRAPHY

Unpublished Documentary Sources

Brasenose College Minute Book, 1896
1871 Census, Knightsbridge, St George's Place
The British Library: Oriental and India Office Collections:
a) European Manuscripts:
MSS Eur: Private Letters from the Earl of Mayo to the Duke of Argyll, 1869.
MSS Eur: Supplementary Layard papers, Vol. I
b) India Office Records:
IOR/L/PS/6; IOR/ L/PS/ 6/565/169; IOR/L/PS/11/162/185; IOR/L/PS/13/180; IOR/L/PS/13/180/1809; IOR/L/PS/438, No.5
Ellison, Francis. 'Family History of the Ellison Family'
Innes, Myriam. 'Family History'
McFarlane, Maynard D. 'Family Record'. n.d.
Merton College Minute Book, 1898
Princess Nusrat Ali Mirza Letter to the Dean, King's College for Women, 31 January 1922, King's College Archive
Parish records, St Mary's Islington
Shepherd, Barrie. 'Family Record'
Stefansson, Vilhjalmur. Vilhjalmur Stefansson papers. Rauner Special Collections, Library Repository. Dartmouth College, Hanover, New Hampshire
Survey of London: Vol. 45, Knightsbridge. Originally published online by London County Council, London, 2000

Published Works

Ballhatchet, Kenneth, *Race, Sex, and Class under the Raj* (London: Weidenfeld & Nicolson, 1980)
Bell, Thomas Evans, *The Bengal Reversion: Another 'Exceptional Case'* (London: Trubner & co, 1872)
Bowie, Ian, McLachlan, Robin, et.al., *Celebrating 100 Harvests: a Centenary History of the Bathurst Agricultural Research Station, 1895–1995* (Bathurst, NSW: NSW Agriculture, 1995)
Bromley High School Magazine, No. 7 (May 1903)
'In Memoriam: Princess Nusrat Ali Mirza', *Bromley High School Magazine,* No. 69 (July 1965)
Cannadine, David, *Ornamentalism* (London: Allen Lane, 2001)
Chaudhury, Sushil, *Dawn*, 6 April 2016

Chesson, F.W., *The Princes of India, Their Rights and Duties* (London: W. Tweedie, 1872)

Collicott, Sylvia L, Connections: Harinhey loval-national-world links (haringey Community Information Services, 1986)

Crichton-Miller, Hugh, *The New Psychology and the Parent* (London: Jarrolds Publishers, 1923)

Dalrymple, William, *The Anarchy: The Relentless Rise of the East India Company* (London: Bloomsbury, 2019)

Das, Neta and Llewellyn-Jones, Rosie, eds., *Murshidabad: Forgotten Capital of Bengal* (Mumbai: Marg Foundation, 2013)

Dawbarn, Charles, *France and the French* (London: Methuen, 1911)

Dawbarn, Charles, *France at Bay* (London, Mills and Boon, 1915)

Dawbarn, Charles, 'The French Woman and the Vote', *Fortnightly Review* (August 1911)

De Lisser, Henry, *In Jamaica and Cuba* (Jamaica Times: Kingston, 1910)

de Waleffe, Maurice, *Quand Paris etait un Paradis* (Paris: Société des editions Denoël, 1947)

Official Catalogue of the Great Exhibition (London: Spicer Brothers, 1851)

Gupta, J.Datta. ed., *West Bengal Records: Murshidabad Nizamut,* Vol. II, 1834–1870

Gupta, J.Datta and Bose, Sanat Kumar, eds., Murshidabad Nizamut: letters issued

Hassan, Hafiz Ahmed, *Pilgrimage to the Caaba and Charing Cross, London* (William Allen 1871)

Higgs, Michelle, *Tracing Your Servant Ancestors* (Barnsley: Pen and Sword Family History, 2012)

Hyam, Ronald, *Empire and Sexuality: The British Experience* (Manchester: Manchester University Press, 1991)

London, H. *Non-white Immigration and the 'White Australia Policy'* (Sydney University Press, 1970)

Mackenzie, Helen, *Storms and Sunshine of a Soldier's Life,* Vol. II (Edinburgh: David Douglas, 1884)

Majumdar, P.C., *The Musnud of Murshidabad 1704–1904* (Murshidabad, 1905)

Mansour Ali Khan, *Memorial from His Highness the Nawab Nazim of Bengal, Bihar and Orissa to His Grace the Duke of Argyll, KT, Her Majesty's Secretary of State for India in Council* (London, 1869)

Marc, Elizabeth, 'Women Want Security', *Daily Mail*, 24 October 1918, p.2

Marc, Elizabeth, 'The Plain Woman's Vote', *Daily Mail,* 18 December 1918, p.4

Marc, Elizabeth, 'Women Who Did Nothing', *Daily Mail,* 12 February 1919, p.4

Marc, Elizabeth, 'Home They Fought For', *Daily Mail,* 26 September 1919, p. 6

Marc, Elizabeth, 'Reading Without Tears', *Home Chat,* 14 February 1920

Marc, Elizabeth, 'Give Your Girl a Career', *Daily Mail,* 18 February 1920, p.6

Marc, Elizabeth, 'Peter on Fibs and Facts', *Home Chat,* 3 July 1920

Marc, Elizabeth, 'Peter on Pluck', *Home Chat,* 29 January 1921. p.164

Marc, Elizabeth, 'Myriam's Easter Egg', *Home Chat,* 15 April 1922. pp. 68–9

Marc, Elizabeth, 'Lonely Hotel Women', Published in *The Daily News*, W.A., 22 May 1922. Originally published in the *Daily Mail*, March 1922

Marc, Elizabeth, 'Should Parents Obey?', *The Daily News* (Perth, WA: 15 June 1922), p.3. republished from the *Daily Mail* (n.d. given).

Marc, Elizabeth, *The Adventures of Conrad the Cock*, by Princess Nusrat (London: Hutchinson, 1922)

Marc, Elizabeth, *The Tale of Tosh and Tim*, by Princess Nusrat (London: Hutchinson, 1922)

Marc, Elizabeth, *The Adventures of Timothy Tinkles: A Little Black Kitten With a Heart of Gold*, by Princess Nusrat (London: Hutchinson, 1922)

Marc, Elizabeth, *Doris and David All Alone*, by Princess Nusrat (London: Hutchinson, 1922)

Marc, Elizabeth, 'The Sunday Taboo', *Pearson's Magazine*, 1923

Marc, Elizabeth, 'The Friendly Arctic', *The Nineteenth Century and After*, October 1923, pp.553–59

Marc, Elizabeth, *With Pucker to the Arctic: a Story for Young Readers* (London: Nelson, 1925)

Marc, Elizabeth, *Lost in the Arctic* (London: Cassell, 1926)

Marc, Elizabeth, *Two in the Bush* (London: Cassell, 1929)

Marc, Elizabeth, *Two Men's Tale* (London: Hutchinson, 1929)

Marc, Elizabeth, *A Man Hunt in the Arctic* (London: Cassell, 1932)

Marc, Elizabeth, *Two Young Adventurers: A Tale of the Australian Bush* (London: Cassell, 1934)

Marc, Elizabeth, *Bush Ragamuffins* (London: Methuen, 1935)

Marc, Elizabeth, 'Interview', *Woman*, June 1936

Metcalf, Thomas R., *Ideologies of the Raj* (Cambridge University Press, 1994)

Miles, Frank and Cranch, Graeme, *Kings College School: the First 150 Years* (King's College School, 1979)

Mirza, Humayun. *From Plassey to Pakistan: the Family History of Iskander Mirza, the First President of Pakistan.* University Press of America (Lanham, Md, 2002)

Mirza, Nusrat Ali, 'Magic I Have Seen', *Daily Mail*, 19 February 1919, p. 4

Mirza, Nusrat Ali, 'Mecca', *Daily Mail*, 1 June 1921, p. 6

Mitchell, R.J. and Leys, M.D.R, *A History of London Life* (London: Longmans, 1958)

Rousselot, Louis, *L'Inde des Rajahs* (Paris: *La Hachette*, 1874)

Stefansson, Viljhamur, *My Life with the Eskimos* (London: Macmillan, 1913)

Stefansson, Viljhamur, *The Friendly Arctic: the Story of Five Years in the Polar Regions* (New York, Macmillan, 1921)

Torrens, Henry W, *A Selection from the Writings, Prose and Poetical*, ed. James Hume (Calcutta: Le Page and Co.)

Torrens, W.F. *Empire in Asia: How We Acquired It: A Book of Confessions* (London: Trubner & Co, 1872)

Trezel, Joe, 'Curiosites Parisiennes: Le Nabab de Bengale', *Le Gaulois*, 1 April 1869

Vanita, Ruth, *Gender, Sex, and the City: Urdu Rekhti Poetry, 1780–1870* (Delhi: Orient Black Swan, 2015)

Visram, Rozina, *Ayars, Lascars and Princes: Indians in Britain 1700–1947* (London: Pluto Press, 1986)

Walsh, J. H.T, *A History of the Murshidabad District* (London, 1902)

White, Jerry, *London in the 19th Century*, (London: Vintage Books, 2008)

Willard, Myra, *The History of Australia's White Immigration Policy* (Melbourne: Melbourne University Press, 1923)

Yates, Edmund, *Edmund Yates, His Recollections and Experiences*, 1884

INDEX